11/20

200+ Original and Adapted
STORY PROGRAM ACTIVITIES

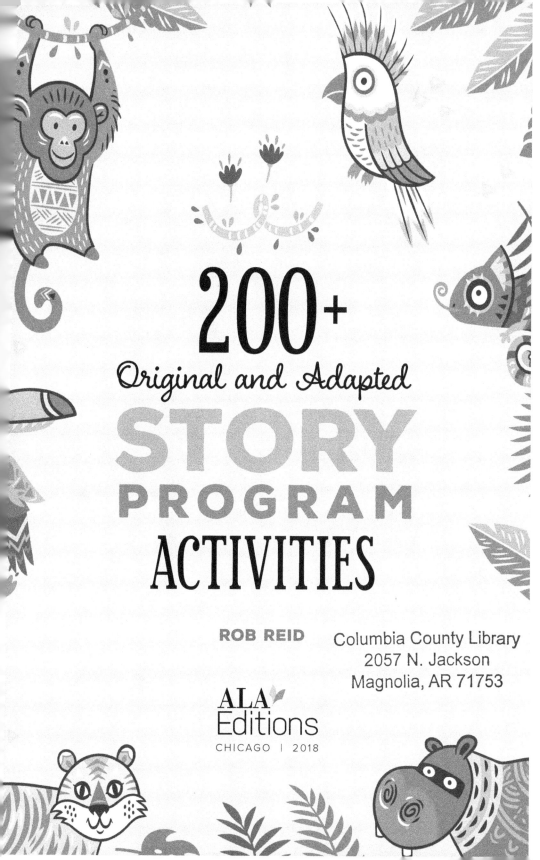

200+
Original and Adapted
STORY
PROGRAM
ACTIVITIES

ROB REID

ALA
Editions
CHICAGO | 2018

ROB REID is the very popular author of numerous books on children's programming for ALA Editions. He has also written resources for Upstart Books and is the author of two picture books. In addition, he has a column in *Book Links* magazine titled "Reid-Aloud Alert." Rob is a senior lecturer at the University of Wisconsin–Eau Claire and conducts workshops across North America on ways to make literature come alive for children.

© 2018 by the American Library Association

Extensive effort has gone into ensuring the reliability of the information in this book; however, the publisher makes no warranty, express or implied, with respect to the material contained herein.

ISBN: 978-0-8389-1738-1 (paper)

Library of Congress Cataloging-in-Publication Data
Names: Reid, Rob, 1955- author.
Title: 200+ original and adapted story program activities / Rob Reid.
Other titles: Two hundred plus original and adapted story program activities
Description: Chicago : ALA Editions, an imprint of the American Library Association, 2018. | Includes bibliographical references and index.
Identifiers: LCCN 2018024987 | ISBN 9780838917381 (print : alk. paper)
Subjects: LCSH: Children's libraries—Activity programs—United States. | Storytelling—United States. | Libraries and preschool children—United States.
Classification: LCC Z718.3 .R435 2018 | DDC 027.62/51—dc23 LC record available at https://lccn.loc.gov/2018024987

Cover design by Kimberly Thornton. Composition by Alejandra Diaz in the Charis SIL, Proxima Nova, and Euphorigenic typefaces.

♾ This paper meets the requirements of ANSI/NISO Z39.48–1992 (Permanence of Paper).

Printed in the United States of America

22 21 20 19 18   5 4 3 2 1

Here ya go, Ru!

contents

MORE FUN   167

THE LITERARY WORLD   207

GOODBYE ACTIVITIES / CLOSINGS   241

acknowledgments

THANKS TO MY wife, Jayne, our four children—Laura, Julia, Alice, and Sam—and our four grandchildren—Parker, Wesley, Harris, and Ruth. I'm so proud of all of you.

Thanks to all the publishers, editors, and staff at ALA Editions with whom I've worked since they invited me to join their family back in 1995 with the publication of my first book, *Children's Jukebox*. Here we are working on our fourteenth book together. Thanks, too, to the American Library Association for inviting me to teach the e-course "Storytime Shenanigans" to librarians all over the world for the past five years. The focus of this class is to learn how to create new story program activities and make one's story programs "the talk of the town."

Thanks to all the publishers, editors, and staff at Upstart Books for inviting me to join their family, first writing regularly for *LibrarySparks* magazine and then writing four books for them, including the picture book *Comin' Down to Storytime*. Its lyrics are reprinted in this collection.

Thanks to Liz Szabla who saw my "Goodbye Rap" and turned it into the picture book *Wave Goodbye*, published by Lee and Low. Its lyrics are reprinted in this collection.

Thanks to Ashley Cordes, Korby Nelson, and Gracie Peterson for their help assembling the material.

And finally, thanks to all the children who joined me for stories and music these past four decades—many of them are now grown up and bringing their own children to my shows.

introduction

I HOPE YOU enjoy reading the 200+ original and adapted story program activities found in this collection and sharing them with children. You will find a variety of types of activities. Most of them are movement and musical activities, but there are also fingerplays, poems, imagination exercises, participation stories, felt stories, spoonerism stories, and even a few library raps.

Many are very simple, like the movement activity "But Mostly I Love You" or the sound effects chant "Happy Birthday in Cow." A few activities are more complex, virtually theatrical productions, such as "The Talent Show ABC," or the participation story "The Biggest, Juiciest Apple in the Whole Orchard," that I use less for the traditional story hour and more for library outreach presentations.

I've had fun writing these activities. They have given me joy the past four decades, sharing them with children as young as preschool age and, for some activities, up through middle school students.

If I remember correctly, the first two activities I created for my story programs as a young children's librarian were "Elephant Hunt," a variation of the popular staple "We're Going on a Bear Hunt" (you'll see I depend on this particular template quite a bit throughout the collection), and "The New Wheels on the Bus," with new verses added to the children's song "The Wheels on the Bus." For the former, I had just learned how to make an impressive elephant trumpeting noise. The idea of leading children in search of an elephant popped into my head. For the latter, again I learned how to make a new sound effect, in this case that of a speeding race car, and wanted to highlight it. Another early creation, the fingerplay "Three Smelly Skunks," came about after I couldn't find a good traditional skunk fingerplay to share with the picture book *Bartholomew the Bossy* by Marjorie Weinman Sharmat, the story of a young skunk. I took the backward-counting format, the kind found in rhymes like "Five Little Monkeys Jumping on the Bed," and voilà! A new story program activity was created. Here I am all these years later, still writing new activities, the latest one—"The Noisy Farmhouse"—created for this book and already "kid-tested" with local youngsters.

Most of these activities have appeared in my books and magazine articles, and my editors and I decided it was time to pull them all together in one collection. The following are new to this book: "The Big Gorilla," "I'm Clean!," "Little Red's Basket of Goodies," "Look Up, Look Down," "Morning Noises," and "Wiggle, Wiggle, Wiggle."

The activities are grouped in the following broad categories: "The Animal World," "My World," "More Fun," and "The Literary World." The collection begins with "Hello Activities/Openings" and ends with "Goodbye Activities/Closings." There are several subcategories in each larger category to help you find activities to fit a specific theme. With that in mind, when looking for activities to fit those specific themes, please note that many activities can fall into several categories and that the "My World," "More Fun," and "The Literary World" sections also have many animal-related activities.

My definitions for the types of activities are as follows:

- Fingerplays are movement activities usually restricted to hand and arm gestures.
- Movement activities use more of the body than hands and arms.
- Musical activities are set to melodies of well-known children's songs (they can easily be found on YouTube) and often double as fingerplays, larger movement activities, or sound effects activities.
- Sound effects activities allow the children to make fun sounds on cue, sometimes with movement.
- Participation stories are oral tales the children can act out while the leader tells the story.
- Felt stories feature felt pieces the leader manipulates while telling an oral tale.
- Imagination exercises have limited movement but ask the children to respond with expressions or lines.
- Spoonerisms are oral stories that transpose letters or parts of words to make a well-known story sound silly.
- Raps are used as rhythmic chants, mostly for library promotional purposes.

Except for the opening and closing activities and the library raps, each activity is accompanied by a recommended picture book to share with children immediately before or after presenting the activity. In a typical story program, I like to read one or two picture books, share an activity, read another picture book, share an activity, and so on. Many of the picture books I originally used for the older activities are no longer in print. I was pleased to find a suitable match for all activities with picture books published between 2012 and 2017.

I believe the picture books are the core of each story program and the activities are the fun glue that holds everything together. Feel free to pick and choose the ones that work best for your own programming style. Adapt them as you see the need and enjoy! Make your story programs "the talk of the town."

The
Activities

HELLO ACTIVITIES / OPENINGS

"HELLO KIDS"

Sound Effects Activity

Have the children repeat the lines after you.

Leader: Hello kids,
Audience: Hello kids,
Leader: Moms and Dads,
Audience: Moms and Dads,
Leader: And everyone else,
Audience: And everyone else,
Leader: And everyone else.
Audience: And everyone else.
Leader: This time, say it with a high voice! (*Say lines with a falsetto voice.*)
Leader: Hello kids,
Audience: Hello kids,
Leader: Moms and Dads,
Audience: Moms and Dads,
Leader: And everyone else,
Audience: And everyone else,
Leader: And everyone else.
Audience: And everyone else.
Leader: Now, say it with a doggy voice! (*Bark the lines.*)
Leader: Woof-woof-woof,
Audience: Woof-woof-woof,
Leader: Woof-woof-woof,
Audience: Woof-woof-woof,
Leader: Woof-woof-woof-woof-woof,
Audience: Woof-woof-woof-woof-woof,
Leader: Woof-woof-woof-woof-woof.
Audience: Woof-woof-woof-woof-woof.

Leader: This time, say it in a very slow voice! (*Draw out each sentence.*)

Leader: Hello . . . kids,

Audience: Hello . . . kids,

Leader: Moms . . . and . . . Dads,

Audience: Moms . . . and . . . Dads,

Leader: And . . . everyone . . . else,

Audience: And . . . everyone . . . else,

Leader: And . . . everyone . . . else.

Audience: And . . . everyone . . . else.

Leader: This time, say it with an underwater voice! (*Run fingers over lips while saying the lines.*)

Leader: Hello kids,

Audience: Hello kids,

Leader: Moms and Dads,

Audience: Moms and Dads,

Leader: And everyone else,

Audience: And everyone else,

Leader: And everyone else.

Audience: And everyone else.

Leader: Now, say it in a loud voice! (*Shout the words.*)

Leader: HELLO KIDS!

Audience: HELLO KIDS!

Leader: MOMS AND DADS!

Audience: MOMS AND DADS!

Leader: AND EVERYONE ELSE!

Audience: AND EVERYONE ELSE!

Leader: AND EVERYONE ELSE!

Audience: AND EVERYONE ELSE!

Leader: That's too loud! Say it again with a softer voice. (*Say lines with a quiet voice.*)

Leader: Hello kids,

Audience: Hello kids,

Leader: Moms and Dads,

Audience: Moms and Dads,

Leader: And everyone else,

Audience: And everyone else,

Leader: And everyone else.

Audience: And everyone else.
Leader: Even quieter! (*Whisper the lines.*)
Leader: Hello kids,
Audience: Hello kids,
Leader: Moms and Dads,
Audience: Moms and Dads,
Leader: And everyone else,
Audience: And everyone else,
Leader: And everyone else.
Audience: And everyone else.
Leader: That's still too loud. Even quieter! (*Silently mouth the words.*)
Leader: (Hello kids,)
Audience: (Hello kids,)
Leader: (Moms and Dads,)
Audience: (Moms and Dads,)
Leader: (And everyone else,)
Audience: (And everyone else,)
Leader: (And everyone else.)
Audience: (And everyone else.)
Leader: Ah, that's music to my ears!

"LOOK UP, LOOK DOWN"

Movement Activity

Have the children repeat the lines after you and imitate your motions.

Leader: Look up, (*Look at the ceiling.*)
Audience: Look up,
Leader: Look down, (*Look at the floor.*)
Audience: Look down,
Leader: Look around and around. (*Swivel head.*)
Audience: Look around and around.
Leader: Look far, (*Point.*)
Audience: Look far,
Leader: Look near, (*Hold hand close to eye and peer at it.*)
Audience: Look near,
Leader: Now everyone is here. (*Hold arms out at sides, palms up.*)
Audience: Now everyone is here.

"SOME OF THESE STORIES"

Poem

This opening poem is especially good if you are going to share some tall tales.

Some of these stories you've heard before,
Some of them will be quite new.
Rest assured that EVERY word is
Absolutely,
Positively,
GUARANTEED
To be . . . almost TRUE! (*Whisper the word "almost."*)

"STORYTELLING WARM-UPS"

Sound Effects Activity

Have the children imitate your motions and sounds. This activity humorously lets the children know that they will be participating throughout the program and that they "need to be warmed up and ready to go."

Let's go through our vowels together. Give me a chorus of "A's." (*Sing a stretched-out "A-A-A-A-A."*)
Now, put your fingers in your mouth, stretch out your lips, look at your neighbor, and give me an "E!" (*Stretch lips and sing "E-E-E-E-E!"*)
Give me a high, falsetto "I." (*Sing a falsetto stretched-out "I-I-I-I-I!"*)
Now, a low, deep "O." (*Sing a low stretched-out "O-O-O-O-O!"*)
Now, a series of "U's." (*Chant each "U" separately: "U-U-U-U-U!"*)
Stretch your jaw muscles this way and that way. (*Put hands on sides of head and tilt head back and forth.*)
Loosen up your cheeks. (*Grab cheeks and move them.*)
Give me a "Cheek Wobble." (*Shake head back and forth and flap cheeks.*)
Give me some "Teeth-Gnashers." (*Gnash teeth.*)
And now for the most important storytelling warm-up—"Tongue Pushups!"
Ready . . . at attention. . . . One! Two! One! Two! (*Stick out tongue and move it up and down.*)
Sideways! One! Two! One! Two! (*Move tongue side to side.*)
Loop-de-loops! (*Move tongue in a clockwise circle.*)
Other way! (*Move tongue in a counter-clockwise circle.*)
Now, we're ready for our first story.

The Animal World

ANIMALS AROUND THE WORLD

"ANIMAL BATHS"

Movement Activity

Ask the children the following questions. Let the children act out how they imagine the animals "take a bath." Movement suggestions are provided. Everyone stands.

Have you ever seen a cat take a bath?
Show me how a cat takes a bath. (*Lick hands as if they are paws.*)
Have you ever seen a robin take a bath?
Show me how a robin takes a bath. (*Mime splashing in a birdbath, arms flapping like wings.*)
Have you ever seen an elephant take a bath?
Show me how an elephant takes a bath. (*Hold arm in front of nose like a trunk. Pretend to spray water out of it.*)
Have you ever seen a dog take a bath?
Show me how a dog takes a bath. (*Move like a dog shaking off water.*)
Have you ever seen a fish take a bath?
Fish don't take baths! Or do they? (*Shrug.*)

PICTURE BOOK MATCH

Baby Animals Take a Bath, written by Marsha Diane Arnold and illustrated by Phyllis Tildes (Charlesbridge, 2017).

> Young animals take baths in different ways. The polar bear cub takes a snow bath, the little hippo has a mud bath, zebra gets a dust bath, tiger cub receives a tongue bath, and sea lion pup is bathed by the sun.

"ANIMAL SIRENS"

Sound Effects Activity

Have the children repeat the sounds after you.

Emergency vehicles all make loud noises so that other vehicles will get
    out of the way.
What does an emergency vehicle sound like?
WEE-O! WEE-O! WEE-O!
Let's pretend that animal emergency vehicles sound like the animals
    driving them.
How might a Mosquito emergency vehicle sound?
BUZZ-O! BUZZ-O! BUZZ-O!
How might a Bird emergency vehicle sound?
TWEET-O! TWEET-O! TWEET-O!
How might a Duck emergency vehicle sound?
QUACK-O! QUACK-O! QUACK-O!
How might a Fish emergency vehicle sound?
GLUB-O! GLUB-O! GLUB-O!
How might a Monkey emergency vehicle sound?
OOH-O! OOH-O! OOH-O!

PICTURE BOOK MATCH

Bug Patrol, written by Denise Dowling Mortensen and illustrated by Cece
    Bell (Clarion, 2013).
        Captain Bob of the Bug Patrol answers the first call of the morning: "Code
        eleven: Donut swarm!" Off goes the Bug Mobile with a loud, "WEE-O!
        WEE-O! WEE-O! WOO!"

"THE BABY BIRD CHOIR"

Sound Effects Activity

Inform the children that they are a choir of baby birds or animals and that they
should make the proper noises when you point to them at the end of each stanza.
Hold a baton—or any stick—to "conduct."

The Baby Bird Choir,
Is lovely to hear,

It goes a lot like this: (*Point to the children and conduct them.*)
Peep! Peep! Peep! Peep! Peep! Peep! Peep!
The Kitty Cat Choir,
Is lovely to hear,
It goes a lot like this: (*Point to the children and conduct them.*)
Meow! Meow! Meow! Meow! Meow! Meow! Meow!
The Puppy Dog Choir,
Is lovely to hear,
It goes a lot like this: (*Point to the children and conduct them.*)
Bow-wow! Bow-wow! Bow-wow-wow!
The Duckling Choir,
Is lovely to hear,
It goes a lot like this: (*Point to the children and conduct them.*)
Quack! Quack! Quack! Quack! Quack! Quack! Quack!
The Mosquito Choir,
Is lovely to hear,
It goes a lot like this: (*Point to the children and conduct them.*)
Buzz! Buzz! Buzz! Buzz! Buzz! Buzz! Buzz!

PICTURE BOOK MATCH

Listen to Our World, written by Bill Martin Jr. and Michael Sampson and
illustrated by Melissa Sweet (Simon and Schuster, 2016).
A trip around the world reveals the sounds of the rain forest with parrots
squawking, Gila monsters hissing in deserts, eagles screeching in the
mountains, and more.

"AN ELEPHANT CAME TO PLAY, PLAY, PLAY" ———

Movement Activity

Have the children repeat the lines after you and imitate your motions. Everyone
stands.

Leader: An elephant came to play, play, play, (*Hold arm in front of nose
to represent an elephant trunk.*)
Audience: An elephant came to play, play, play,
Leader: He's big, and large, and gray, gray, gray. (*Hold arms outstretched
at sides to show size of the elephant.*)

Audience: He's big, and large, and gray, gray, gray.

Leader: A rhino came to play, play, play, (*Hold hand in front of nose to represent a rhino horn.*)

Audience: A rhino came to play, play, play,

Leader: She's big, and large, and gray, gray, gray. (*Hold arms outstretched at sides to show size of the rhino.*)

Audience: She's big, and large, and gray, gray, gray.

Leader: A hippo came to play, play, play, (*Shake hips.*)

Audience: A hippo came to play, play, play,

Leader: He's big, and large, and gray, gray, gray. (*Hold arms outstretched at sides to show size of the hippo.*)

Audience: He's big, and large, and gray, gray, gray.

Leader: All three came to play, play, play, (*Make an elephant trunk, followed by a rhino horn, and then followed by shaking hips.*)

Audience: All three came to play, play, play,

Leader: They're big, and large, and gray, gray, gray. (*Hold arms outstretched at sides to show size of the animals.*)

Audience: They're big, and large, and gray, gray, gray.

PICTURE BOOK MATCH

Petal and Poppy, written by Lisa Clough and illustrated by Ed Briant (Houghton Mifflin Harcourt, 2014).

> An elephant named Petal drives a rhino named Poppy crazy with her tuba playing: "BAH-BWAB-BAAH!" When Poppy gets lost on a boat in the fog, the sounds of Petal's tuba reunites them.

"FIVE LITTLE ALLIGATORS" ──────────────

Movement Activity

This activity is modeled after the fingerplay "Five Little Monkeys Swinging from a Tree." Have the children imitate your motions. Everyone stands.

Five little gators floating 'neath a tree, (*Hold up five fingers.*)

Teasing Big Gorilla, "You can't catch me!" (*Shake pointer finger on "You can't catch me!"*)

Big Gorilla snuck around as quiet as could be, (*Put pointer finger to lips to signal "be quiet."*)

And grabbed one gator from beneath that tree. (*Make a grabbing motion with one hand.*)

Four little gators floating 'neath a tree, (*Hold up four fingers.*)

Teasing Big Gorilla, "You can't catch me!" (*Shake pointer finger on "You can't catch me!"*)

Big Gorilla snuck around as quiet as could be, (*Put pointer finger to lips to signal "be quiet."*)

And grabbed one gator from beneath that tree. (*Make a grabbing motion with one hand.*)

Three little gators floating 'neath a tree, (*Hold up three fingers.*)

Teasing Big Gorilla, "You can't catch me!" (*Shake pointer finger on "You can't catch me!"*)

Big Gorilla snuck around as quiet as could be, (*Put pointer finger to lips to signal "be quiet."*)

And grabbed one gator from beneath that tree. (*Make a grabbing motion with one hand.*)

Two little gators floating 'neath a tree, (*Hold up two fingers.*)

Teasing Big Gorilla, "You can't catch me!" (*Shake pointer finger on "You can't catch me!"*)

Big Gorilla snuck around as quiet as could be, (*Put pointer finger to lips to signal "be quiet."*)

And grabbed one gator from beneath that tree. (*Make a grabbing motion with one hand.*)

One little gator floating 'neath a tree, (*Hold up one finger.*)

Teasing Big Gorilla, "You can't catch me!" (*Shake pointer finger on "You can't catch me!"*)

Big Gorilla snuck around as quiet as could be, (*Put pointer finger to lips to signal "be quiet."*)

And grabbed one gator from beneath that tree. (*Make a grabbing motion with one hand.*)

No little gators floating 'neath that tree, (*Shake head.*)

No little gators singing, "Can't catch me!" (*Shrug shoulders.*)

Big Gorilla looked around as quiet as could be, (*Hand over eyes, look around.*)

Then sat right down and rested 'neath that tree. (*Smile, nod, and sit down.*)

PICTURE BOOK MATCH

Snappsy the Alligator (Did Not Ask to Be in This Book), written by Julie
Falatko and illustrated by Tim Miller (Viking, 2016).

> According to the book's narrator, Snappsy is a big, mean alligator.
> Snappsy eats his peanut butter sandwich, reads a book, and basically
> wants the narrator of the book to buzz off.

"I KNOW A COWBOY, I KNOW A COWGIRL"

Sound Effects Activity

Pause before the last word in each stanza and let the children respond with the
proper animal sound.

I know a Cowboy named Gene,
I know a Cowgirl named Sue,
They're in charge of a herd of cows,
The cows go . . . "Moo!"
I know a Horse-boy named Hank,
I know a Horse-girl named Renee,
They're in charge of a herd of horses,
The horses go . . . "Neigh!"
I know a Snake-boy named Sam,
I know a Snake-girl named Miss,
They're in charge of a herd of snakes,
The snakes go . . . "Hiss!"
I know a Coyote-boy named Larry,
I know a Coyote-girl named Lou,
They're in charge of a herd of coyotes,
The coyotes go . . . "Arrrrroooo!"

PICTURE BOOK MATCH

I Wanna Be a Cowgirl, written by Angela DiTerlizzi and illustrated by
Elizabet Vukovic (Beach Lane, 2017).

> A girl living in town dreams about moving to a ranch and becoming a
> cowgirl. She hangs gloves from the clothesline and pretends to milk the
> cows. She brushes her dog and pretends to shear the sheep.

"A LITTLE BEAR CUB CLIMBED UP A TREE" ———————

Movement/Sound Effects Activity

Have the children imitate your motions. Everyone stands.

In North America:
A little bear cub climbed up a tall tree, (*Mime climbing.*)
The cub looked around, (*Swivel head.*)
And what did she see?
She saw one wolf! (*Hold up one finger and howl.*)
In Africa:
A little lion cub climbed up a tall tree, (*Mime climbing.*)
The cub looked around, (*Swivel head.*)
And what did he see?
He saw two elephants! (*Hold up two fingers and make a trumpeting noise.*)
In Australia:
A little koala cub climbed up a tall tree, (*Mime climbing.*)
The cub looked around, (*Swivel head.*)
And what did she see?
She saw three kangaroos! (*Hold up three fingers and hop.*)
In South America:
A little parrot chick flew up a tall tree, (*Mime flying.*)
The chick looked around, (*Swivel head.*)
And what did he see?
He saw four snakes! (*Hold up four fingers and hiss.*)
In the Pacific Ocean:
A little whale calf swam down into the sea, (*Mime swimming.*)
The calf looked around, (*Swivel head.*)
And what did she see?
She saw five sharks! (*Hold up five fingers, then make shark jaws with
    arms.*)

PICTURE BOOK MATCH

Where, Oh Where, Is Baby Bear? written and illustrated by Ashley Wolff
(Beach Lane, 2017).
> Mama Bear keeps looking for her cub. Baby Bear is up in a tree, behind a
> waterfall, between cattails in a pond, and on top of a boulder. When they
> return to their cave, Baby Bear asks, "Where, oh where, is Mama Bear?"

"LOOKING FOR POLAR BEARS" ————————————

Movement/Sound Effects Activity

This activity is modeled after the movement activity "We're Going on a Bear Hunt." Have the children slap their legs to simulate walking and ask them to repeat the lines after you and imitate your motions.

Chorus:
Leader: We're looking for polar bears. *(Slap legs.)*
Audience: We're looking for polar bears.
Leader: We're going to find a big one.
Audience: We're going to find a big one.
Leader: We're not afraid.
Audience: We're not afraid.
Leader: Are you? I'm not!
Audience: Are you? I'm not!

Leader: We need to put on our snowshoes. (*Stop slapping legs and mime putting on snowshoes.*)
Audience: We need to put on our snowshoes.
Leader: Let's go! (*Slap legs.*)
Audience: Let's go!

Chorus:
Leader: We're looking for polar bears.
Audience: We're looking for polar bears.
Leader: We're going to find a big one.
Audience: We're going to find a big one.
Leader: We're not afraid.
Audience: We're not afraid.
Leader: Are you? I'm not!
Audience: Are you? I'm not!

Leader: Here's a little hill. (*Stop slapping legs and point.*)
Audience: Here's a little hill.
Leader: Can't go under it, (*Make a down-and-up curve with hand.*)
Audience: Can't go under it,
Leader: Can't go around it. (*Make a straightforward curve with hand.*)
Audience: Can't go around it.

Leader: We'll have to climb over it. (*Make an up-and-down curve with hand.*)

Audience: We'll have to climb over it.

Leader: Careful, it's slippery! (*Slap slowly as if climbing is an effort; huff and puff.*)

Audience: Careful, it's slippery!

Chorus:

Leader: We're looking for polar bears.

Audience: We're looking for polar bears.

Leader: We're going to find a big one.

Audience: We're going to find a big one.

Leader: We're not afraid.

Audience: We're not afraid.

Leader: Are you? I'm not!

Audience: Are you? I'm not!

Leader: We're at the top of the hill. (*Stop slapping legs.*)

Audience: We're at the top of the hill.

Leader: We'll have to get down there. (*Point.*)

Audience: We'll have to get down there.

Leader: Let's take off our snowshoes. (*Mime removing snowshoes.*)

Audience: Let's take off our snowshoes.

Leader: We'll have to slide. (*Move body side to side and shout, "Wheee!"*)

Audience: We'll have to slide.

Leader: Put our snowshoes back on. (*Mime putting on snowshoes.*)

Audience: Put our snowshoes back on.

Chorus:

Leader: We're looking for polar bears. (*Slap legs.*)

Audience: We're looking for polar bears.

Leader: We're going to find a big one.

Audience: We're going to find a big one.

Leader: We're not afraid.

Audience: We're not afraid.

Leader: Are you? I'm not!

Audience: Are you? I'm not!

Leader: Here's some open water. (*Stop slapping legs and point.*)
Audience: Here's some open water.
Leader: Can't go under it. (*Make a down-and-up curve with hand.*)
Audience: Can't go under it.
Leader: Can't go around it. (*Make a straightforward curve with hand.*)
Audience: Can't go around it.
Leader: We'll have to go on the top of it. (*Make an up-and-down curve with hand.*)
Audience: We'll have to go on the top of it.
Leader: Let's take off our snowshoes. (*Mime removing snowshoes.*)
Audience: Let's take off our snowshoes.
Leader: Here's a kayak. (*Mime paddling kayak.*)
Audience: Here's a kayak.
Leader: Paddle, paddle, paddle, paddle.
Audience: Paddle, paddle, paddle, paddle.
Leader: Finally! Here's land! (*Point.*)
Audience: Finally! Here's land!
Leader: Let's put on our snowshoes. (*Mime putting on snowshoes.*)
Audience: Let's put on our snowshoes.

Chorus:
Leader: We're looking for polar bears. (*Slap legs.*)
Audience: We're looking for polar bears.
Leader: We're going to find a big one.
Audience: We're going to find a big one.
Leader: We're not afraid.
Audience: We're not afraid.
Leader: Are you? I'm not!
Audience: Are you? I'm not!

Leader: Uh-oh! Snowstorm! (*Stop slapping legs and point.*)
Audience: Uh-oh! Snowstorm!
Leader: It's hard to see! (*Squint and put hands near eyes.*)
Audience: It's hard to see!
Leader: Here's shelter! (*Point.*)
Audience: Here's shelter!

Leader: It's a snow den.

Audience: It's a snow den.

Leader: Let's crawl in. (*Mime crawling.*)

Audience: Let's crawl in.

Leader: Whew! That was close. (*Wipe brow.*)

Audience: Whew! That was close.

Leader: I think there's something in here with us. (*Look around.*)

Audience: I think there's something in here with us.

Leader: I feel something furry! Is it your coat? (*Hold out hands as if feeling something.*)

Audience: I feel something furry! Is it your coat?

Leader: I see two eyes. Are they yours? (*Point.*)

Audience: I see two eyes, Are they yours?

Leader: I see big teeth. They're too big for you! (*Point.*)

Audience: I see big teeth. They're too big for you!

Leader: It's a polar bear! Run! (*Slap legs quickly.*)

Audience: It's a polar bear! Run!

Leader: Take off our snowshoes and into the kayak! (*Mime removing snowshoes and paddling kayak.*)

Audience: Take off our snowshoes and into the kayak!

Leader: We're on the other side!

Audience: We're on the other side!

Leader: Put our snowshoes back on. (*Mime putting on snowshoes.*)

Audience: Put our snowshoes back on.

Leader: Climb the hill! (*Slap legs slowly; huff and puff.*)

Audience: Climb the hill!

Leader: Take off our snowshoes. (*Mime taking off snowshoes.*)

Audience: Take off our snowshoes.

Leader: Slide down the other side. (*Move side to side and shout "Wheee!"*)

Audience: Slide down the other side.

Leader: Whew! We're safe! (*Wipe brow.*)

Audience: Whew! We're safe!

Leader: I wasn't afraid. Were you?

Audience: I wasn't afraid. Were you?

All: NO!

She'll Be Coming Up the Mountain, written by Kim Norman and illustrated by Liza Woodruff (Sterling, 2016).

> Polar Bear's friends prepare a welcome home party in her honor. Moose, Seal, and others put up a banner, knit Polar Bear a sweater, and "play music, tapping icicles and drums."

"MY BEST FRIEND"

Movement/Sound Effects Activity

Have the children imitate your motions. Everyone stands.

My best friend is a Snake!
Here are two things we can do:
We can slide on the grass, (*Get down on your belly.*)
And stick out our tongues, (*Stick tongue in and out quickly.*)
That's what best friends do. (*Get into a sitting position.*)
My best friend is a Monkey!
Here are two things we can do:
We can scratch ourselves, (*Scratch all over.*)
And go "ooh-ooh-ooh," (*Make monkey noises.*)
That's what best friends do.
My best friend is a Beaver!
Here are two things we can do:
We can chew on wood, (*Make chewing motions.*)
And slap our tails, (*Slap hands on floor.*)
That's what best friends do.
My best friend is a Hippo!
Here are two things we can do;
We can float real low, (*Get down on belly with eyes peering over hands.*)
And open our mouth wide, (*Open mouth wide.*)
That's what best friends do.
My best friend is a Sloth!
Here are two things we can do:
We can hang upside-down, (*Flip over on back with arms in the air, as if hanging from a branch.*)

And move r-r-r-e-e-e-a-a-1-1-1 sl-oooooo-www, (*Stand up slowly.*)
That's what best friends do. (*Applaud.*)

Are You a Monkey? A Tale of Animal Charades, written and illustrated by
Marine Rivoal and translated by Maria Tunney (Phaidon Press, 2017).
    The animals play a game of charades with each other. The parrot fluffs
    its head feathers to resemble a lion, a crocodile sticks its head in the
    ground pretending to be an ostrich, and the ostrich bends its neck back
    to imitate an elephant.

"THE NOT-SO-ITSY-BITSY HIPPO"

Movement Activity

Have the children imitate you making large, oversized versions of the traditional
"Itsy-Bitsy Spider" fingerplay motions. Recite the lines with a loud voice. Rush the
"Not-So-Itsy-Bitsy Hippo" lines to add to the comedic effect.

The Not-So-Itsy-Bitsy Hippo went up the water spout, (*Walk fingers
    upward.*)
Down came the rain and washed the hippo out, (*Wiggle fingers downward.*)
Out came the sun and dried up all the rain, (*Make a circle with hands
    overhead.*)
And the Not-So-Itsy-Bitsy Hippo went up the spout again. (*Walk fingers
    upward again.*)

Big Little Hippo, written and illustrated by Valeri Gorbachev (Sterling,
2017).
    Little Hippo's family members are bigger than he is, the crocodile is
    bigger, the giraffe is bigger, "and, of course, giant Elephant was much,
    much, MUCH bigger." Little Hippo feels better when he helps little
    beetles and they call him Big Hippo.

"OVER IN THE CREEK"

Musical/Movement Activity

Sing to the first melodic part of the song "Over in the Meadow." Have the children imitate your motions.

Over in the creek,
Swimming all around, (*Make little swimming motions with hands as if a tiny fish is swimming.*)
Swam a tiny minnow, (*Indicate an inch-length with thumb and pointer finger.*)
Moving up and down. (*Resume swimming motions.*)
Over in the pond,
Swimming all around, (*Make slightly larger swimming motions with hands.*)
Swam a little sunfish, (*Indicate a foot-length with both hands.*)
Moving up and down. (*Resume swimming motions.*)
Over in the lake,
Swimming all around, (*Make slightly larger swimming motions with hands.*)
Swam a good-sized musky, (*Indicate a yard-length with both hands.*)
Moving up and down. (*Resume swimming motions.*)
Over in the sea,
Swimming all around, (*Make even larger swimming motions with hands.*)
Swam a great big shark, (*Spread both hands as wide apart as possible.*)
Moving up and down. (*Resume swimming motions.*)
Over in the ocean,
Swimming all around, (*Make oversized swimming motions with hands.*)
Swam a gigantic whale, (*Look all around the room.*)
Moving up and down. (*Resume swimming motions.*)

PICTURE BOOK MATCH

Agua, Agüita / Water, Little Water, written by Jorge Tetl Argueta and illustrated by Felipe Ugalde Alcántara (Piñata, 2017).

> A drop of water sings, "I am a tiny drop." It becomes a river, then a lake, and next an ocean before climbing to the sky and returning as rain.

"TINY LITTLE FROGS" ————————————————————

Movement/Sound Effects Activity

Have the children imitate your sounds and motions. Everyone stands.

Tiny little frogs,
Jumping up and down, (*Jump.*)
Making funny sounds, (*Make a frog noise like "Ribbit" and "Croak."*)
Tiny little frogs.
Tiny little calves,
Leaping up and down, (*Leap.*)
Making funny sounds, (*Make a calf noise like "Moo" and "Maa."*)
Tiny little calves.
Tiny little ducklings,
Waddling all around, (*Waddle with arms tucked in like wings.*)
Making funny sounds, (*Make a duckling noise like "Quack."*)
Tiny little ducklings.
Tiny little owls,
Swooping all around, (*Hold arms out like wings and swoop around the room.*)
Making funny sounds, (*Make an owl noise like "Hoot."*)
Tiny little owls.
Tiny little monkeys,
Swinging all around, (*Mime swinging from branch to branch.*)
Making funny sounds, (*Make a monkey noise like "Ooh-Ooh" or "Screech."*)
Tiny little monkeys.
Tiny little mice,
Scurrying all around, (*Get down on all fours, making little darting movements.*)
Making funny sounds, (*Make a mouse noise like "Squeak."*)
Tiny little mice.

PICTURE BOOK MATCH

When I Grow Up, written and illustrated by Anita Bijsterbosch (Clavis, 2017).

> The little lion growls softly now, but when it grows up, it will roar. Little crocodile will be able to jump into deep water when it grows up, little toucan will be able to fly, little giraffe will be able to reach up high with its long neck, little snake will be able to wrap around big trees, and little elephant will use its "trunk to spray everything and everyone!"

"THE UNDERWATER PARADE" ——————————————

Movement/Sound Effects Activity

Have the children imitate your motions. Everyone stands and marches in place.

The underwater parade,
There's ten in a line, (*Hold up ten fingers.*)
A shark is getting close—GULP! (*Clap.*)
And now there are nine. (*Hold up nine fingers.*)
The underwater parade,
There's nine—don't call them bait,
A shark is getting close—GULP! (*Clap.*)
And now there are eight. (*Hold up eight fingers.*)
The underwater parade,
There's three less than eleven,
A shark is getting close—GULP! (*Clap.*)
And now there are seven. (*Hold up seven fingers.*)
The underwater parade,
They're all doing tricks,
A shark is getting close—GULP! (*Clap.*)
And now there are six. (*Hold up six fingers.*)
The underwater parade,
They're taking a dive,
A shark is getting close—GULP! (*Clap.*)
And now there are five. (*Hold up five fingers.*)
The underwater parade,
They're near the ocean floor,
A shark is getting close—GULP! (*Clap.*)
And now there are four. (*Hold up four fingers.*)
The underwater parade,
They're swimming out to sea,
A shark is getting close—GULP! (*Clap.*)
And now there are three. (*Hold up three fingers.*)
The underwater parade,
They're playing peek-a-boo,
A shark is getting close—GULP! (*Clap.*)
And now there are two. (*Hold up two fingers.*)
The underwater parade,
They're having lots of fun,

A shark is getting close—GULP! (*Clap.*)
And now there is one. (*Hold up one finger.*)
The underwater parade,
The shark sees a whale,
The shark decides it's over,
That's the end of this tale! (*Wave goodbye.*)

PICTURE BOOK MATCH

One Lonely Fish: A Counting Book with Bite!, concept by Andie Mansfield
  and illustrated by Thomas Flintham (Bloomsbury, 2017).
    A sequence of fish line up to swallow each other. Funny-shaped pages
    add to the concept. The tenth fish has its mouth wide enough to sur-
    round all the other fish.

"USE, USE, USE YOUR MIND—MOVE"

Musical Activity

Sing to the tune of "Row, Row, Row Your Boat." Have the children imitate your
motions. Everyone stands.

Use, use, use your mind,
To a special groove,
Imagine you're an Alligator,
Show me how you move. (*Make alligator jaws out of arms and "snap" them.*)
Use, use, use your mind,
To a special groove,
Imagine you're a Butterfly,
Show me how you move. (*Flap arms as you move slowly around the room.*)
Use, use, use your mind,
To a special groove,
Imagine you're a Hummingbird,
Show me how you move. (*Flap arms very quickly and dart around the room.*)
Use, use, use your mind,
To a special groove,
Imagine you're a Lobster,
Show me how you move. (*Click thumbs on both hands as if they are claws.*)
Use, use, use your mind,

To a special groove,
Imagine you're a Turtle,
Show me how you move. (*Get on all fours and move slowly around the
     room.*)
Use, use, use your mind,
To a special groove,
Imagine you're a Cheetah,
Show me how you move. (*Run quickly back and forth.*)

PICTURE BOOK MATCH

Still a Gorilla!, written by Kim Norman and illustrated by Chad Geran
     (Orchard, 2016).
> Willy the gorilla has many questions. If he struts and roars, will he be
> a lion? If he jumps around, does that mean he is now a kangaroo? He
> learns that the answer to all his questions is, "No. Still a gorilla."

BIRDS

"FIVE LITTLE HUNGRY BIRDS"

Movement Activity

Have the children imitate your motions. Everyone stands.

Five little hungry birds, (*Flap arms as wings.*)
Looking for food to eat, (*Look downward and move head back and forth.*)
One found a juicy worm, (*Pretend to grab the worm with beak.*)
Mmm . . . mmm . . . what a treat! (*Smile and rub belly.*)
Four little hungry birds, (*Flap arms as wings.*)
Looking for food to eat, (*Look downward and move head back and forth.*)
One found a ripe blackberry, (*Pretend to grab the blackberry with beak.*)
Mmm . . . mmm . . . what a treat! (*Smile and rub belly.*)
Three little hungry birds, (*Flap arms as wings.*)
Looking for food to eat, (*Look downward and move head back and forth.*)
One found a ripe red cherry, (*Pretend to grab the cherry with beak.*)
Mmm . . . mmm . . . what a treat! (*Smile and rub belly.*)
Two little hungry birds, (*Flap arms as wings.*)
Looking for food to eat, (*Look downward and move head back and forth.*)
One found a sunflower seed, (*Pretend to grab the sunflower seed with beak.*)
Mmm . . . mmm . . . what a treat! (*Smile and rub belly.*)
One little hungry bird, (*Flap arms as wings.*)
Looking for food to eat, (*Look downward and move head back and forth.*)
It found a tasty bug, (*Pretend to grab the bug with beak.*)
Mmm . . . mmm . . . what a treat! (*Smile and rub belly.*)
No little hungry birds, (*Shake head and pat belly.*)
Looking for food to eat, (*Point to mouth and shake head again.*)
It won't be long before they're back, (*Flap arms as wings.*)
Looking for tasty treats. (*Look downward and move head back and forth.*)

North, South, East, West, written by Margaret Wise Brown and illustrated
by Greg Pizzoli (Harper, 2017).

> A bird heads north where everything is white. She next heads south
> where it's hot. After visiting the west, she heads back home to the east
> and hatches little birds. They, in turn, wonder if they will fly "North,
> South, East, or West."

"FLAP YOUR WINGS" ——————————————————————

Movement/Sound Effects Activity

Have the children imitate your motions. Pause before the last word in each stanza
and let the children respond with the answer. Everyone stands.

Flap your wings, (*Flap arms.*)
It's time to fly,
Spread your wings, (*Move in circles with outstretched arms.*)
We're way up high.
Now we're landing in a tree, (*Bend knees and fold arms into body.*)
Here's my sound,
You know it's me.
"Whoo! Whoo!"
What am I?
Audience: An owl!
Flap your wings, (*Flap arms.*)
It's time to fly,
Spread your wings, (*Move in circles with outstretched arms.*)
We're way up high.
Now we're landing in a tree, (*Bend knees and fold arms into body.*)
Here's my sound,
You know it's me.
"Caw! Caw!"
What am I?
Audience: A crow!
Flap your wings, (*Flap arms.*)
It's time to fly,
Spread your wings, (*Move in circles with outstretched arms.*)
We're way up high.

Now we're landing in a tree, (*Bend knees and fold arms into body.*)
Here's my sound,
You know it's me.
"Polly wants a cracker!"
What am I?
Audience: A parrot!
Flap your wings, (*Flap arms.*)
It's time to fly,
Spread your wings, (*Move in circles with outstretched arms.*)
We're way up high.
Now we're landing near a tree, (*Bend knees and fold arms into body.*)
Here's my sound,
You know it's me.
"Quack! Quack!"
What am I?
Audience: A duck!

PICTURE BOOK MATCH

Hooray for Birds!, written and illustrated by Lucy Cousins (Candlewick, 2017).

> Imagine being a bird and making noises like "Cock-a-doodle-doo" or "Cheep, cheep, cheep." Imagine waddling like a penguin, running like an ostrich, or standing on one leg like a flamingo. After a busy day of imagining, it's time to say good night like an owl.

"THE MORE WE TWEET TOGETHER"

Musical Activity

Sing to the tune of "The More We Get Together." Everyone joins in with the bird noises at the end of each stanza.

The more we tweet together, together, together,
The more we tweet together, the happier we'll be.
For your friends are my friends, and my friends are your friends,
The more we tweet together, the happier we'll be.
"Tweet, tweet, tweet, tweet."
The more we hoot together, together, together,
The more we hoot together, the happier we'll be.

For your friends are my friends and my friends are your friends,
The more we hoot together, the happier we'll be.
"Hoot, hoot, hoot, hoot."
The more we caw together, together, together,
The more we caw together, the happier we'll be.
For your friends are my friends and my friends are your friends,
The more we caw together, the happier we'll be.
"Caw, caw, caw, caw."

PICTURE BOOK MATCH

Home Tweet Home, written and illustrated by Courtney Dicmas (Doubleday, 2015).
> The nest is too crowded for Pippi and Burt. They live with several broth-
> ers and sisters—"Edgar, Maude, Rupert, Helena, Winnie, Cecil, Beatrix,
> Rosalie." Pippi and Burt fly all over the world looking for a new nest
> before agreeing that their old nest is the best.

"THE PENGUIN"

Felt Story

Make an all-white felt penguin with the following colored tuxedo shapes to place
on it: red, yellow, green with orange stripes, plaid, and black.

A penguin walked into a clothing store. (*Place penguin on felt board.*)
He said, "Do you have anything colorful I can wear?"
"We sure do," said the storekeeper. "We have a new line of colorful
tuxedos. Let's try on this red one." (*Place the red tux on the penguin.*)
"Hmmm, not bad," said the penguin. "Hey, kids. Do you think I look
good in red?"
(*Shake head so children will respond, "NO!" If they say "YES" during the
story sequence, have the penguin say, "I think I'll try on another color
anyway."*)
"Let me try on another outfit," said the penguin to the storekeeper.
The storekeeper said, "Let's try on this yellow one." (*Place the yellow tux
on the penguin.*)
"Hmmm, not bad," said the penguin. "Hey, kids. Do you think I look
good in yellow?"

(*Shake head so children will respond, "NO!"*)

"Let me try on another outfit," said the penguin to the storekeeper.

The storekeeper said, "Let's try on this green-and-orange-striped one."
(*Place the green tux with orange stripes on the penguin.*)

"Hmmm, not bad," said the penguin. "Hey, kids. Do you think I look
good in green-and-orange stripes?"

(*Shake head so children will respond, "NO!"*)

"Let me try on another outfit," said the penguin to the storekeeper.

The storekeeper said, "Let's try on this plaid one." (*Place the plaid tux on
the penguin.*)

"Hmmm, not bad," said the penguin. "Hey, kids. Do you think I look
good in plaid?"

(*Shake head so children will respond, "NO!"*)

"Let me try on another outfit," said the penguin to the storekeeper.

The storekeeper said, "Let's try on this black one." (*Place the black tux
on the penguin.*)

"Hmmm, not bad," said the penguin. "Hey, kids. Do you think I look
good in black?"

(*If the kids mostly respond with "YES," have the penguin thank the kids. If
the kids respond mostly with "NO," remove the black tux and have the
penguin say, "I guess I'll just go with white."*)

PICTURE BOOK MATCH

Pip the Little Penguin, written by Roger Priddy and illustrated by Lindsey
Sagar (Priddy, 2016).

> Pip the penguin wants to be blue like a whale, green like a crocodile,
> red like a fox, orange like an orangutan, purple like a butterfly, pink
> like a pig, brown like a bear, and yellow like a lion. When he sees a
> black-and-white zebra, a panda, and a skunk, Pip learns "that being
> yourself is the way to be."

"THE PENGUINS ALL MARCH IN A LINE"
Musical/Movement Activity

Sing to the tune of "The Ants Go Marching." Everyone stands and marches around
the room, waddling like penguins.

The penguins all march in a line, hurrah, hurrah,
The penguins all march in a line, hurrah, hurrah,
The penguins all march in a line,
They wave their flippers at the same time, (*Wave hands.*)
Yes, the penguins all march in a line.

PICTURE BOOK MATCH

***Waddle! Waddle!*,** written and illustrated by James Proimos (Scholastic, 2015).

> A penguin is looking for a friend who dances. He waddles around and finds a penguin who sings and one who plays the horn, but no dancer. The penguin sees his reflection and realizes that *he* is the dancing friend.

"THE QUACKER CHOIR"

Musical/Movement Activity

Have the children "quack" to the melody of any popular children's song, such as "Mary Had a Little Lamb" and "Old MacDonald Had a Farm." Instead of singing the words, simply say "quack" for each word. Everyone stands and "waddles" around the story program space like ducks.

PICTURE BOOK MATCH

Monkey and Duck Quack Up!, written by Jennifer Hamburg and illustrated by Edwin Fotheringham (Scholastic, 2015).

> Monkey wants to win a rhyming contest, but his best friend Duck responds to each verse with a "Quack." Monkey cleverly writes a poem with words that rhyme with "Quack."

DINOSAURS AND PREHISTORIC MAMMALS

"IF A DINOSAUR SAYS 'ROAR!'"

Sound Effects Activity

Have the children repeat the lines after you.

Leader: If a dinosaur says, "Roar!"
Audience: If a dinosaur says, "Roar!"
Leader: It really means, "I want more!"
Audience: It really means, "I want more!" (*Make an aside on this last line and say, "More friends, that is . . . ."*)
Leader: If a dinosaur says, "Wobba-wobba-hey!"
Audience: If a dinosaur says, "Wobba-wobba-hey!"
Leader: It really means, "Let's go out and play!"
Audience: It really means, "Let's go out and play!"
Leader: If a dinosaur says, "Boogaloo!"
Audience: If a dinosaur says, "Boogaloo!"
Leader: It really means, "I love you!"
Audience: It really means, "I love you!"
Leader: If a dinosaur says, "Burp!"
Audience: If a dinosaur says, "Burp!"
Leader: Well . . . all it means is "Burp!"
Audience: Well . . . all it means is "Burp!"

PICTURE BOOK MATCH

No Honking Allowed!, written by Stephanie Calmenson and illustrated by AntonGionata Ferrari (Holiday House, 2017).
> Two dinosaurs, Rex and Stego, go for a ride in a red convertible. They hear the "Vroom" of the engine and the "Screeechhh" of the brakes.

"THE SAUROPOD"

Movement Activity

Have the children imitate your motions. Everyone stands.

A sauropod's head, (*Point to head.*)
Is way up high, (*Look upward.*)
It looks to me, (*Point upward.*)
Like it touches the sky.
Its body is big, (*Hold out arms in large semicircle.*)
And it's very strong, (*Make a muscle.*)
And its neck, (*Point to neck.*)
Is very, very, very, very, (*Put hands together and slowly move them apart
    vertically on each "very."*)
Very, very, very, very,
Very, very, very, very,
LONG!

PICTURE BOOK MATCH

Mamasaurus, written and illustrated by Stephan Lomp (Chronicle, 2016).
    Babysaurus slides down his mother's back and lands in a pile of leaves.
    "He could not see his Mamasaurus anywhere." He asks other dinosaurs
    if they have seen his mother. The descriptions of what mothers look like
    are different for each dinosaur.

"THE TRICERATOPS"

Movement Activity

Have the children imitate your motions. Everyone stands.

The three-horned dino is called triceratops, (*Hold up three fingers.*)
It has one horn in the middle, (*Point to your nose.*)
And two more on top, (*Touch two spots on forehead.*)
This dino doesn't flop, (*Sit.*)
This dino doesn't hop, (*Stand and hop.*)
'Cause when it moves around, it goes clippity-clop. (*Gallop around the
    room.*)

PICTURE BOOK MATCH

The Three Triceratops Tuff, written and illustrated by Stephen Shaskan
(Beach Lane, 2013).

> The Tuff brothers, Stanley, Rufus, and Bob, look for some grub. A mean
> Tyrannosaurus rex stands between the brothers and their meal. The two
> younger brothers make it past the T. rex, and Bob sends the bully "clear
> out of the valley," never to be seen again.

"THE WOOLLY MAMMOTH"

Movement Activity

This activity is modeled after the movement activity "An Elephant Goes Like This
and That." Have the children imitate your motions. Everyone stands.

A woolly mammoth goes like this and that, (*Sway back and forth.*)
He's terribly huge, (*Hold arms out to show the size of the mammoth.*)
He's terribly fat, (*Hold hands in front of stomach.*)
Don't mess with Woolly, I hate to harp, (*Shake finger as if scolding.*)
But its tusks are very, very sharp! (*Pull back finger quickly as if poked by
   a tusk.*)

PICTURE BOOK MATCH

How to Wash a Woolly Mammoth, written by Michelle Robinson and illustrated by Kate Hindley (Holt, 2014).

> A girl provides the reader with step-by-step directions on how to wash
> a woolly mammoth, starting with filling the bathtub and adding bubble
> bath. Getting the woolly mammoth into the tub can be tricky, but "when
> all else fails, there is always cake" as a bribe.

FARMS

"A COW HAS A HORN"

Fingerplay

Have the children imitate your motions.

A cow has a horn here, (*Hold up right hand with forefinger in the air.*)
And she has a horn there, (*Hold up pinkie finger. Hold down two middle fingers with thumb to make horns.*)
And in between: some fur. (*Pet the two middle fingers as if petting the cow's head.*)
You need to be careful, (*Shake forefinger of left hand as if warning someone.*)
She doesn't poke you, (*Point the "horns" sideways with a jabbing motion.*)
When you go to milk her. (*Turn right hand so the "horns" are pointing downward and become "udders." Grab them with left hand as if milking the cow.*)

PICTURE BOOK MATCH

That's Not My Cow, written by Fiona Watt and illustrated by Rachel Wells (EDC, 2015).

> This tactile board book informs the reader "that's not my cow. Its ears are too soft." We then feel the cloth ears. We also learn the cow's udder is too smooth, "its horns are too shiny," and "its hooves are too bumpy." We know the right cow when we see and feel its fluffy tail.

"THE FARM ANIMALS INTRODUCE THEMSELVES" ————

Sound Effects Activity

Pause before the last word in each stanza and let the children respond with the animal sounds.

I am a Cow,
Yes, it's true.
I am a Cow,
And I say . . . "Moo!"
I am a Horse,
And that's okay.
I am a Horse,
And I say . . . "Neigh!"
I am a Sheep,
Well, la-de-da.
I am a Sheep,
And I say . . . "Baa!"
I am a Duck,
And that's a fact.
I am a Duck,
And I say . . . "Quack!"
I am a Chicken,
I'm not a Duck.
I am a Chicken,
And I say . . . "Cluck!"

PICTURE BOOK MATCH

Goose on the Farm, written and illustrated by Laura Wall (Harper, 2016).
Goose joins Sophie on a trip to the farm and meets the other animals. The mother hen clucks and chases Goose from her eggs. Pig oinks a greeting and an invitation to play in the mud. Cow moos when Goose bumps into her. Goat leads Goose to the other farm animals where they all make sounds and sing a silly song.

"THE FARM ANIMALS SING OLD MACDONALD" ————

Musical Activity

Sing to the tune of "Old MacDonald Had a Farm." Have the children sing like the different animals.

How would a duck sing "Old MacDonald Had a Farm"?
Quack quack quack quack quack quack quack,
Quack quack quack quack quack.
Quack quack quack quack quack quack quack quack,
Quack quack quack quack quack.
How would a cow sing "Old MacDonald Had a Farm"?
Moo moo moo moo moo moo moo,
Moo moo moo moo moo.
Moo moo moo moo moo moo moo moo,
Moo moo moo moo moo.
How would a pig sing "Old MacDonald Had a Farm"?
Oink oink oink oink oink oink oink,
Oink oink oink oink oink.
Oink oink oink oink oink oink oink oink,
Oink oink oink oink oink.
(*Add new verses with horses singing with "Neigh" sounds, sheep singing with*
"Baa" sounds, and so on.)

PICTURE BOOK MATCH

The Farmer's Away! Baa! Neigh!, written and illustrated by Anne Vittur
Kennedy (Candlewick, 2014).

While the farmer is working in the field, the animals have fun playing
in a creek, having a picnic, going down a roller coaster, water-skiing,
flying in the air, and dancing. Their pleasure is shown entirely through
neighs, baas, quacks, tweets, arfs, oinks, and clucks.

"HAPPY BIRTHDAY IN COW"

Musical Activity

Sing to the tune of "Happy Birthday." Have the children sing like a cow.

How does a cow sing "Happy Birthday"?
Moo moo moo moo to you,
Moo moo moo moo to you,
Moo moo moo moo dear __, (*Pick a name.*)
Moo moo moo moo to you.
(*Add new verses as if other animals were singing "Happy Birthday," such as a snake— "Hiss hiss hiss hiss to you . . ."—and an owl—"Whoo whoo whoo whoo to you . . ."*)

PICTURE BOOK MATCH

Click, Clack, Surprise!, written by Doreen Cronin and illustrated by Betsy Lewin (Atheneum, 2016).
> The farm animals, including the cows, sheep, pigs, chickens, and mice, are all invited to Little Duck's birthday party under the maple tree. Little Duck imitates each animal as they clean themselves.

"THE NOISY FARMHOUSE"

Participation Story

This story is inspired by the folktale known by various titles, such as "Too Much Noise." Have the children imitate your sounds and motions. This adaptation is dedicated to my grandmother Hazel Goff, who ran a farmhouse with four kids, including my mother.

It was very noisy inside Hazel's farmhouse.
Her husband was busy hammering. "Bam! Bam! Bam!" (*Mime hammering while saying, "Bam! Bam! Bam!"*)
Her mother-in-law was busy vacuuming. "Whrr! Whrr! Whrr!" (*Mime using a vacuum cleaner while saying, "Whrr! Whrr! Whrr!"*)
Her four children were busy playing. "Scream! Scream! Scream!" (*Wave arms in the air while shaking head and yelling, "Scream! Scream! Scream!"*)
All Hazel wanted was some peace and quiet.

She occasionally drove into town to the public library to escape the noise.

While there were noises coming from the story room, the library had a "Quiet Area."

Hazel loved reading in the "Quiet Area."

She thought, "Oh, this is so peaceful and quiet."

One day, she was talking to the librarian about her noisy farmhouse.

She told the librarian that she enjoyed being at the library because at home . . .

Her husband was always hammering. "Bam! Bam! Bam!" (*Mime hammering while saying, "Bam! Bam! Bam!"*)

Her mother-in-law was always vacuuming. "Whrr! Whrr! Whrr!" (*Mime using a vacuum cleaner while saying, "Whrr! Whrr! Whrr!"*)

And her four children were always playing. "Scream! Scream! Scream!" (*Wave arms in the air while shaking head and yelling, "Scream! Scream! Scream!"*)

The librarian said, "I think I can help. I remember reading a story that reminds me of your situation."

Hazel was very interested.

The librarian said, "When you go home, bring all of your chickens into the house."

Hazel thought it was a very strange suggestion, but since she had such a high opinion of the librarian, she followed this advice.

Hazel's chickens went, "Cluck! Cluck! Cluck!" (*Mime walking like a chicken while saying, "Cluck! Cluck! Cluck!"*)

Her husband hammered. "Bam! Bam! Bam!" (*Mime hammering while saying, "Bam! Bam! Bam!"*)

Her mother-in-law vacuumed. "Whrr! Whrr! Whrr!" (*Mime using a vacuum cleaner while saying, "Whrr! Whrr! Whrr!"*)

And her four children played. "Scream! Scream! Scream!" (*Wave arms in the air while shaking head and yelling, "Scream! Scream! Scream!"*)

Hazel made another trip to the library. She told the librarian it was noisier than ever at her farmhouse. The librarian said, "When you go home, bring all of your pigs into the house."

Hazel thought it was a very strange suggestion, but since she had such a high opinion of the librarian, she followed this advice.

Hazel's pigs went, "Oink! Oink! Oink! (*Mime rooting like a pig while saying, "Oink! Oink! Oink!"*)

Her chickens went, "Cluck! Cluck! Cluck!" (*Mime walking like a chicken while saying, "Cluck! Cluck! Cluck!"*)

Her husband hammered. "Bam! Bam! Bam!" (*Mime hammering while saying "Bam! Bam! Bam!"*)

Her mother-in-law vacuumed. "Whrr! Whrr! Whrr!" (*Mime using a vacuum cleaner while saying, "Whrr! Whrr! Whrr!"*)

And her four children played. "Scream! Scream! Scream!" (*Wave arms in the air while shaking head and yelling, "Scream! Scream! Scream!"*)

Hazel made another trip to the library. She told the librarian it was noisier than ever at her farmhouse. The librarian said, "When you go home, bring all of your cows into the house."

Hazel thought it was a very strange suggestion, but since she had such a high opinion of the librarian, she followed this advice.

Hazel's cows went, "Moo! Moo! Moo!" (*Mime chewing cud while saying, "Moo! Moo! Moo!"*)

Her pigs went, "Oink! Oink! Oink!" (*Mime rooting like a pig while saying, "Oink! Oink! Oink!"*)

Her chickens went, "Cluck! Cluck! Cluck!" (*Mime walking like a chicken while saying, "Cluck! Cluck! Cluck!"*)

Her husband hammered. "Bam! Bam! Bam!" (*Mime hammering while saying, "Bam! Bam! Bam!"*)

Her mother-in-law vacuumed. "Whrr! Whrr! Whrr!" (*Mime using a vacuum cleaner while saying, "Whrr! Whrr! Whrr!"*)

And her four children played. "Scream! Scream! Scream!" (*Wave arms in the air while shaking head and yelling, "Scream! Scream! Scream!"*)

Hazel made another trip to the library. She told the librarian it was noisier than ever at her farmhouse. The librarian said, "When you go home, bring your rooster into the house."

Hazel thought it was a very strange suggestion, but since she had such a high opinion of the librarian, she followed this advice.

Hazel's rooster went, "Cock-a-Doodle-Doo!" (*Mime strutting like a rooster while saying, "Cock-a-Doodle-Doo!"*)

Her cows went, "Moo! Moo! Moo!" (*Mime chewing cud while saying, "Moo! Moo! Moo!"*)

Her pigs went, "Oink! Oink! Oink!" (*Mime rooting like a pig while saying, "Oink! Oink! Oink!"*)

Her chickens went, "Cluck! Cluck! Cluck!" (*Mime walking like a chicken while saying, "Cluck! Cluck! Cluck!"*)

Her husband hammered. "Bam! Bam! Bam!" (*Mime hammering while saying, "Bam! Bam! Bam!"*)

Her mother-in-law vacuumed. "Whrr! Whrr! Whrr!" (*Mime using a vacuum cleaner while saying, "Whrr! Whrr! Whrr!"*)

And her four children played. "Scream! Scream! Scream!" (*Wave arms in the air while shaking head and yelling, "Scream! Scream! Scream!"*)

Hazel made another trip to the library. She told the librarian it was noisier than ever at her farmhouse.

The librarian said, "When you go home, remove the rooster from your house. (*Mime strutting like a rooster while saying, "Cock-a-Doodle-Doo!"*)

Remove the cows from your house. (*Mime chewing cud while saying, "Moo! Moo! Moo!"*)

Remove the pigs from your house. (*Mime rooting like a pig while saying, "Oink! Oink! Oink!"*)

And remove the chickens from your house." (*Mime walking like a chicken while saying, "Cluck! Cluck! Cluck!"*)

Hazel thought they were very strange suggestions, but remember, she did have a high opinion of the librarian, and she followed this advice.

When she was done, Hazel listened.

She heard her husband hammering. "Bam! Bam! Bam!" (*Mime hammering while saying "Bam! Bam! Bam!"*)

She heard her mother-in-law vacuuming. "Whrr! Whrr! Whrr!" (*Mime using a vacuum cleaner while saying, "Whrr! Whrr! Whrr!"*)

She heard her four children playing. "Scream! Scream! Scream!" (*Wave arms in the air while shaking head and yelling, "Scream! Scream! Scream!"*)

Hazel smiled and thought, "Oh, the farmhouse is so peaceful and quiet."

PICTURE BOOK MATCH

Farmer Falgu Goes on a Trip, written by Chitra Soundar and illustrated by Kanika Nair (Karadi Tales, 2016).

> "Cluck cluck! Moo moo! Woof woof! Quack quack! Farmer Falgu's farm was noisy." He goes on a trip in search of silence. His trip is so noisy that he realizes, "My farm is not noisy. It is happy!"

"OLD MACDONALD HAD AN OWL" ——————————

Musical/Movement Activity

Sing to the tune of "Old MacDonald Had a Farm." Have the children imitate your sounds and motions. Inform them that everything on this farm begins with the letter O.

Old MacDonald had a farm, E-I-E-I-O.
And on this farm, he had an Owl, E-I-E-I-O.
With a "Whoo-Whoo" here and a "Whoo-Whoo" there, (*Flap arms.*)
Here a "Whoo," there a "Whoo," everywhere a "Whoo-Whoo,"
Old MacDonald had an Owl, E-I-E-I-O.
And on this farm, he had an Ogre, E-I-E-I-O.
With an "Aargh-Aargh" here and an "Aargh-Aargh" there, (*Make fierce gestures with hands and fierce expressions.*)
Here an "Aargh," there an "Aargh," everywhere an "Aargh-Aargh,"
Old MacDonald had an Ogre, E-I-E-I-O.
And on this farm, he had an Octopus, E-I-E-I-O.
With a "Hug-Hug" here and a "Hug-Hug" there, (*Hug self.*)
Here a "Hug," there a "Hug," everywhere a "Hug-Hug,"
Old MacDonald had an Octopus, E-I-E-I-O.
And on this farm, he had an Onion, E-I-E-I-O.
With a "Waah-Waah" here and a "Waah-Waah" there, (*Put hands near eyes to mime crying.*)
Here a "Waah," there a "Waah," everywhere a "Waah-Waah,"
Old MacDonald had an Onion, E-I-E-I-O.
And on this farm, he had an Opera, E-I-E-I-O.
With a "Laaa!" here and a "Laaa!" there, (*Hold out arms and belt out a loud "Laaa!"*)
Here a "Laaa!," there a "Laaa!," everywhere a "Laaa!"
Old MacDonald had an Opera, E-I-E-I-O.

PICTURE BOOK MATCH

Señor Pancho Had a Rancho, written by René Colato Laínez and illustrated by Elwood Smith (Holiday House, 2013).

> Señor Pancho is a neighbor to Old MacDonald. On his rancho, he has *un gallo* (rooster), *un perro* (dog), *una oveja* (sheep), *un caballo* (horse), *un pollito* (chick), and *una vaca* (cow). They all dance together with English and Spanish animal sounds.

"OLD MACDONALD HAD A PIG"

Sing to the tune of "Old MacDonald Had a Farm." Ask the children what kinds of noises pigs make. Although many will probably respond with "oink" noises, let them know after the first verse that pigs make other noises as well. Have the children imitate your sounds.

Old MacDonald had a farm, E-I-E-I-O.
And on his farm, he had a pig, E-I-E-I-O.
With an "Oink-Oink" here, and an "Oink-Oink" there,
Here an "Oink," there an "Oink," everywhere an "Oink-Oink,"
Old MacDonald had a farm, E-I-E-I-O.
And on his farm, he had another pig, E-I-E-I-O.
With a "Grunt-Grunt" here, and a "Grunt-Grunt" there,
Here a "Grunt," there a "Grunt," everywhere a "Grunt-Grunt,"
Old MacDonald had a farm, E-I-E-I-O.
And on his farm, he had another pig, E-I-E-I-O.
With a "Squeal-Squeal" here, and a "Squeal-Squeal" there,
Here a "Squeal," there a "Squeal," everywhere a "Squeal-Squeal,"
Old MacDonald had a farm, E-I-E-I-O.
And on his farm, he had another pig, E-I-E-I-O.
With a "Snort-Snort" here, and a "Snort-Snort" there,
Here a "Snort," there a "Snort," everywhere a "Snort-Snort,"
Old MacDonald had a farm, E-I-E-I-O.
(*This idea works with other animals that make a variety of sounds, like
dogs—"Woof," "Bark," "Ruff"—cats—"Meow," "Purr," "Rarrr"—and
frogs—"Croak," "Ribbit."*)

PICTURE BOOK MATCH

Big Pigs, written and illustrated by Leslie Helakoski (Boyds Mills, 2014).
Three young pigs sneak into a garden, gobble a row of vegetables, and sink into the mud to act like big pigs. Mama Pig asks, "Are you the pigs who sneaked into the garden, ate all the food, and dragged half the mudhole into the yard?" and then she congratulates them.

"A PIG IN A POND"

Movement Activity

This activity is modeled after camp activities. Teach the children to stand every time there is a word that begins with the letter P and to sit when followed by another word beginning with P. Say the chant slowly to allow for the constant up-and-down movements. An alternative method is to have the children raise and lower their hands.

A *P*ig in a *P*ond,
A *P*ig in a *P*ond,
How *P*reposterous to have,
A *P*ig in a *P*ond.
A *P*ython, a *P*ossum, or *P*uffin *P*erhaps?
A *P*eacock? A *P*enguin? A *P*ronghorn? No chance!
But a *P*ig in a *P*ond,
A *P*ig in a *P*ond,
I'm tickled *P*ink to think,
Of a *P*ig in a *P*ond.

PICTURE BOOK MATCH

Ribbit!, written by Rodrigo Folgueira and illustrated by Poly Bernatene (Knopf, 2012).

> A pink pig shows up at the frog pond and says, "Ribbit!" The frogs are confused, and the other animals find the whole situation amusing. The next time we see the pig, he is in a tree with birds and is singing, "Tweet!"

"P-O-R-K-Y"

Musical Activity

Sing to the tune of "Bingo." As you and the children sing each stanza, replace a letter with an "oink" sound.

There was a farmer had a pig and Porky was its name-o,
P-O-R-K-Y, P-O-R-K-Y, P-O-R-K-Y, and Porky was its name-o.
There was a farmer had a pig and Porky was its name-o,
(*Oink!*)-O-R-K-Y, (*Oink!*)-O-R-K-Y, (*Oink!*)-O-R-K-Y, and Porky was its name-o.

There was a farmer had a pig and Porky was its name-o,
(*Oink! Oink!*)-R-K-Y, (*Oink! Oink!*)-R-K-Y, (*Oink! Oink!*)-R-K-Y, and
    Porky was its name-o.
There was a farmer had a pig and Porky was its name-o,
(*Oink! Oink! Oink!*)-K-Y, (*Oink! Oink! Oink!*)-K-Y, (*Oink! Oink! Oink!*)-
    K-Y, and Porky was its name-o.
There was a farmer had a pig and Porky was its name-o,
(*Oink! Oink! Oink! Oink!*)-Y, (*Oink! Oink! Oink! Oink!*)-Y, (*Oink! Oink!*
    Oink! Oink!)-Y, and Porky was its name-o.
There was a farmer had a pig and Porky was its name-o,
(*Oink! Oink! Oink! Oink! Oink!*), (*Oink! Oink! Oink! Oink! Oink!*),
(*Oink! Oink! Oink! Oink! Oink!*),
And Porky was its name-o.

PICTURE BOOK MATCH

Is That Wise, Pig?, written and illustrated by Jan Thomas (Beach Lane, 2016).
    When Mouse makes soup, Pig wants to add umbrellas and galoshes.
    Mouse and Cow repeatedly ask, "Is that wise, Pig?" Pig eventually adds
    nine carrots but also invites ten hungry pig friends.

"TEN IN THE FIELD"

Musical Activity

Sing to the tune of "Ten in the Bed." Have the children imitate your motions.

There were ten in the field and the farmer called out, "Moo-ve over!"
    (*Hold up ten fingers.*)
They all moved over, one went into the barn,
There were nine in the field and the farmer called out, "Moo-ve over!"
    (*Hold up nine fingers.*)
They all moved over, one went into the barn,
There were eight in the field and the farmer called out, "Moo-ve over!"
    (*Hold up eight fingers.*)
They all moved over, one went into the barn,
There were seven in the field and the farmer called out, "Moo-ve over!"
    (*Hold up seven fingers.*)
They all moved over, one went into the barn,

There were six in the field and the farmer called out, "Moo-ve over!"
   (*Hold up six fingers.*)
They all moved over, one went into the barn,
There were five in the field and the farmer called out, "Moo-ve over!"
   (*Hold up five fingers.*)
They all moved over, one went into the barn,
There were four in the field and the farmer called out, "Moo-ve over!"
   (*Hold up four fingers.*)
They all moved over, one went into the barn,
There were three in the field and the farmer called out, "Moo-ve over!"
   (*Hold up three fingers.*)
They all moved over, one went into the barn,
There were two in the field and the farmer called out, "Moo-ve over!"
   (*Hold up two fingers.*)
They all moved over, one went into the barn,
There was one in the field and the farmer called out, "Moo-ve over!"
   (*Hold up one finger.*)
So that one moved over, she went into the barn,
There were none in the field and the farmer called out, (*Cup hands to mouth.*)
"Moo-vie Time!"

PICTURE BOOK MATCH

In, Over and On the Farm, written and illustrated by Ethan Long (G. P.
   Putnam's Sons, 2015).
      Cow, Pig, Hen, and Goat climb *in* and *out* of the chicken coop. The goat
      shows the hen how to jump *over* a fence. Finally, the animals demonstrate
      that they are *on* the tractor, until they are *off* and land in a mud puddle.

"TRIP-TRAP, TRIP-TRAP, WHO'S THAT?" ——————

Movement Activity

Have the children imagine they are trolls waiting under a bridge like in the story
"The Three Billy Goats Gruff." Teach them to say, "Trip-trap, trip-trap, who's that?"
They can then shout out the answer to the leader's riddles.

All: Trip-trap, trip-trap, (*Slap legs.*)
Who's that? (*Cup hand by ear.*)

Leader: It has horns, gives milk, and moos.
Kids: A cow!
All: Trip-trap, trip-trap, (*Slap legs.*)
Who's that? (*Cup hand by ear.*)
Leader: It is one of the tallest animals on a farm and can gallop.
Kids: A horse!
All: Trip-trap, trip-trap, (*Slap legs.*)
Who's that? (*Cup hand by ear.*)
Leader: It goes "oink-oink."
Kids: A pig!
All: Trip-trap, trip-trap, (*Slap legs.*)
Who's that? (*Cup hand by ear.*)
Leader: It goes "cluck-cluck."
Kids: A chicken!
All: Trip-trap, trip-trap, (*Slap legs.*)
Who's that? (*Cup hand by ear.*)
Leader: It flies and quacks.
Kids: A duck!
All: Trip-trap, trip-trap, (*Slap legs.*)
Who's that? (*Cup hand by ear.*)
Leader: It has horns and stars in the story "The Three Billy Goats Gruff."
Kids: A goat!

PICTURE BOOK MATCH

What Is Chasing Duck?, written and illustrated by Jan Thomas (Houghton Mifflin Harcourt, 2017).
> Something is chasing Duck. Sheep is nervous about what it could be and runs behind Duck. They are joined by Donkey and Dog. They find out that Squirrel was running after Duck to give him a turnip.

"WHO EATS CORN?"

Sound Effects Activity

Have the children respond with the correct animal sound.

Leader: Who eats corn? Horses eat corn!
How does a horse say, "Yum! Yum!"?
Audience: "Neigh! Neigh!"

Leader: Who eats corn? Cows eat corn!
How does a cow say, "Yum! Yum!"?
Audience: "Moo! Moo!"
Leader: Who eats corn? Pigs eat corn!
How does a pig say, "Yum! Yum!"?
Audience: "Oink! Oink!"
Leader: Who eats corn? Goats eat corn!
How does a goat say, "Yum! Yum!"?
Audience: "Maa! Maa!"
Leader: Who eats corn? Chickens eat corn!
How does a chicken say, "Yum! Yum!"?
Audience: "Cluck! Cluck!"
Leader: Who eats corn? Geese eat corn!
How does a goose say, "Yum! Yum!"?
Audience: "Honk! Honk!"
Leader: Who eats corn? People eat corn!
How does a person say, "Yum! Yum!"?
Audience: "Yum! Yum!"

PICTURE BOOK MATCH

Anywhere Farm, written by Phyllis Root and illustrated by G. Brian Karas
(Candlewick, 2017).
You can plant a seed anywhere. "Here's all that you need: soil, and
sunshine, some water, a seed." You can plant "corn in a horn" or "kale
in a pail." Pretty soon, the anywhere farm is everywhere.

INSECTS AND SPIDERS

"A FLY IS BUZZING 'ROUND MY HEAD"

Movement Activity

Have the children imitate your motions. Everyone stands.

A fly is buzzing 'round my toes, (*Wave hands around toes.*)
'Round my toes, 'round my toes,
A fly is buzzing 'round my toes,
And I can't catch it!
A fly is buzzing 'round my knees, (*Wave hands around knees.*)
'Round my knees, 'round my knees,
A fly is buzzing 'round my knees,
And I can't catch it!
A fly is buzzing 'round my tummy, (*Wave hands around tummy.*)
'Round my tummy, 'round my tummy,
A fly is buzzing 'round my tummy,
And I can't catch it!
A fly is buzzing 'round my neck, (*Wave hands around neck.*)
'Round my neck, 'round my neck,
A fly is buzzing 'round my neck,
And I can't catch it!
A fly is buzzing 'round my head, (*Wave hands around head.*)
'Round my head, 'round my head,
A fly is buzzing 'round my head,
And I can't catch it!
A fly is buzzing 'round my mouth, (*Wave hands around mouth.*)
'Round my mouth, 'round my mouth,
A fly is buzzing 'round my mouth,
Gulp! Caught it! (*Make an exaggerated gulp and smile.*)

The House That Zack Built, written and illustrated by Alison Murray (Candlewick, 2016).

> Zack is making a house out of wooden blocks at his farm. A fly makes a buzzing noise as it goes by. A chain reaction starts with a cat chasing the fly and involves a cow, a dog, and some lambs. Zack fixes the mess, takes a deep breath, and blows the fly away.

"THE MOSQUITO WAVE"

Movement Activity

Lead the audience in a cheer, as if at a sporting event.

Leader: Give me an M!
Audience: M!
Leader: Give me an O!
Audience: O!
Leader: Give me an S!
Audience: S!
Leader: Give me a Q!
Audience: Q!
Leader: Give me a U!
Audience: U!
Leader: Give me an I!
Audience: I!
Leader: Give me a T!
Audience: T!
Leader: Give me an O!
Audience: O!
Leader: What does it spell?
Audience: MOSQUITO!
Leader: What does it spell?
Audience: MOSQUITO!!
Leader: What does it spell?
Audience: MOSQUITO!!! (*Have everyone scream and wave their hands frantically as if waving away a pesky mosquito.*)

Mosquitoes Can't Bite Ninjas, written and illustrated by Jordan P. Novak (Bloomsbury, 2017).

> Mosquitoes bite swimmers, chefs, "old ladies with blue hair," and babies. But mosquitoes are not sneaky enough nor are they quick enough to bite ninjas. Sometimes, a ninja will bite a mosquito.

"SPIDER HERE, SPIDER THERE"

Movement Activity

Have children hold up one hand and wiggle their fingers to represent the spider. Have them imitate your motions. Everyone stands.

Spider here, (*Place hand on one shoulder.*)
Spider there, (*Place hand on other shoulder.*)
This little spider, (*Hold hand out front.*)
Is everywhere. (*Place hand all over body rapidly.*)
He's on my knee, (*Hand on knee.*)
He's on my toes, (*Hand on toes.*)
He's on my belly, (*Hand on belly.*)
He's on my nose. (*Hand on nose.*)
He's on my head, (*Hand on top of head.*)
But then he fled, (*Hold out arm and point toward door.*)
I bet he's off, (*Hand over eyes peering in the distance.*)
To spin his web. (*Wiggle fingers on both hands and wave hands around each other.*)

Walter's Wonderful Web, written and illustrated by Tim Hopgood (Farrar, Straus and Giroux, 2016).

> Walter the spider makes wibbly-wobbly webs that blow away in the wind. A determined Walter "makes a small web in the shape of a triangle." He battles the wind and makes webs in the shape of a square, a rectangle, a diamond, and, finally, a circle.

"TEN LITTLE FIREFLIES" ——————————————————————

Fingerplay

Have the children imitate your motions.

Ten little fireflies, (*Wiggle all ten fingers.*)
Shimmering oh so bright,
Two opened their wings, (*Wiggle both thumbs.*)
And flew flickering in the night. (*Tuck thumbs into palms.*)
Eight little fireflies, (*Wiggle eight fingers.*)
Shimmering oh so bright,
Two opened their wings, (*Wiggle both pinkie fingers.*)
And flew flickering in the night. (*Hold pinkie fingers with thumbs. The
    other six fingers are upright.*)
Six little fireflies, (*Wiggle all six fingers.*)
Shimmering oh so bright,
Two opened their wings, (*Wiggle both ring fingers.*)
And flew flickering in the night. (*Hold pinkie fingers and ring fingers with
    thumbs. The other four fingers are upright.*)
Four little fireflies, (*Wiggle all four fingers.*)
Shimmering oh so bright,
Two opened their wings, (*Wiggle both middle fingers.*)
And flew flickering in the night. (*Hold all fingers except pointer fingers
    with thumbs. The pointer fingers are upright.*)
Two little fireflies, (*Wiggle both fingers.*)
Shimmering oh so bright,
They opened their wings, (*Continue wiggling both fingers.*)
And flew flickering in the night. (*Make two fists.*)
No little fireflies, (*Look at hands and shake head.*)
Shimmering oh so bright,
It's time to go to bed,
And sleep all night. (*Put palms together and rest head on them as if
    sleeping.*)

PICTURE BOOK MATCH

Lucy's Light, written by Margarita del Mazo and illustrated by Silvia Álva-
    rez (Cuento de Luz SL, 2015).
    A tiny firefly named Lucy is anxious about joining her family on their

nighttime journey to the forest. Grandma Firefly informs Lucy that the big light in the sky is the moon. Lucy learns that "my light is important."

"THIS FUNNY BUG" ————————————————————

Movement Activity

Everyone stands. Have the children bend over and point as if seeing something tiny on the ground.

This funny bug,
Is a teeny-tiny bug,
I'll give it some food,
And a great big hug.
Fun!
This funny bug, (*Straighten up just a little, look straight ahead, and point.*)
Is a medium-sized bug,
I'll give it some food,
And a great big hug.
Fun!
This funny bug, (*Have everyone look slightly higher and point.*)
Is a great big bug,
I'll give it some food,
And a great big hug.
Fun!
This scary bug, (*Look straight up overhead and point.*)
Is a HUGE GIGANTIC BUG!
I won't give it food,
And I won't give a hug!
Run! (*Run in place.*)

PICTURE BOOK MATCH

Bring Me a Rock!, written and illustrated by Daniel Miyares (Simon and Schuster, 2016).

A grasshopper demands that the other insects bring him a big rock for his "majestic pedestal." When the towering throne starts to fall, a little bug supports the structure with its puny pebble. In the end, all the insects get thrones the same size as each other's.

INTO THE WOODS

"BABY BEAR ROARS"

Musical Activity

Sing to the tune of "Mary Had a Little Lamb." Have the children imitate the sounds after you.

Baby bears make quiet roars, quiet roars, quiet roars,
Baby bears make quiet roars,
Let's hear your bear cub roar. (*Make a quiet roaring noise.*)
But when they grow, they roar real loud, roar real loud, roar real loud,
When they grow, they roar real loud,
Let's hear your great big roar. (*Make a loud roar.*)

PICTURE BOOK MATCH

The Hide-and-Scare Bear, written and illustrated by Ivan Bates (Templar, 2016).
A bear likes to play a game he calls hide and scare. He surprises the
other forest animals with a loud "ROAR" and laughs as they run away.
A rabbit teaches the bear to be kind.

"THE BEAR CUBS' HUNT"

Movement/Sound Effects Activity

This movement activity is based on the popular story program activity "We're Going on a Bear Hunt." This version is done from the bear cubs' perspectives. Have the children slap their legs as if walking through the woods and imitate all other motions.

Chorus:
We're going on a bear hunt, (*Slap legs.*)
Gonna have a lot of fun,
What a big adventure,
C'mon everyone.

'Bye warm cave. (*Stop slapping legs and wave.*)
Through tall grass. (*Move hands as if parting tall grass.*)
Swish-swish, swish-swish.

Chorus:
We're going on a bear hunt, (*Slap legs.*)
Gonna have a lot of fun,
What a big adventure,
C'mon everyone.

Into the stream. It's very wet. (*Stop slapping legs and mime swimming.*)
Splash-splash, splash-splash.

Chorus:
We're going on a bear hunt, (*Slap legs.*)
Gonna have a lot of fun,
What a big adventure,
C'mon everyone.

Hollow log. Grubs inside. (*Stop slapping legs, crouch, and pretend to crawl.*)
Crawl-crawl, crawl-crawl.

Chorus:
We're going on a bear hunt, (*Slap legs.*)
Gonna have a lot of fun,
What a big adventure,
C'mon everyone.

Up a tree. What can we see? (*Stop slapping legs and mime climbing up a tree.*)
Climb-climb, climb-climb.
What's that smell? (*Sniff.*)
It sure smells good.
Down we go. (*Mime climbing down a tree.*)
There's some food. Let's go eat. (*Point.*)
Wait. What's that?
Two legs, two arms, a face.
People! (*Shout.*)
Run! (*Slap legs quickly.*)

Through the log. Crawl-crawl-crawl. (*Mime crawling.*)
Across the stream. Swim-swim-swim. (*Mime swimming.*)
Through the grass. Swish-swish-swish. (*Mime parting the grass.*)
Almost there. (*Slap legs quickly.*)
Back in the cave. Safe at last. (*Take a deep breath and wipe brow.*)
We went on a bear hunt.
What a big adventure.

PICTURE BOOK MATCH

A Brave Bear, written by Sean Taylor and illustrated by Emily Hughes
(Candlewick, 2016).
> One hot day, a bear cub and his father head for the river. On the way,
> they go through tall grass, jump across rocks, and cross a log. When the
> cub falls, the father bear encourages the little one.

"FIVE LITTLE QUIET RACCOONS" ————————————

Fingerplay

Have the children imitate your motions.

Five little quiet raccoons, (*Hold up five fingers.*)
Sneaking 'round all day,
One grabbed my favorite hat, (*Grab imaginary hat off head.*)
And then it ran away!
Four little quiet raccoons, (*Hold up four fingers.*)
Sneaking 'round all day,
One grabbed my favorite bear, (*Make a grabbing motion.*)
And then it ran away!
Three little quiet raccoons, (*Hold up three fingers.*)
Sneaking 'round all day,
One grabbed my favorite ball, (*Make a grabbing motion.*)
And then it ran away!
Two little quiet raccoons, (*Hold up two fingers.*)
Sneaking 'round all day,
One grabbed my favorite book, (*Make a grabbing motion.*)
And then it ran away!
One little quiet raccoon, (*Hold up one finger.*)

Saw what went on that day,
Showed me where the others hid, (*Point.*)
I got everything back today! (*Hold hands up in the air in celebration.*)

Secret Pizza Party, written by Adam Rubin and illustrated by Daniel Salm-
ieri (Dial, 2013).

> A pizza-loving raccoon sneaks around, trying to throw a secret pizza party
> where he'd be the guest of honor. He dresses up like a human, goes into
> Uncle Mark's Pizza Parlor, and makes it back home with a pizza. That's
> when he notices several humans throwing their own secret pizza party.

"I WAS WALKING IN THE WOODS"

Fingerplay/Sound Effects Activity

Have the children imitate your motions. Pause at the end of each stanza to allow
the children to make the appropriate animal noises.

I was walking in the woods when I saw ten wolves, (*Hold up ten fingers.*)
Ten wolves I saw and this is what they said: "Howl!"
I was walking in the woods when I saw nine bears, (*Hold up nine fingers.*)
Nine bears I saw and this is what they said: "Grrr!"
I was walking in the woods when I saw eight turkeys, (*Hold up eight
    fingers.*)
Eight turkeys I saw and this is what they said: "Gobble-gobble!"
I was walking in the woods when I saw seven owls, (*Hold up seven fingers.*)
Seven owls I saw and this is what they said: "Hoot-hoot!"
I was walking in the woods when I saw six bobcats, (*Hold up six fingers.*)
Six bobcats I saw and this is what they said: "Ree-ow!"
I was walking in the woods when I saw five eagles, (*Hold up five fingers.*)
Five eagles I saw and this is what they said: "Screech!"
I was walking in the woods when I saw four crows, (*Hold up four fingers.*)
Four crows I saw and this is what they said: "Caw-caw!"
I was walking in the woods when I saw three moose, (*Hold up three fingers.*)
Three moose I saw and this is what they said: "Maa-aaa!"

I was walking in the woods when I saw two mice, (*Hold up two fingers.*)
Two mice I saw and this is what they said: "Squeak!"
I was walking in the woods when I saw one skunk, (*Hold up one finger.*)
One skunk I saw and this is what *I* said: "Run!"

PICTURE BOOK MATCH

Jo MacDonald Hiked in the Woods, written by Mary Quattlebaum and
   illustrated by Laura J. Bryant (Dawn, 2013).
      Jo hikes in the woods with her grandfather. They hear a woodpecker
      "with a rat-tat here and a rat-tat there." She even hears a skunk "with
      a pad-pad here and a pad-pad there."

"MY BUNNY HOPS INTO ITS BURROW" ————————————
Musical/Movement Activity

This activity is modeled after the musical camp adaptation of "My Bonnie Lies Over
the Ocean." Teach the children to stand every time there is a word that begins with
the letter B and to sit when followed by another word beginning with B. Say the
chant slowly to allow for the constant up-and-down movements. An alternative
method is to have the children raise and lower their hands.

My bunny hops into its burrow,
My bunny hops wild and free,
My bunny hops into its burrow,
Oh, bring back my bunny to me.
Bring back, bring back, oh, bring back my bunny to me, to me,
Bring back, bring back, oh, bring back my bunny to me.

PICTURE BOOK MATCH

Hop, written and illustrated by Jorey Hurley (Simon and Schuster, 2016).
      Bunnies not only hop, but they listen as well. They follow each other,
      nibble, graze, and play. When danger is near, they freeze, run, warn,
      and hide. They also jump, snuggle, and finally sleep.

"OVER IN THE FOREST"

Musical/Movement Activity

Sing to the tune of "Over in the Meadow." Have the children imitate your sounds and motions. Everyone stands.

Over in the forest underneath a tall tree,
Was a mama black bear and her little cubbies three.
"Growl!" said the mama,
"We'll growl!" said the three,
And they growled and were glad underneath that tall tree. (*Growl.*)
Over in the forest halfway up that tall tree,
Was a mama woodpecker and her little fledglings three.
"Hammer!" said the mama,
"We'll hammer!" said the three,
And they hammered and were glad halfway up that tall tree. (*Mime
    hammering by touching nose to palm of hand and moving head back
    and forth.*)
Over in the forest near the top of that tree,
Was a mama flying squirrel and her little squirrels three.
"Soar!" said the mama,
"We'll soar!" said the three,
And they soared and were glad near the top of that tree. (*Hold out arms
    and twirl.*)

PICTURE BOOK MATCH

Side by Side, written by Rachel Bright and illustrated by Debi Gliori (Scho-
    lastic, 2015).
    Little Mouseling has a big heart but often finds herself alone. She encoun-
    ters several woodland creatures while searching for a new friend.

"A RABBIT"

Movement Activity

Have the children imitate your motions. Everyone stands.

A rabbit has two long ears, (*Hold up two fingers behind your head for
    bunny ears.*)
A rabbit has a wiggly nose, (*Wiggle your nose.*)

A rabbit has a bushy tail, (*Tap your backside.*)
That shakes wherever he goes. (*Shake bottom.*)

The Wonderful Habits of Rabbits, written by Douglas Florian and illustrated by Sonia Sanchez (Little Bee, 2016).

> There are many things rabbits like to do. They leap, dig holes, smell flowers, and are good at "finding lost things that were buried for years." Rabbits especially have the best hops.

"THE RACCOONS' HUNT"

Movement/Sound Effects Activity

This activity is modeled after the traditional movement activity "We're Going on a Bear Hunt." Have the children slap their legs to simulate walking, repeat the lines after you, and imitate your motions. Inform the children that they are raccoons.

Leader: We're going on a hunt for food.
Audience: We're going on a hunt for food.
Leader: We're creeping past a human's house.
Audience: We're creeping past a human's house.
Leader: Ssshhh! (*Stop slapping legs and make a shushing noise with finger to lips.*)
Audience: Ssshhh!
Leader: We need to be quiet.
Audience: We need to be quiet.
Leader: What's that? (*Cup ear with hand.*)
Audience: What's that?
Leader: Bark! Bark! Bark! Bark! Bark! Bark!
Audience: Bark! Bark! Bark! Bark! Bark! Bark!
Leader: Oh no! A dog!
Audience: Oh no! A dog!
Leader: Run away! (*Slap legs quickly.*)
Audience: Run away!
Leader: Whew, that was TOO close. (*Stop slapping legs and wipe brow.*)
Audience: Whew, that was TOO close.
Leader: Let's try again.
Audience: Let's try again.

Leader: We're going on a hunt for food. (*Slap legs.*)

Audience: We're going on a hunt for food.

Leader: We're creeping past a human's house.

Audience: We're creeping past a human's house.

Leader: Ssshhh! (*Stop slapping legs and make a shushing noise with finger to lips.*)

Audience: Ssshhh!

Leader: We need to be quiet.

Audience: We need to be quiet.

Leader: What's that? (*Cup ear with hand.*)

Audience: What's that?

Leader: Honk! Honk! Honk! Honk! Honk! Honk!

Audience: Honk! Honk! Honk! Honk! Honk! Honk!

Leader: Oh no! A car!

Audience: Oh no! A car!

Leader: Run away! (*Slap legs quickly.*)

Audience: Run away!

Leader: Whew, that was TOO close. (*Stop slapping legs and wipe brow.*)

Audience: Whew, that was TOO close.

Leader: Let's try again.

Audience: Let's try again.

Leader: We're going on a hunt for food. (*Slap legs.*)

Audience: We're going on a hunt for food.

Leader: We're creeping past a human's house.

Audience: We're creeping past a human's house.

Leader: Ssshhh! (*Stop slapping legs and make a shushing noise with finger to lips.*)

Audience: Ssshhh!

Leader: We need to be quiet.

Audience: We need to be quiet.

Leader: What's that? (*Cup ear with hand.*)

Audience: What's that?

Leader: Hey, it's a trash can!

Audience: Hey, it's a trash can!

Leader: Oops, oops, we knocked it over!

Audience: Oops, oops, we knocked it over!

Leader: Crash! Crash! Rattle! Bang!

Audience: Crash! Crash! Rattle! Bang!

Leader: Oh well. (*Shrug shoulders.*)
Audience: Oh well.
Leader: Let's eat!
Audience: Let's eat!
Leader: Please pass the fish heads.
Audience: Please pass the fish heads.
Leader: Yum! Yum! (*Mime eating.*)
Audience: Yum! Yum!

PICTURE BOOK MATCH

Hungry Roscoe, written and illustrated by David J. Plant (Flying Eye, 2015).
Roscoe discovers that the local zoo has plenty of food. The zookeeper
has his eye out for Roscoe and chases him away. The young raccoon
finally earns the friendship of the zookeeper after a tricky encounter
with several monkeys.

"THERE MAY BE WILDLIFE NEAR"
Sound Effects Activity

Tell the children you are all going to take a pretend walk in the North American
woods. Pause after each "I hear a" line and let the audience respond with the
correct answer.

Look around,
What do you see?
There may be wildlife near.
I don't see anything,
But this is what I hear—"Rib-it!"
I hear a: Frog!
Look around,
What do you see?
There may be wildlife near.
I don't see anything,
But this is what I hear—"Caw!"
I hear a: Crow!
Look around,
What do you see?

There may be wildlife near.
I don't see anything,
But this is what I hear—"Howl!"
I hear a: Wolf!
Look around,
What do you see?
There may be wildlife near.
I don't see anything,
But this is what I hear—"Roar!"
I hear a: Bear!
Look around,
What do you see?
There may be wildlife near.
I don't see anything,
But this is what I hear—"Whoo-whoo!"
I hear an: Owl!

PICTURE BOOK MATCH

Hoot and Peep, written and illustrated by Lita Judge (Dial, 2016).
> Older brother Hoot knows everything there is about being an owl. He tries to impart his wisdom to his little sister Peep. However, when he teaches her to go "Hooo," Peep goes "Schweeepty peep!"

"THERE WERE TEN BUNNIES HOPPING" ————————

Fingerplay

Have a volunteer come to the front and hold up ten fingers. Have the volunteer move her or his fingers up and down as if they are bunnies hopping. Everyone else can do the same from their seats.

There were ten bunnies hopping,
Hopping all around.
There were ten bunnies hopping,
Hopping safe and sound.
(*Have a second volunteer come to the front and join the first.*)
There were twenty bunnies hopping,
Hopping all around.

There were twenty bunnies hopping,
Hopping safe and sound.
(*Have a third volunteer come to the front and join the other two.*)
There were thirty bunnies hopping,
Hopping all around.
There were thirty bunnies hopping,
Hopping safe and sound.
(*Have all the other children stand and recite the following verse.*)
There were MANY bunnies hopping,
Hopping all around.
There were MANY bunnies hopping,
Hopping safe and sound.

PICTURE BOOK MATCH

Bunny Dreams, written and illustrated by Peter McCarty (Holt, 2016).
   Several bunnies hop all around. They know how to eat vegetables and
   how to run from the farmer's dog. They snuggle down into tunnels
   underground and dream wild dreams.

"THREE LITTLE SMELLY SKUNKS" ───────────────────

Fingerplay

Have the children imitate your motions.

Three little smelly skunks, (*Hold up three fingers.*)
Sleeping in their smelly bunks, (*Lay head on hands.*)
Didn't hear an owl sneak in. (*Point to ear and then flap arms like wings.*)
A "Whoo-whoo" woke them quick as a wink! (*Look surprised.*)
One forgot to spray its stink, (*Point to head and then hold nose.*)
Now there are two smelly skunks. (*Hold up two fingers.*)
Two little smelly skunks, (*Hold up two fingers.*)
Sleeping in their smelly bunks, (*Lay head on hands.*)
Didn't hear a human sneak in. (*Point to ear.*)
A "Gotcha" woke them quick as a wink! (*Look surprised.*)
One forgot to spray its stink, (*Point to head and then hold nose.*)
Now there is one smelly skunk. (*Hold up one finger.*)
One little smelly skunk, (*Hold up one finger.*)

Sleeping in its smelly bunk, (*Lay head on hands.*)
Didn't hear a dog sneak in. (*Point to ear.*)
A "Woof-woof" woke it quick as a wink! (*Look surprised.*)
It remembered to spray its stink, (*Point to head, nod head, and then hold nose.*)
Now there is one smelly dog. (*Howl like a dog.*)

PICTURE BOOK MATCH

Who Wants a Hug?, written and illustrated by Jeff Mack (Harper, 2015). Skunk tries to make Bear smell bad with a rotten mackerel, a bag of garbage, and a stinky balloon. Skunk's plans backfire, and he smells even worse than ever.

"WE'RE GOING TO EXPLORE A CAVE"

Movement Activity

This activity is modeled after the traditional movement activity "We're Going on a Bear Hunt." Have the children slap their legs to simulate walking, repeat the lines after you, and imitate your motions. Everyone stands.

Chorus:
We're going to explore a cave today.
We're going to explore a cave.
Let's go!

It's dark in here. (*Stop slapping legs.*)
Turn on your lights. (*Mime turning on headlamps.*)

Chorus:
We're going to explore a cave today. (*Slap legs.*)
We're going to explore a cave.
Let's go!

Careful! Tight squeeze. Go sideways. (*Stop slapping legs, turn sideways, and shuffle a few feet to mime squeezing though a narrow passage.*)

Chorus:
We're going to explore a cave today. (*Slap legs.*)
We're going to explore a cave.
Let's go!
Look there! Underground pond. Let's swim. (*Stop slapping legs and make swimming motions for a few seconds.*)

Chorus:
We're going to explore a cave today. (*Slap legs.*)
We're going to explore a cave.
Let's go!

Watch out! Low ceiling. Watch your head. (*Stop slapping legs, get down on hands and knees, and crawl around for a few seconds. Then stand.*)

Chorus:
We're going to explore a cave today. (*Slap legs.*)
We're going to explore a cave.
Let's go!

Wow! A big room. Look around. (*Stop slapping legs and point upward.*)
Wait! What's that flapping sound? (*Hold hand to ear.*)
Bats! (*Make a frightened face and swat the air overhead.*)
Let's get out of here! (*Slap legs.*)
Low ceiling! (*Stop slapping legs and crawl.*)
Underground pond! (*Stand and mime swimming.*)
Tight squeeze! (*Shuffle sideways and then slap legs.*)
We're out of the cave! (*Stop slapping legs.*)
Turn off your lights. (*Mime turning off lights.*)
Look! The bats followed us! (*Point.*)
They're catching bugs.
'Bye bats. (*Wave.*)
'Bye cave. (*Continue waving.*)
We explored a cave today,
We explored a cave.
Whew! (*Wipe forehead.*)

PICTURE BOOK MATCH

A Dark, Dark Cave, written by Eric Hoffman and illustrated by Corey R.
Tabor (Viking, 2016).

Two imaginative kids explore a cave. "Bats in flight disappear from
sight." The cave turns out to be blankets covering chairs in the children's
bedroom.

"WE'RE TAKING A WALK IN THE WOODS"

Musical/Movement Activity

Sing to the tune of "The Bear Went Over the Mountain." Have the children walk in a
circle or, if there is not enough room, walk in place. Have them imitate your motions.

We're taking a walk in the woods,
We're taking a walk in the woods,
We're taking a walk in the woods,
On this gorgeous day.
We're taking a hop in the woods, (*Hop.*)
We're taking a hop in the woods,
We're taking a hop in the woods,
On this gorgeous day.
We're doing a dance in the woods, (*Dance.*)
We're doing a dance in the woods,
We're doing a dance in the woods,
On this gorgeous day.
We're taking a jog in the woods, (*Jog.*)
We're taking a jog in the woods,
We're taking a jog in the woods,
On this gorgeous day.
We're scaring all the wildlife, (*Look around and point.*)
We're scaring all the wildlife,
We're scaring all the wildlife,
By hopping, (*Hop.*)
Dancing, (*Dance.*)
And jogging (*Jog.*)
In the woods.

(*Spoken:*) Oh dear, I'm sorry we scared them. I hope the wildlife come
   back.
(*Whisper.*)
We're taking a walk in the woods, (*Walk.*)
We're taking a walk in the woods,
We're taking a walk in the woods,
On this gorgeous day.

PICTURE BOOK MATCH

All Ears, All Eyes, written by Richard Jackson and illustrated by Katherine
   Tillotson (Atheneum, 2017).
   > An owl goes "hoot" as the light in the forest dims. A porcupine "scoots
   > between roots." Bats whirl around. Other woodland creatures settle in
   > for the evening.

"WHAT DID I SEE AT THE POND?"

Movement Activity

Everyone stands. Have the children imitate your motions and walk on tiptoes as
you recite the words.

As quiet, as quiet, as quiet as I could be,
I went to the pond and what did I see?
I saw lots of wildlife but then—they saw me!
The frogs jumped into the water! (*Jump.*)
The turtles fell into the water! (*Get down on all fours and fall on side.*)
The beaver slapped the water with his tail! (*Slap the floor behind you.*)
The fish darted under the surface of the water! (*Hold palms together,
   move hands quickly.*)
The ducks flew into the air! (*Flap arms and stand. Move around as if
   flying and then pause before the next line.*)
The pond was empty, as empty as could be.
But I sat very quietly and what did I see?
One by one, the wildlife returned to me.
The frog jumped back on the lily pad! (*Jump.*)
The turtles climbed up on a log! (*Get down on the floor and mime climbing.*)

The beaver began to chew on a stick! (*Hold hands up to mouth and make chewing motions.*)

The fish swam slowly once more! (*Palms together, move hands slowly.*)

And the ducks flew back! (*Stand up, "fly" around, and sit.*)

PICTURE BOOK MATCH

On Duck Pond, written by Jane Yolen and illustrated by Bob Marstall (Cornell Lab, 2017).

> The quiet of the pond is "shattered by a raucous call" as several ducks arrive, splash, chitter, and chatter. Fish, turtles, and frogs are upset by the commotion. Once the ducks move on, "the pond grew mirrored, still," and the other wild things return to Duck Pond.

PETS

"DOG COMMANDS" ———————————

Fingerplay

Have the children imitate your motions.

My little dog can run and play, (*Make a fist and move it back and forth.*)
My little dog can sit and stay. (*Hold up palm in a stop signal.*)
My little dog loves to play catch, (*Make mouth shape with hand and shut it as if catching a ball in its "mouth."*)
My little dog can run and fetch. (*Move fist back and forth.*)
She rolls over, then on two legs stands, (*Move hand in circle, then hold two fingers downward.*)
I ask for her paw and she shakes my hand. (*Hold out hand and move it up and down as if shaking another's hand.*)
When I say "Sit," my dog takes a seat, (*Place hand on lap.*)
She barks on command and gets a treat. (*Everyone barks, makes a mouth shape again, and "eats" the imaginary treat.*)

PICTURE BOOK MATCH

How to Be a Dog, written and illustrated by Jo Williamson (Little Bee, 2015).
A dog greets the reader with "A very big Woof to all you dogs!" Don't tell people, but dogs need to learn how to pick the right human, greet visitors, "be less friendly to strangers," choose where to go to the bathroom, play games, and "be very happy in your new home."

"DOGS AND CATS AND GUINEA PIGS" ———————————

Musical Activity

Sing to the tune of "Head, Shoulders, Knees, and Toes." Sing the song slowly. Before sharing this activity with the children, teach them the following actions to accompany each animal.

Dogs: Pant with tongues hanging out.
Cats: Lick the backs of hands as if cleaning them.
Guinea Pigs: Blink and look around as if just waking up.
Birds: Flap arms.
Fish: Purse lips and move hands behind ears as if they are gills.
Snakes: Flick tongues in and out.
Mice: Move hands behind ears as if cleaning them.
Dogs and cats and guinea pigs, guinea pigs.
Dogs and cats and guinea pigs, guinea pigs.
Birds and fish and snakes and mice.
Dogs and cats and guinea pigs, guinea pigs.

PICTURE BOOK MATCH

Some Pets, written by Angela Di Terlizza and illustrated by Brendan Wenzel (Beach Lane, 2016).

> All kinds of pets are on display at the city park pet show. Some of the pets play, some slither, and other pets "drool on their kibbles." "Some pets SQUEAL. Some pets SQUAWK. Some pets SQUEAK."

"FIVE LITTLE CATS"

Fingerplay

(Have the children imitate your motions.)

One cat, one little cat, (*Hold up one finger.*)
One little cat is sleeping. (*Purr.*)
Two cats, two little cats, (*Hold up two fingers.*)
Two little cats are sleeping. (*Purr.*)
Three cats, three little cats. (*Hold up three fingers.*)
Three little cats are sleeping. (*Purr.*)
Four cats, four little cats, (*Hold up four fingers.*)
Four little cats are sleeping. (*Purr.*)
Five cats, five little cats, (*Hold up five fingers.*)
Five little cats are . . . (*Pause.*) . . . LEAPING! (*Meow loudly.*)

Lola Gets a Cat, written by Anna McQuinn and illustrated by Rosalind
Beardshaw (Charlesbridge, 2017).

> Lola loves her toy cats and feels she's ready to take care of a real cat.
> She and her family visit a pet shelter and "before Lola can decide, one
> little cat chooses her!" Lola names the cat "*Makeda.* It is the name of
> an African queen."

"GUESS MY FRIEND"

Poem

Pause at the proper place in the last line of each stanza and let the children respond
with the correct animal.

I have a friend, his name is Mark,
My friend Mark, he likes to bark.
I have a friend, his name is Mark,
Mark is a (*pause*) *dog* who likes to bark.
I have a friend, her name is Patches,
My friend Patches purrs and scratches.
I have a friend, her name is Patches,
Patches is a (*pause*) *cat* who purrs and scratches.
I have a friend, his name is Ty,
My friend Ty, he loves to fly.
I have a friend, his name is Ty,
Ty is a (*pause*) *bird,* who loves to fly.

Emerson Barks, written and illustrated by Liza Woodruff (Holt, 2016).

> Eva's dog Emerson barks a lot. Her neighbor, Miss Cross, is angry because
> Emerson's barking caused her cat Kissy to run away. Emerson's barking
> leads everyone to Kissy . . . and her new kittens.

"HOW MUCH IS THAT TURTLE IN THE WINDOW?" ——————

Musical Activity

Sing to the tune of "How Much Is That Doggie in the Window?" While the leader sings, the children can act like the animals being sung about, as if they are on display in a window.

How much is that turtle in the window?
The one with the shell and the tail?
How much is that turtle in the window?
I sure hope that turtle's for sale.
How much is that kitten in the window?
The one with the nice furry tail?
How much is that kitten in the window?
I sure hope that kitten's for sale.
How much is that bunny in the window?
The one with the cotton-ball tail?
How much is that bunny in the window?
I sure hope that bunny's for sale.
How much is that snake in the window?
The one with the long, long tail?
How much is that snake in the window?
I sure hope that snake is for sale.

PICTURE BOOK MATCH

Alfie (The Turtle That Disappeared), written and illustrated by Thyra
    Heder (Abrams, 2017).
        A little girl named Nia gets her pet turtle Alfie from the pet store on
        her sixth birthday. On Nia's seventh birthday, Alfie disappears. We then
        hear Alfie's side of the story.

"I HAVE FLEAS" ————————————————————————

Movement/Sound Effects Activity

Have the children imitate your sounds and motions.

I'm a dog and I have fleas,
I must scratch my ears. "Arrrooooo!" (*Scratch behind ears with left hand
    and howl.*)

I'm a dog and I have fleas,
I must scratch my back, (*Scratch back with right hand.*)
And ears, (*Scratch behind ears.*)
"Arrrooooo!" (*Howl.*)
I'm a dog and I have fleas,
I must scratch my leg, (*Pretend to bite one leg.*)
And back, (*Scratch back.*)
And ears, (*Scratch behind ears.*).
"Arrrooooo!" (*Howl.*)
I'm a dog and I have fleas,
I must scratch my rear, (*Stand up and wiggle hips.*)
And leg, (*Bite leg.*)
And back, (*Scratch back.*)
And ears, (*Scratch behind ears.*).
"Arrrooooo!" (*Howl.*)
Thank goodness! (*Come to a complete stop.*)
I think they're gone! (*Slowly, give a little scratch behind one ear.*)

PICTURE BOOK MATCH

The Flea, written by Laurie Cohen and illustrated by Marjorie Béal
(Owlkids, 2014).
> A flea, thinking he is too little, climbs until he reaches a cloud. A bear
> spots the flea and calls him "teeny-tiny." The flea jumps down on the
> bear. He makes the bear "scratch and scratch . . . And that's when he
> realized it. He was big. A big nuisance."

"I KNOW AN OLD LADY WHO HAD A PET FLY"

Musical Fingerplay

Sing to the tune of "I Know an Old Lady Who Swallowed a Fly." Have the children imitate your motions.

I know an old lady who had a pet fly, (*Move hand around as if it is a fly.*)
I don't know why she had a pet fly,
I wonder why. (*Shrug.*)
I know an old lady who had a pet spider, (*Wiggle fingers.*)
That wiggled and jiggled and tickled around her. (*Shake body.*)
She had a pet spider to play with the fly, (*Move hand around.*)

I don't know why she had a pet fly,
I wonder why. (*Shrug.*)
I know an old lady who had a pet cat, (*Lick back of hand like a cat.*)
Imagine that, she had a pet cat.
She had a pet cat to play with the spider, (*Wiggle fingers.*)
That wiggled and jiggled and tickled around her, (*Shake body.*)
She had a pet spider to play with the fly, (*Move hand around.*)
I don't know why she had a pet fly,
I wonder why. (*Shrug.*)
I know an old lady who had a pet dog, (*Pant like a dog with tongue
    hanging out.*)
She went for a jog with her little pet dog, (*Jog in place.*)
She had a pet dog to play with the cat, (*Lick back of hand.*)
She had a pet cat to play with the spider, (*Wiggle fingers.*)
That wiggled and jiggled and tickled around her, (*Shake body.*)
She had a pet spider to play with the fly, (*Move hand around.*)
I don't know why she had a pet fly,
I wonder why. (*Shrug.*)
I know an old lady who had a pet skunk, (*Hold nose.*)
Who'd have thunk that she had a pet skunk?
She had a pet skunk that went "Spritz! Splash! Splat!"
That's the end of that.

PICTURE BOOK MATCH

The Skunk, written by Mac Barnett and illustrated by Patrick McDonnell
    (Roaring Brook, 2015).
> A skunk shows up on a man's doorstep. The skunk follows the man all
> over town, even following in a taxi cab. Later, the man misses the skunk
> and starts following it.

"MY DOG IS A NOISY DOG" ————————————————

Sound Effects Activity

(*Have the children imitate your sounds.*)
My dog is a noisy dog,
He barks and barks all day. (*Bark.*)
My dog is a noisy dog,

He growls and growls all day. (*Growl.*)
My dog is a noisy dog,
He whines and whines all day. (*Whine.*)
My dog is a noisy dog,
He pants and pants all day. (*Pant.*)
My dog is a noisy dog,
He slurps and slurps all day. (*Slurp.*)
My dog is a noisy dog,
He snores and snores all day—and night! (*Snores.*)

PICTURE BOOK MATCH

Dog Rules, written and illustrated by Jef Czekaj (Balzer and Bray, 2016).
> A cat tries to trick two dogs to raise a baby dog, although the baby is really a bird. They teach it to "Grrrr." The baby tweets. They try to get it to bark. The baby tweets. When the cat appears, the baby gives it a loud "WOOF!"

"MY LITTLE KITTEN RAN AWAY"

Musical Activity

Sing to the tune of "Bingo." Have the children imitate your sounds and motions.

My little kitten ran away,
Oh where, oh where is she?
Kitty! Clap, clap, clap! (*Shout "Kitty" with cupped hands and then clap three times in rhythm to the "Bingo" song.*)
Kitty! Clap, clap, clap!
Kitty! Clap, clap, clap!
My kitty's back with me!
My little puppy ran away,
Oh where, oh where is he?
Puppy! Clap, clap, clap! (*Shout "Puppy" with cupped hands and then clap three times in rhythm to the "Bingo" song.*)
Puppy! Clap, clap, clap!
Puppy! Clap, clap, clap!
My puppy's back with me!

They All Saw a Cat, written and illustrated by Brendan Wenzel, (Chronicle, 2016).

> A child sees a nice, friendly cat. A dog sees a skinny, suspicious cat. A fish sees a gigantic blob with eyes. A mouse sees a monster. We also see the perspectives of a fox, bee, bird, flea, snake, skunk, worm, and bat. Finally, the cat sees itself in a puddle of water.

"WHAT KIND OF SOUND DOES A CAT MAKE?" ———————

Sound Effects Activity

Have the children repeat each line after you.

Leader: What kind of sound does a cat make?
Audience: What kind of sound does a cat make?
Leader: A cat can sound like this . . .
Audience: A cat can sound like this . . .
Leader: "Meow!"
Audience: "Meow!"
Leader: Sometimes a cat goes, "Meow."
Audience: Sometimes a cat goes, "Meow."
Leader: What kind of sound does a cat make?
Audience: What kind of sound does a cat make?
Leader: A cat can sound like this . . .
Audience: A cat can sound like this . . .
Leader: "Rrrrow!"
Audience: "Rrrrow!"
Leader: Sometimes a cat howls.
Audience: Sometimes a cat howls.
Leader: What kind of sound does a cat make?
Audience: What kind of sound does a cat make?
Leader: A cat can sound like this . . .
Audience: A cat can sound like this . . .
Leader: "Hiss! Spit! Hiss!"
Audience: "Hiss! Spit! Hiss!"
Leader: Sometimes a cat hisses and spits.
Audience: Sometimes a cat hisses and spits.
Leader: What kind of sound does a cat make?

Audience: What kind of sound does a cat make?
Leader: A cat can sound like this . . .
Audience: A cat can sound like this . . .
Leader: "Purrrrrrr."
Audience: "Purrrrrrr."
Leader: Sometimes a cat purrs.
Audience: Sometimes a cat purrs.

PICTURE BOOK MATCH

Meow!, written and illustrated by Victoria Ying (Harper, 2017).
> With just one word, "Meow," we follow a kitten throughout its day. Its "meow" means different things, like "Want to play?" and "I'm mad." The kitten's parents yell, "MEOW!!" and send it to a timeout chair.

ZOOS

"ANIMAL PHOTO POSES"

Movement Activity

Have the children pose like each animal you mention. Tell them you are going to take pictures of them, while they pose, with your pretend camera. Everyone stands.

Pink Flamingo . . . (*Turn head and rest it on shoulder. Stand on one leg.*)
Green Turtle . . . (*Get on all fours and scrunch head into shoulders.*)
Gray Elephant . . . (*Hold arm upraised in front of nose to represent a trunk.*)
Blue Peacock . . . (*Hold hands behind bottom with thumbs intertwined and fingers extended outward.*)
Brown Moose . . . (*Put thumbs on each side of head with fingers extended outward.*)

PICTURE BOOK MATCH

Wild About Us!, written by Karen Beaumont and illustrated by Janet Stevens (Houghton Mifflin Harcourt, 2015).
>Animals pose for the reader and celebrate what makes them unique. Warty Warthog shows off its tusks, Crocodile is proud of his "toothy grin," Rhino loves her "wrinkly skin," and Elephant unfurls his long nose.

"THE ANIMALS IN THE ZOO"

Musical Activity

Sing to the tune of "The Wheels on the Bus." Have the children imitate the sounds with you.

The monkeys in the zoo go, "Ooh-ooh-ooh!
Ooh-ooh-ooh! Ooh-ooh-ooh!"
The monkeys in the zoo go, "Ooh-ooh-ooh!"

Every single day.
The lions in the zoo go, "Roar-roar-roar!
Roar-roar-roar! Roar-roar-roar!"
The lions in the zoo go, "Roar-roar-roar!"
Every single day.
The parrots in the zoo go, "Squawk-squawk-squawk!
Squawk-squawk-squawk! Squawk-squawk-squawk!"
The parrots in the zoo go, "Squawk-squawk-squawk!"
Every single day.
The hippos in the zoo go, "Yawn-yawn-yawn!
Yawn-yawn-yawn! Yawn-yawn-yawn!"
The hippos in the zoo go, "Yawn-yawn-yawn!"
Every single day.
The beavers in the zoo go, "Timmmberrr!
Timmmberrr! Timmmberrr!"
The beavers in the zoo go, "Timmmberrr!"
Every single day.

PICTURE BOOK MATCH

Peek-a-Boo Zoo!, written and illustrated by Jane Cabrera (Little Bee, 2017).
A young lemur discovers several animals in the zoo. Through cutout
holes, it finds a panda bear cub and its mother, a blue parrot, a joey
and its kangaroo mother, a monkey, and, for the final discovery, a wide
array of zoo creatures.

"DOOT DOOT ZOO"

Movement Activity

This activity is modeled after the camp activity "Baby Shark." Have the children
chant the words with you while making the motions. Yell the word "zoo" louder
than the other words. Everyone stands.

Rattlesnake! Doot-doot-doodley-ZOO! (*Hold up fist and shake it as if it is
a rattlesnake tail.*)
Rattlesnake! Doot-doot-doodley-ZOO!
Chimpanzee! Doot-doot-doodley-ZOO! (*Hold up arms overhead and swing
them back and forth.*)

Chimpanzee! Doot-doot-doodley-ZOO!

Crocodile! Doot-doot-doodley-ZOO! (*Move arms up and down as if they are crocodile jaws.*)

Crocodile! Doot-doot-doodley-ZOO!

Kangaroo! Doot-doot-doodley-ZOO! (*Hop in place.*)

Kangaroo! Doot-doot-doodley-ZOO!

Mountain goat! Doot-doot-doodley-ZOO! (*Make horns with fingers.*)

Mountain goat! Doot-doot-doodley-ZOO!

Elephant! Doot-doot-doodley-ZOO! (*Put arm in front of nose as if it is a trunk.*)

Elephant! Doot-doot-doodley-ZOO!

That's all! Doot-doot-doodley-ZOO!

For today! Doot-doot-doodley-ZOO!

PICTURE BOOK MATCH

Oh, Nuts!, written by Tammi Sauer and illustrated by Dan Krall (Bloomsbury, 2012).

> Three chipmunks—Cutesy, Blinky, and Bob—live in a zoo, but the humans don't pay attention to them. The chipmunks dress up, play music, and outperform the other animals to no avail. They eventually decide that it is okay to be ignored.

"ELEPHANT HUNT"

Movement Activity

This activity is modeled after the movement activity "We're Going on a Bear Hunt." Have the children slap their legs to simulate walking during the chorus and imitate your motions.

Chorus:

We're going on an elephant hunt, Boom-Boom, (*Slap legs.*)

We're going on an elephant hunt, Boom-Boom,

We'll stomp and sway and (*trumpeting noise*) all day,

We're going on an elephant hunt.

Where are we going to find an elephant? At the zoo! Let's go!

Chorus:
We're going on an elephant hunt, Boom-Boom, (*Slap legs.*)
We're going on an elephant hunt, Boom-Boom,
We'll stomp and sway and (*trumpeting noise*) all day,
We're going on an elephant hunt.

Stop! Look over there . . . in the children's zoo . . . in that big mud
    puddle . . . (*Stop slapping legs and point.*)
Something big and gray. Maybe it's an elephant. Let's go over. (*Slap legs.*)
Hope you don't mind walking in the mud. (*Make squishing noises.*)
Get your cameras out. (*Stop slapping legs and hold up a pretend camera.*)
Ready! Aim! WAIT! Listen! (*Make pig noises.*)
That's not an elephant. That's a . . . (*The children shout, "Pig!"*)
Let's go to another part of the zoo.
Oh wait, look at our feet. What a mess. Just scrape the mud off with
    your hands. (*Mime scraping the mud off.*)
Oh no, look at our hands. What a mess. Just wipe it off on your shirt.
    (*Mime wiping mud off hands.*)
Wipe them on your neighbor's shirt. (*Wipe hands on neighbor's back.*)
Let's go to another part of the zoo.

Chorus:
We're going on an elephant hunt, Boom-Boom, (*Slap legs.*)
We're going on an elephant hunt, Boom-Boom,
We'll stomp and sway and (*trumpeting noise*) all day,
We're going on an elephant hunt.

Stop! Look over there . . . by that big tank of water . . . (*Stop slapping
    legs and point.*)
Something big and gray. Maybe it's an elephant.
Let's tiptoe and get a closer look. (*Instead of slapping legs, gently tap legs
    with pointer fingers.*)
(*Whisper*) Tiptoe, tiptoe.
Get your cameras out. (*Stop tapping legs and hold up a pretend camera.*)
Ready! Aim! WAIT! (*Make the barking sound of a seal—"Ark! Ark! Ark!"*)
That's not an elephant! That's a . . . (*The children shout, "Seal!"*)
Let's go to another part of the zoo.

Uh-oh, look at the time! We'll never make it at this rate.
We'll have to go faster.

Chorus:
We're going on an elephant hunt, Boom-Boom, (*Slap legs slightly faster
than before.*)
We're going on an elephant hunt, Boom-Boom,
We'll stomp and sway and (*trumpeting noise*) all day,
We're going on an elephant hunt.

Faster!

Chorus:
We're going on an elephant hunt, Boom-Boom, (*Slap legs faster than
before.*)
We're going on an elephant hunt, Boom-Boom,
We'll stomp and sway and (*trumpeting noise*) all day,
We're going on an elephant hunt.

FASTER!

Chorus:
We're going on an elephant hunt, Boom-Boom, (*Slap legs even faster.*)
We're going on an elephant hunt, Boom-Boom,
We'll stomp and sway and (*trumpeting noise*) all day,
We're going on an elephant hunt.

I need to rest against this big gray wall. (*Stop slapping legs and "gasp for
breath." Stand with arms outstretched leaning against "the gray wall."
Pause until the children yell that the wall is an elephant.*)
This wall is an elephant? Let's get out of here! Run! (*Slap legs quickly.
After a few seconds, hold up hands for all to stop.*)
Didn't you always want to scream in a library?
Whew, we're safe. Wait a minute! We forgot something.
(*Audience yells out that we forgot to take a picture!*)
You know what that means, don't you? It means . . .

Chorus:
We're going on an elephant hunt, Boom-Boom, (*Slap legs.*)
We're going on an elephant hunt, Boom-Boom,
We'll stomp and sway and (*trumpeting noise*) all day,
We're going on an elephant hunt.

TOMORROW! (*Stop slapping legs and throw arms up in the air.*)

PICTURE BOOK MATCH

Ellie, written and illustrated by Mike Wu (Hyperion, 2015).
When the zookeeper announces that the zoo is closing, Ellie the Elephant wonders how she can help. She and the zookeeper discover that she's a talented artist. "Word spread of Ellie's talents." Thanks to Ellie, the zoo remains "open for good!"

"FIVE LITTLE MONKEYS SWINGING IN THE ZOO" ————

Fingerplay

This activity is modeled after the fingerplay "Five Little Monkeys Jumping on the Bed." Have the children imitate your motions.

Five little monkeys swinging in the zoo, (*Make overhead arm-over-arm swinging motions.*)
One escaped and bid, "Adieu!" (*Blow a kiss.*)
Call the zookeeper—she'll know what to do, (*Mime calling on a phone.*)
She'll say, "Lock that cage, (*Mime locking a door.*)
While they're swinging in the zoo!" (*Shake finger as if scolding.*)
Four little monkeys swinging in the zoo, (*Make overhead arm-over-arm swinging motions.*)
One escaped and bid, "Adieu!" (*Blow a kiss.*)
Call the zookeeper—she'll know what to do, (*Mime calling on a phone.*)
She'll say, "Lock that cage, (*Mime locking a door.*)
While they're swinging in the zoo!" (*Shake finger as if scolding.*)
Three little monkeys swinging in the zoo, (*Make overhead arm-over-arm swinging motions.*)
One escaped and bid, "Adieu!" (*Blow a kiss.*)
Call the zookeeper—she'll know what to do, (*Mime calling on a phone.*)
She'll say, "Lock that cage, (*Mime locking a door.*)

While they're swinging in the zoo!" (*Shake finger as if scolding.*)
Two little monkeys swinging in the zoo, (*Make overhead arm-over-arm swinging motions.*)
One escaped and bid, "Adieu!" (*Blow a kiss.*)
Call the zookeeper—she'll know what to do, (*Mime calling on a phone.*)
She'll say, "Lock that cage, (*Mime locking a door.*)
While they're swinging in the zoo!" (*Shake finger as if scolding.*)
One little monkey swinging in the zoo, (*Make overhead arm-over-arm swinging motions.*)
It escaped and bid, "Adieu!" (*Blow a kiss.*)
Call the zookeeper—she'll know what to do, (*Mime calling on a phone.*)
She'll say, "I guess we can go home now." (*Shrug and smile.*)

PICTURE BOOK MATCH

Manners Are Not for Monkeys, written by Heather Tekavec and illustrated by David Huyck (Kids Can, 2016).

Monkeys emulate well-behaved human children. The monkeys stop swinging, they no longer screech, and they stop making a mess. When a group of rowdy children show up, the zookeeper frees the monkeys and puts the rowdy human children in the monkey cage.

"MARY HAD A LITTLE ZOO"

Musical/Movement Activity

Sing to the tune of "Mary Had a Little Lamb." Have the children get down on the ground on all fours and imitate your motions.

Mary had a little zoo, little zoo, little zoo,
Mary had a little zoo, she had a little zoo.
And in her zoo, she had a giraffe, had a giraffe, had a giraffe,
And in her zoo, she had a giraffe, it looked a lot like this . . . (*Stretch necks.*)
Mary had a little zoo, little zoo, little zoo,
Mary had a little zoo, she had a little zoo.
And in her zoo, she had a hippo, had a hippo, had a hippo,
And in her zoo, she had a hippo, it looked a lot like this . . . (*Open mouth wide.*)
Mary had a little zoo, little zoo, little zoo,

Mary had a little zoo, she had a little zoo.

And in her zoo, she had a rhino, had a rhino, had a rhino,

And in her zoo, she had a rhino, it looked a lot like this . . . (*Hold up one hand on nose as if it is a horn.*)

PICTURE BOOK MATCH

A Hippo in Our Yard, written and illustrated by Liza Donnelly (Holiday House, 2016).

> Sally discovers a hippo in her family's yard. Mom doesn't believe her. Sally comes back and reports there is a tiger in their tree, zebras in their garage, and koalas in their hammock.

"OLD MACDONALD ABC"

Musical/Movement Activity

Sing to the tune of "Old MacDonald Had a Farm." Have the children imitate your sounds and motions.

Old MacDonald had a farm, E-I-E-I-O.

And on her farm, she had an Alligator, E-I-E-I-O.

With a "Snap-Snap" here and a "Snap-Snap" there, (*Hold arms straight out and clap hands.*)

Here a "Snap," there a "Snap," everywhere a "Snap-Snap,"

Old MacDonald had a farm, E-I-E-I-O.

And on her farm, she had a Badger, E-I-E-I-O.

With a "Dig-Dig" here and a "Dig-Dig" there (*Mime a digging motion with hands.*)

Here a "Dig," there a "Dig," everywhere a "Dig-Dig,"

Old MacDonald had a farm, E-I-E-I-O.

And on her farm, she had a Crab, E-I-E-I-O.

With a "Click-Clack" here and a "Click-Clack" there, (*Form claws with hands. Open and shut the thumb.*)

Here a "Click," there a "Clack," everywhere a "Click-Clack,"

Old MacDonald had a farm, E-I-E-I-O.

And on her farm, she had a Dolphin, E-I-E-I-O.

With an "Eee-Eee" here and an "Eee-Eee" there, (*Hold head up as if sticking it out of the water while making the sound.*)

Here an "Eee," there an "Eee," everywhere an "Eee-Eee,"
Old MacDonald had a farm, E-I-E-I-O.
And on her farm, she had an Elephant, E-I-E-I-O.
With a "Trumpet-Trumpet" here and a "Trumpet-Trumpet" there, (*Hold arm in front of nose.*)
Here a "Trumpet," there a "Trumpet," everywhere a "Trumpet-Trumpet,"
Old MacDonald had a farm, E-I-E-I-O.
And on her farm, she had a Frog, E-I-E-I-O.
With a "Croak-Croak" here and a "Croak-Croak" there, (*Puff cheeks.*)
Here a "Croak," there a "Croak," everywhere a "Croak-Croak,"
Old MacDonald had a farm, E-I-E-I-O.
And on her farm, she had a Gorilla, E-I-E-I-O.
With a "Thump-Thump" here and a "Thump-Thump" there, (*Beat chest with hands.*)
Here a "Thump," there a "Thump," everywhere a "Thump-Thump,"
Old MacDonald had a farm, E-I-E-I-O.
And on her farm, she had a Hyena, E-I-E-I-O.
With a "Whee-Hee" here and a "Whee-Hee" there, (*Slap leg with hand while laughing.*)
Here a "Whee," there a "Hee," everywhere a "Whee-Hee,"
Old MacDonald had a farm, E-I-E-I-O.
And on her farm, she had an Iguana, E-I-E-I-O.
With a "Gulp-Gulp" here and a "Gulp-Gulp" there, (*Roll out tongue and slowly gulp.*)
Here a "Gulp," there a "Gulp," everywhere a "Gulp-Gulp,"
Old MacDonald had a farm, E-I-E-I-O.
And on her farm, she had a Jaguar, E-I-E-I-O.
With a "Growl-Growl" here and a "Growl-Growl" there, (*Make a mean face and growl.*)
Here a "Growl," there a "Growl," everywhere a "Growl-Growl,"
Old MacDonald had a farm, E-I-E-I-O.
And on her farm, she had a Kangaroo, E-I-E-I-O.
With a "Hop-Hop" here and a "Hop-Hop" there, (*Hop in place.*)
Here a "Hop," there a "Hop," everywhere a "Hop-Hop,"
Old MacDonald had a farm, E-I-E-I-O.
And on her farm, she had a Llama, E-I-E-I-O.
With a "Spit-Spit" here and a "Spit-Spit" there, (*Mime spitting.*)
Here a "Spit," there a "Spit," everywhere a "Spit-Spit,"

Old MacDonald had a farm, E-I-E-I-O.

And on her farm, she had a Monkey, E-I-E-I-O.

With an "Ooh-Ooh" here and an "Ooh-Ooh" there, (*Wave arms in the air.*)

Here an "Ooh," there an "Ooh," everywhere an "Ooh-Ooh,"

Old MacDonald had a farm, E-I-E-I-O.

And on her farm, she had a Narwhal, E-I-E-I-O.

With a "Grunt-Grunt" here and a "Grunt-Grunt" there, (*Hold arm out on head like a long horn.*)

Here a "Grunt," there a "Grunt," everywhere a "Grunt-Grunt,"

Old MacDonald had a farm, E-I-E-I-O.

And on her farm, she had an Octopus, E-I-E-I-O.

With a "Hug-Hug" here and a "Hug-Hug" there, (*Hug yourself.*)

Here a "Hug," there a "Hug," everywhere a "Hug-Hug,"

Old MacDonald had a farm, E-I-E-I-O.

And on her farm, she had a Penguin, E-I-E-I-O.

With a "Waddle-Waddle" here and a "Waddle-Waddle" there, (*Waddle in place.*)

Here a "Waddle," there a "Waddle," everywhere a "Waddle-Waddle,"

Old MacDonald had a farm, E-I-E-I-O.

And on her farm, she had a Quail, E-I-E-I-O.

With a "Bob-WHITE" here and a "Bob-WHITE" there, (*Bob head up and down and emphasize "WHITE" on the call.*)

Here a "Bob," there a "WHITE," everywhere a "Bob-WHITE,"

Old MacDonald had a farm, E-I-E-I-O.

And on her farm, she had a Rattlesnake, E-I-E-I-O.

With a "Shake-Shake" here and a "Shake-Shake" there, (*Shake fist to simulate a rattle.*)

Here a "Shake," there a "Shake," everywhere a "Shake-Shake,"

Old MacDonald had a farm, E-I-E-I-O.

And on her farm, she had a Seal, E-I-E-I-O.

With an "Orp-Orp" here and an "Orp-Orp" there, (*Clap the backs of your hands together.*)

Here an "Orp," there an "Orp," everywhere an "Orp-Orp,"

Old MacDonald had a farm, E-I-E-I-O.

And on her farm, she had a Trumpeter Swan, E-I-E-I-O.

With a "Honk-Honk" here and a "Honk-Honk" there, (*Stretch neck and flap arms.*)

Here a "Honk," there a "Honk," everywhere a "Honk-Honk,"

Old MacDonald had a farm, E-I-E-I-O.

And on her farm, she had a Ural Owl, E-I-E-I-O.

With a "Whoo-Whoo" here and a "Whoo-Whoo" there, (*Blink and turn head around.*)

Here a "Whoo," there a "Whoo," everywhere a "Whoo-Whoo,"

Old MacDonald had a farm, E-I-E-I-O.

And on her farm, she had a Vulture, E-I-E-I-O.

With a "Soar-Soar" here and a "Soar-Soar" there, (*Hold arms out as wings and move in a circle.*)

Here a "Soar," there a "Soar," everywhere a "Soar-Soar,"

Old MacDonald had a farm, E-I-E-I-O.

And on her farm, she had a Wolf, E-I-E-I-O.

With a "Howl-Howl" here and a "Howl-Howl" there, (*Lift head back to howl.*)

Here a "Howl," there a "Howl," everywhere a "Howl-Howl,"

Old MacDonald had a farm, E-I-E-I-O.

And on her farm, she had a Xenarthra, E-I-E-I-O. (*Stop and explain that a sloth is a member of the superorder Xenarthra. The name is pronounced "ZEN-are-thra."*)

With a "Snore-Snore" here and a "Snore-Snore" there, (*Close eyes and hold hands overhead as if grasping a branch.*)

Here a "Snore," there a "Snore," everywhere a "Snore-Snore,"

Old MacDonald had a farm, E-I-E-I-O.

And on her farm, she had a Yak, E-I-E-I-O.

With a "Snort-Snort" here and a "Snort-Snort" there, (*Shake head and make chewing motions.*)

Here a "Snort," there a "Snort," everywhere a "Snort-Snort,"

Old MacDonald had a farm, E-I-E-I-O.

(*Spoken*) Wait!

Old MacDonald didn't have a farm.

She had a ZOO! (*Slap forehead.*)

PICTURE BOOK MATCH

The ABC Animal Orchestra, written and illustrated by Donald Saaf (Holt, 2015).

Several animals demonstrate the alphabet while singing and playing musical instruments. An aardvark plays an accordion, a butterfly plucks her banjo, and a chimpanzee crashes his cymbals. After a zebra strums her zither, "the animal orchestra plays all together!"

"THE ZOO ANIMALS INTRODUCE THEMSELVES" ───────
Sound Effects Activity

Pause before the last word in each stanza and let the children fill in the proper animal sounds.

I am a Monkey,
Yes, it's true,
I am a Monkey,
And I say . . . "Ooh-ooh!"
I am a Tiger,
Whom you all adore,
I am a Tiger,
And I say . . . "Roar!"
I am a Snake,
Look at this,
I am a Snake,
And I say . . . "Hiss!"
I am an Owl,
I thought you knew,
I am an Owl,
And I go . . . "Whoo-whoo!"
I am a Wolf,
I'm on the prowl,
I am a Wolf,
And I go . . . "Howl!"

PICTURE BOOK MATCH

The Opposite Zoo, written and illustrated by Il Sung Na (Knopf, 2016).
Monkey sees some zoo animals that are awake and others that are asleep. Some animals are hairy, and some are bald. The giraffe is tall, and the boar is short. Monkey continues to explore the animals in the zoo.

My
World

BEDTIME AND MORNING TIME

"ANIMAL SNORES"

Sound Effects Activity

Ask the children what it sounds like when people snore. Then ask them what they think it would sound like if a dog snored. Have everyone join you with the following animal snores.

Dog snore: "Snore . . . woof, woof, woof . . . Snore . . . woof, woof, woof."
Cat snore: "Snore . . . meow, meow, meow . . . Snore . . . meow, meow, meow."
Cow snore: "Snore . . . moo, moo, moo . . . Snore . . . moo, moo, moo."
Chicken snore: "Snore . . . cluck, cluck, cluck . . . Snore . . . cluck, cluck, cluck."
Pig snore: "Snore . . . oink, oink, oink . . . Snore . . . oink, oink, oink."
Elephant snore: "Snore . . . (*trumpeting noise*) . . . Snore . . . (*trumpeting noise*).

PICTURE BOOK MATCH

I Will Take a Nap!, written and illustrated by Mo Willems (Hyperion, 2015). Gerald the elephant is cranky and tries to take a nap, but he is constantly interrupted by Piggy. After arguing with his friend, Piggy decides to take a nap as well. His snoring keeps Gerald awake. "SNORE! Snurk. Snurk. Snurk. Snurk. Puff. Mmmmmmm . . . SNORE!"

"BUSY DAY"

Fingerplay

Have the children imitate your motions and say "Shhh" on the last line.

Here they are,
My family and friends, (*Hold up five fingers.*)

They had a busy day. (*Wiggle fingers.*)
Now they all
Are going to bed, (*Bend fingers down.*)
And this is what they say:
"Shhhh . . ." (*Finger to lips.*)

Feet, Go to Sleep, written by Barbara Bottner and illustrated by Maggie
Smith (Knopf, 2015).

Fiona tells her toes to go to sleep and then her feet. As she lies in bed,
she remembers what her toes and feet did during her busy day. Fiona
continues this exercise with her knees, legs, tummy, shoulders, arms,
hands, fingers, mouth, ears, and, finally, her eyes.

"FIVE LITTLE MONKEYS JUMPING SO HIGH"

Fingerplay

This fingerplay is modeled after the fingerplay "Five Little Monkeys Jumping on the
Bed." Have everyone imitate your motions.

Five little monkeys jumping on the bed, (*Hold up five fingers on one hand
and bounce that hand on the palm of the other hand.*)
One bounced higher, "Watch!" she said. (*Hold up one finger and raise it
overhead.*)
That little monkey jumped so high,
She disappeared into the sky-y-y! (*Peer upward with hand shading eyes.
Shrug.*)
Four little monkeys jumping on the bed, (*Hold up four fingers on one
hand and bounce that hand on the palm of the other hand.*)
One bounced higher, "Watch!" he said. (*Hold up one finger and raise it
overhead.*)
That little monkey jumped so high,
He disappeared into the sky-y-y! (*Peer upward with hand shading eyes.
Shrug.*)
Three little monkeys jumping on the bed, (*Hold up three fingers on one
hand and bounce that hand on the palm of the other hand.*)

One bounced higher, "Watch!" she said. (*Hold up one finger and raise it overhead.*)

That little monkey jumped so high,

She disappeared into the sky-y-y! (*Peer upward with hand shading eyes. Shrug.*)

Two little monkeys jumping on the bed, (*Hold up two fingers on one hand and bounce that hand on the palm of the other hand.*)

One bounced higher, "Watch!" he said. (*Hold up one finger and raise it overhead.*)

That little monkey jumped so high,

He disappeared into the sky-y-y! (*Peer upward with hand shading eyes. Shrug.*)

One little monkey jumping on the bed, (*Hold up one finger on one hand and bounce that hand on the palm of the other hand.*)

One bounced higher, "Watch!" she said. (*Hold up one finger and raise it overhead.*)

That little monkey jumped so high,

She disappeared into the sky-y-y! (*Peer upward with hand shading eyes. Shrug.*)

No little monkeys jumping on the bed, (*Look around and shrug shoulders.*)

If you look hard and lift your head, (*Look upward.*)

You'll see a speck beneath the moon,

Those monkeys hitched a ride in a hot air balloon! (*Point with a big smile.*)

PICTURE BOOK MATCH

Spunky Little Monkey, written by Bill Martin Jr. and Michael Sampson and illustrated by Brian Won (Scholastic, 2017).

> When the little monkey won't get out of bed, Mama calls the doctor, and he says, "Apple juice, orange juice, gooseberry pies—Monkey needs some exercise!" Monkey leaps up and claps, stomps, shakes his hips, to get "ready for the day."

"FIVE WOLVES IN THE BED"

Musical/Movement Activity

(Sing to the tune of "Ten in the Bed." Have the children imitate your motions and sounds.)

Five wolves in the bed, (*Hold up five fingers.*)
And a little one said, "Howl!" (*Point face upward and howl.*)
So, they all rolled over, (*Roll hands over each other.*)
And one fell out.
Four wolves in the bed, (*Hold up four fingers.*)
And a little one said, "Howl!" (*Point face upward and howl.*)
So, they all rolled over, (*Roll hands.*)
And one fell out.
Three wolves in the bed, (*Hold up three fingers.*)
And a little one said, "Howl!" (*Point face upward and howl.*)
So, they all rolled over, (*Roll hands.*)
And one fell out.
Two wolves in the bed, (*Hold up two fingers.*)
And a little one said, "Howl!" (*Point face upward and howl.*)
So, they all rolled over, (*Roll hands.*)
And one fell out.
One wolf in the bed, (*Hold up one finger.*)
And the little one said, "Howl!" (*Point face upward and howl.*)
So, she rolled over, (*Roll hands.*)
And she fell out.
There were none in the bed . . . (*Lift hands and shrug shoulders.*)
(*Spoken*) They were all asleep on the floor. (*Close eyes, put head on
    hands, and make snoring noises.*)

PICTURE BOOK MATCH

Little Wolf's First Howling, written by Laura McGee Kvasnosky and illus-
    trated by Kate Harvey McGee. Candlewick, 2017.
        After his father shows him proper wolf-howling techniques, Little Wolf
        adds some jazz be-bop scatting to his unique howls. The father tries to
        correct Little Wolf's unusual style of howling. In the end, Little Wolf
        wins his father's approval.

"I'M NOT SLEEPY"

Movement/Sound Effects Activity

Have the audience members either sit on the floor or in chairs pretending they are sitting up in bed. Have them repeat the lines after you and imitate your motions.

Leader: I'm not sleepy,
Audience: I'm not sleepy,
Leader: Blinking my eyes. (*Blink eyes.*)
Audience: Blinking my eyes.
Leader: I'm not sleepy,
Audience: I'm not sleepy,
Leader: Wiggling my feet, (*Wiggle feet.*)
Audience: Wiggling my feet,
Leader: Blinking my eyes. (*Wiggle feet, blink eyes.*)
Audience: Blinking my eyes.
Leader: I'm not sleepy,
Audience: I'm not sleepy,
Leader: Waving my hands, (*Wave hands.*)
Audience: Waving my hands,
Leader: Wiggling my feet, (*Wave hands, wiggle feet.*)
Audience: Wiggling my feet,
Leader: Blinking my eyes. (*Wave hands, wiggle feet, blink eyes.*)
Audience: Blinking my eyes.
Leader: I'm not sleepy,
Audience: I'm not sleepy,
Leader: Tossing my head, (*Move head.*)
Audience: Tossing my head,
Leader: Waving my hands, (*Move head, wave hands.*)
Audience: Waving my hands,
Leader: Wiggling my feet, (*Move head, wave hands, wiggle feet.*)
Audience: Wiggling my feet,
Leader: Blinking my eyes. (*Move head, wave hands, wiggle feet, blink eyes.*)
Audience: Blinking my eyes.
Leader: I'm VERY sleepy!
Audience: I'm VERY sleepy!
Leader: I'm going to yawn, (*Yawn.*)
Audience: I'm going to yawn,

Leader: I'm going to snore. (*Snore.*)
Audience: I'm going to snore. (*Close eyes, slump in chair, and pretend to be asleep.*)

PICTURE BOOK MATCH

Twenty Yawns, written by Jane Smiley and illustrated by Lauren Castillo (Two Lions, 2016).

> Lucy is wide awake. She gathers her stuffed animals and places them in bed. She imagines them and even the moon yawning. "Then she gave one last yawn . . . and fell asleep."

"MORNING NOISES"

Movement/Sound Effects Activity

Have the children repeat the lines after you and imitate your motions.

Leader: We're still asleep. (*Head on hands.*)
Audience: We're still asleep.
Leader: Snore! Snore! Snore!
Audience: Snore! Snore! Snore!
Leader: The alarm clock rings. (*Open eyes and wave hands.*)
Audience: The alarm clock rings.
Leader: Ring! Ring! Ring!
Audience: Ring! Ring! Ring!
Leader: Stretch and yawn! (*Stretch and say the line while yawning.*)
Audience: Stretch and yawn!
Leader: Stretch! Stretch! Stretch!
Audience: Stretch! Stretch! Stretch!
Leader: Time to eat! (*Mime eating.*)
Audience: Time to eat!
Leader: Chomp! Chomp! Chomp!
Audience: Chomp! Chomp! Chomp!
Leader: Juice or milk? (*Mime drinking.*)
Audience: Juice or milk?
Leader: Gulp! Gulp! Gulp!
Audience: Gulp! Gulp! Gulp!
Leader: Brush our teeth! (*Mime brushing teeth.*)

Audience: Brush our teeth!
Leader: Brush! Brush! Brush!
Audience: Brush! Brush! Brush!
Leader: Out the door! (*Position body as if ready to run.*)
Audience: Out the door!
Leader: ZOOOOOOM!
Audience: ZOOOOOOM!

PICTURE BOOK MATCH

Good Morning to Me!, written and illustrated by Lita Judge (Atheneum, 2015).
A parrot named Beatrix wakes the other pets in the house, including Mouse and Kitty. A dog named Grace enters the picture along with Goldfish. Chaos erupts until Beatrix promises to "be a good birdie." She almost succeeds.

"THERE WAS WHO IN THE BED?"

Musical/Movement Activity

Sing to the tune of "Ten in the Bed." Let the audience guess the mystery animal for each verse. Have them imitate your motions.

There were five in the bed, (*Hold up five fingers.*)
And the little one said, "Who is it? Who is it?" (*Shrug shoulders.*)
(*Spoken*) I have spots and a long neck and I eat leaves from the tops of trees.
Audience: A giraffe!
So, they all rolled over, (*Twirl hands over each other.*)
And Giraffe fell out.
There were four in the bed, (*Hold up four fingers.*)
And the little one said, "Who is it? Who is it?" (*Shrug shoulders.*)
(*Spoken*) I am gray and I have a long nose also known as a trunk.
Audience: An elephant!
So, they all rolled over, (*Twirl hands over each other.*)
And Elephant fell out.
There were three in the bed, (*Hold up three fingers.*)
And the little one said, "Who is it? Who is it?" (*Shrug shoulders.*)
(*Spoken*) I am gray and have a sharp horn near the end of my nose.

Audience: A rhino!
So, they all rolled over, (*Twirl hands over each other.*)
And Rhino fell out.
There were two in the bed, (*Hold up two fingers.*)
And the little one said, "Who is it? Who is it?" (*Shrug shoulders.*)
(*Spoken*) I climb in trees, swing from branch to branch, and love bananas.
Audience: A monkey!
So, they all rolled over, (*Twirl hands over each other.*)
And Monkey fell out.
There was one in the bed, (*Hold up one finger.*)
And the little one said, "Who is it? Who is it?" (*Shrug shoulders.*)
(*Spoken*) I am green and have a big mouth that snaps shut.
Audience: A crocodile!
So, they all rolled over, (*Twirl hands over each other.*)
And Crocodile fell out.
There were none in the bed, (*Hold up fist.*)
And the little one said, "Now I can finally get some sleep!"

PICTURE BOOK MATCH

Go Sleep in Your Own Bed!, written by Candace Fleming and illustrated by
   Lori Nichols (Schwartz and Wade, 2017).

> The pig finds the cow in his sty. The cow returns to her stall, only to find
> a hen. Each animal returns to its correct sleeping spot to find another
> animal already there until the kitty, who was kicked out of the dog's
> house, sleeps in a little girl's bed.

"WHEN BEARS WAKE UP"

Movement Activity

Have the children imitate your motions.

When bears wake up, they shake their head, (*Shake head.*)
They stretch their paws, crawl out of bed. (*Stretch paws, crawl a few feet,
   and sit.*)
When birds wake up, they shake their head, (*Shake head.*)
They flap their wings, fly out of bed. (*Stand, flap arms, fly in a circle,
   and sit.*)

When snakes wake up, they shake their head, (*Shake head.*)
They stretch their tongues, slither out of bed. (*Move tongue in and out,
    crawl a few feet, and sit.*)
When kangaroos wake up, they shake their head, (*Shake head.*)
They pat their pouch, jump out of bed. (*Pat tummy, stand, jump up and
    down, and sit.*)
When elephants wake up, they shake their head, (*Shake head.*)
They stretch their trunk, lumber out of bed. (*Hold arm in front of nose,
    stand, move side to side, and sit.*)
When peacocks wake up, they shake their head, (*Shake head.*)
They flap their tails, run out of bed. (*Stand, splay hands near bottom, run
    in a circle, and sit.*)

PICTURE BOOK MATCH

I'm Awake!, written and illustrated by Maxwell Eaton III (Knopf, 2017).
    A young hamster wakes up before his father and tries to make pancakes.
    He makes a mess and lets the neighborhood animals inside. It's not until
    he does an impression of his father that he falls back asleep.

"WHILE WE SLEEP"

Sound Effects Activity

Have the children imitate your sounds.

While we sleep, the owls do play,
And this is what those little owls say,
"Whoo-whoo! Whoo-whoo!"
While we sleep, the crickets do play,
And this is what those little crickets say,
"Chirp-chirp! Chirp-chirp!"
While we sleep, the frogs do play,
And this is what those little frogs say,
"Rib-it, croak! Rib-it, croak!"
While we sleep, the wolves do play,
And this is what those little wolves say,
"Howwwl! Howwwl!"

Night Animals, written and illustrated by Gianna Marino (Viking, 2015).
> Possum tells Skunk that he's afraid of night animals. They encounter a wolf and a bear who are also afraid of night animals. They settle down once a bat informs them that they are night animals. But then they run into some humans.

"YAWN AND STRETCH"

Movement/Sound Effects Activity

This activity is modeled after the nursery rhyme "The Grand Old Duke of York." Have the children imitate your sounds and motions.

You tired girls and boys,
You "yawn" the biggest yawn, (*Yawn.*)
Your hands go way up high, (*Stretch both arms overhead.*)
And back down with a sigh, (*Lower arms and sigh.*)
And when they're up, they're up, (*Stretch arms overhead again.*)
And when they're down, they're down, (*Lower arms.*)
And when you "yawn" again and again, (*Yawn.*)
They're neither up, (*Point up with one finger.*)
Nor down. (*Point down with the same finger.*)
(*Aside*) Because they're covering your mouth! (*Yawn and cover mouth with both hands.*)

Everyone Is Yawning, written and illustrated by Anita Bijsterbosch (Clavis, 2016).
> This lift-the-flap book features several animals smiling at the reader. When flaps are lifted, the animals, including a pig, a snake, a bunny, and more, are yawning with wide-open mouths. A human child is last, and an owl warns us to be quiet so all can fall asleep.

CLOTHING

"THE BUNDLE-UP DANCE" ─────────────

Musical/Movement Activity

Sing to the tune of "Baby Shark." Have the children imitate your motions. Everyone stands.

Bundle-up, doot-doot-doodley-doot,
Bundle-up, doot-doot-doodley-doot.
Snow pants, doot-doot-doodley-doot, (*Mime putting on snow pants.*)
Snow pants, doot-doot-doodley-doot.
Winter coat, doot-doot-doodley-doot, (*Mime putting on winter coat.*)
Winter coat, doot-doot-doodley-doot.
Two boots, doot-doot-doodley-doot, (*Mime putting on boots.*)
Two boots, doot-doot-doodley-doot.
Warm hat, doot-doot-doodley-doot, (*Mime putting on hat.*)
Warm hat, doot-doot-doodley-doot.
Long scarf, doot-doot-doodley-doot, (*Mime wrapping scarf around neck.*)
Long scarf, doot-doot-doodley-doot.
Two gloves, doot-doot-doodley-doot, (*Mime putting on gloves.*)
Two gloves, doot-doot-doodley-doot.
Let's play, doot-doot-doodley-doot, (*Dance in place.*)
In the snow, doot-doot-doodley-doot.
Bundle-up, doot-doot-doodley-doot.
Oh yeah, doot-doot-doodley-doot.

PICTURE BOOK MATCH

Little Penguins, written by Cynthia Rylant and illustrated by Christian Robinson (Schwartz and Wade, 2016).

> When the penguins see it snowing outside, they put on their mittens, scarves, socks, and boots. They play outside in the deep snow. When they return home, they take their winter clothes off and put on their jammies.

"DOES YOUR SCARF HANG LOW?" ———————————

Musical/Movement Activity

Sing to the tune of "Do Your Ears Hang Low?" Have several scarves for the children to put on and do the motions with you. If you have a large audience, ask the few with scarves to join you in front and have everyone else mime having a scarf. Place your scarf around your neck and move the ends to the lyrics as you sing.

Does your scarf hang low? (*Drape scarf around neck with the ends of the scarf hanging down.*)
Does it wobble to-and-fro? (*Flap the ends of the scarf.*)
Can you tie it in a knot? (*Mime tying the ends in a knot on top of your head.*)
Can you tie it in a bow? (*Mime tying the ends in a bow in front of your neck.*)
Can you throw it over your shoulder (*Throw one end of the scarf over one of your shoulders.*)
Like a Continental soldier? (*Salute.*)
Does your scarf hang low? (*Drop the ends of the scarf straight down again.*)

PICTURE BOOK MATCH

Lost. Found., written by Marsha Diane Arnold and illustrated by Matthew Cordell (Roaring Brook, 2015).
> Bear's red scarf is lost, and two raccoons find it. They fight over it and lose it. Several other animals find the scarf and eventually lose it until it returns to Bear . . . all unraveled. Bear and the animals repair the scarf and, when they share it, it is "Found."

"DRESSING FOR THE WEATHER" ———————————

Movement Activity

This activity is inspired by all the locations in the country where the residents say, "If you don't like the weather, just wait a few minutes and it will change." Have the children imitate your motions. Everyone stands.

Let's go for a pretend walk.
Look out the window. (*Peer.*)
I think it's raining.

There's no lightning or thunder, so we can walk in the rain.
Put on your boots. (*Mime putting on boots.*)
Put on your raincoat. (*Mime putting on coat.*)
Put on your rain hat. (*Mime putting on hat.*)
Go outside and open your umbrella. (*Mime opening an umbrella.*)
Splash in the puddles. (*Jump up and down.*)
Oh no, the rain is turning to snow.
Back inside. (*Walk in place.*)
Close your umbrella. (*Stop walking and mime closing umbrella.*)
Take off your rain hat. (*Mime removing hat.*)
Take off your raincoat. (*Mime removing coat.*)
Take off your boots. (*Mime removing boots.*)
Put on your snow pants. (*Mime putting on pants.*)
Put on your boots. (*Mime putting on boots.*)
Put on your winter coat. (*Mime putting on coat.*)
Put on your winter hat. (*Mime putting on hat.*)
Put on your mittens. (*Mime putting on mittens.*)
Put on your scarf. (*Mime putting on scarf.*)
Back outside. (*Walk like you are all bundled up.*)
Let's build a snowman. (*Mime playing in the snow.*)
The snow is melting! It's getting hot.
Back inside. (*Walk in place.*)
Take off your scarf. (*Stop walking and mime removing scarf.*)
Take off your mittens. (*Mime removing mittens.*)
Take off your hat. (*Mime removing hat.*)
Take off your coat. (*Mime removing coat.*)
Take off your boots. (*Mime removing boots.*)
Take off your snow pants. (*Mime removing pants.*)
Put on your short pants. (*Mime putting on pants.*)
Put on your Hawaiian shirt. (*Mime putting on shirt.*)
Put on your flip-flops. (*Mime putting on flip-flops.*)
Put on your sunglasses. (*Mime putting on glasses.*)
Let's go outside. (*Walk in place.*)
Oh no. It's starting to rain. (*Stop walking and hold out hand.*)
Do we have to do this all over again? (*Shrug shoulders.*)
Let's go back inside for now and read another book. (*Wave folks to join you.*)

The Thing About Yetis, written and illustrated by Vin Vogel (Dial, 2015).
Yetis love winter. They go sliding, build snow castles, ice-skate "Yeti style" (on their stomachs), and "make the best snowballs on the planet." However, sometimes they can't get warm enough and they "get downright crabby." That's when they miss summer.

"IF YOUR CLOTHES HAVE ANY RED"

Movement Activity

Sing to the tune of "If You're Happy and You Know It." There are several versions of this activity that directs children to touch their shoe and touch their head. My directions are a little goofier. Everyone sits. They stand only if they are wearing the article of clothing mentioned. Then they sit again until the next verse that applies to them.

If your clothes have any yellow, any yellow,
If your clothes have any yellow, any yellow,
If your clothes have any yellow . . . turn your body into Jell-O, (*Shake body.*)
If your clothes have any yellow, any yellow.
If your clothes have any brown, any brown,
If your clothes have any brown, any brown,
If your clothes have any brown . . . stand right up and turn around, (*Turn in a circle.*)
If your clothes have any brown, any brown.
If your clothes have any blue, any blue,
If your clothes have any blue, any blue,
If your clothes have any blue . . . stick your nose inside your shoe, (*Take off shoe and hold it up to face.*)
If your clothes have any blue, any blue.
If your clothes have any pink, any pink,
If your clothes have any pink, any pink,
If your clothes have any pink . . . give us all a great big wink, (*Wink.*)
If your clothes have any pink, any pink.
If your clothes have any white, any white,
If your clothes have any white, any white,
If your clothes have any white . . . give your neighbor a great big fright—BOO! (*Face neighbor and say "Boo!"*)
If your clothes have any white, any white.

Green Pants, written and illustrated by Kenneth Kraegel (Candlewick, 2017).

> Jameson only wears green pants. When his cousin Armando and Armando's fiancé, Jo, ask him to be in their wedding, he says, "Absolutely." He then learns that he must wear black pants with his tuxedo. In the end, Jameson works out a fun solution to his desire to only wear green pants.

"IF YOU'RE WEARING A SHIRT"

Movement Activity

Everyone sits. They stand only if they are wearing the article of clothing mentioned. Then they sit again until the next verse that applies to them. Give them ample time to perform each action.

If you're wearing a shirt . . . stand and pretend you're digging in the dirt. (*Stand and mime digging.*)

If you're wearing any pants . . . stand and do a little dance. (*Stand and dance in place.*)

If you're wearing a hat . . . stand and meow like a cat. (*Stand and meow.*)

If you're wearing a ring . . . stand and let me hear you sing. (*Stand and sing "La, La, La."*)

If you're wearing a dress . . . stand and nod your head yes. (*Stand and nod yes.*)

If you're wearing any underwear . . . (*Big pause.*) . . . That's okay, you just sit there.

Maggie and Michael Get Dressed, written and illustrated by Denise Fleming (Holt, 2016).

> Michael tells his pet dog Maggie that he's putting on yellow socks. Maggie runs away with them. Maggie helps choose the color of Michael's shirt, pants, sneakers, and hat. Of course, there's white underwear.

"THE THREE LITTLE KITTENS WEREN'T THE ONLY ONES TO LOSE THINGS"

Fingerplay

This fingerplay is modeled after the nursery rhyme "Three Little Kittens Lost Their Mittens." Have the children imitate your sounds and motions.

Three little kittens lost their mittens, (*Hold up three fingers.*)
And they began to cry,
"Meow, meow, meow, meow, (*Make meowing sounds while wiggling fists on eyes.*)
Why, oh why, oh why?" (*Hold up hands, palms upward, sad expression on face.*)
Three little ants lost their pants, (*Hold up three fingers.*)
And they began to cry,
"Bibbly-boo, bibbly-boo, (*Make antennae with fingers while making these nonsensical sounds.*)
Why, oh why, oh why?" (*Hold up hands, palms upward, sad expression on face.*)
Three little apes lost their capes, (*Hold up three fingers.*)
And they began to cry,
"Ooh-ooh-ooh, ooh-ooh-ooh, (*Scratch head while making the noise.*)
Why, oh why, oh why?" (*Hold up hands, palms upward, sad expression on face.*)
Three little bats lost their caps, (*Hold up three fingers.*)
And they began to cry,
"Flip-flap, flip-flap, (*Make wings out of hands.*)
Why, oh why, oh why?" (*Hold up hands, palms upward, sad expression on face.*)
Three little doves lost their gloves, (*Hold up three fingers.*)
And they began to cry,
"Coo-coo, coo-coo, (*Bob head back and forth while crying with fists on eyes.*)
Why, oh why, oh why?" (*Hold up hands, palms upward, sad expression on face.*)
Three little goats lost their coats, (*Hold up three fingers.*)
And they began to cry,
"Baa-baa, baa-baa, (*Make baa-like sounds while wiggling fists on eyes.*)
Why, oh why, oh why?" (*Hold up hands, palms upward, sad expression on face.*)

Three little llamas lost their pajamas, (*Hold up three fingers.*)
And they began to cry,
"Bleat, bleat, bleat, bleat, (*Make bleating sounds while wiggling fists on eyes.*)
Why, oh why, oh why?" (*Hold up hands, palms upward, sad expression on face.*)
Three little flies lost their ties, (*Hold up three fingers.*)
And they began to cry,
"Buzz, buzz, buzz, buzz, (*Make buzzing sounds while wiggling fists on eyes.*)
Why, oh why, oh why?" (*Hold up hands, palms upward, sad expression on face.*)
They searched and they tossed and they found what they lost! (*Look around with hand over eyes.*)
They all made a great big sigh, (*Sigh.*)
Their spirits did shine and they all got in line, (*Smile.*)
And ate a great big piece of pie. (*Mime taking a bite out of a piece of pie.*)

PICTURE BOOK MATCH

We Found a Hat, written and illustrated by Jon Klassen (Candlewick, 2016).

> Two turtles find a hat. Although the hat looks good on both, they decide to leave the hat where they found it. Even though they are keeping a close eye on each other, both turtles are tempted to return to the hat.

FAMILY AND FRIENDS

"FIVE LITTLE KIDDOS" ————————————————

Fingerplay

Have the children imitate your motions.

Five little kiddos, (*Hold up five fingers.*)
Rolling in the mud, (*Twirl hands.*)
Mama picked up one kid, (*Grab back of shirt and yank up.*)
And dumped him in the tub. (*Hold nose, take a deep breath, and close eyes.*)
Four little kiddos, (*Hold up four fingers.*)
Rolling in the mud, (*Twirl hands.*)
Papa picked up one kid, (*Grab back of shirt and yank up.*)
And dumped her in the tub. (*Hold nose, take a deep breath, and close eyes.*)
Three little kiddos, (*Hold up three fingers.*)
Rolling in the mud, (*Twirl hands.*)
Mama picked up one kid, (*Grab back of shirt and yank up.*)
And dumped her in the tub. (*Hold nose, take a deep breath, and close eyes.*)
Two little kiddos, (*Hold up two fingers.*)
Rolling in the mud, (*Twirl hands.*)
Papa picked up one kid, (*Grab back of shirt and yank up.*)
And dumped him in the tub. (*Hold nose, take a deep breath, and close eyes.*)
One little kiddo, (*Hold up one finger.*)
Rolling in the mud, (*Twirl hands.*)
His parents picked him up, (*Grab back of shirt and yank up.*)
And dumped him in the tub. (*Hold nose, take a deep breath, and close eyes.*)
Five little kiddos, (*Hold up five fingers.*)
Splashing with bathtub toys, (*Pretend to splash.*)
Smiling 'cause they know they are, (*Big smile.*)
Squeaky-clean girls and boys! (*Rub skin and say "Squeak-squeak."*)

Dirt + Water = Mud, written and illustrated by Katherine Hannigan (Greenwillow, 2016).

> A girl and her dog make a big mud puddle in the yard and dive in. They both roll around in it: "MUD + SPLASH + SPLATTER = VERY MUCKY." They wash off with the garden hose and move on to another backyard adventure.

"THE ITSY-BITSY BABY"

Musical Activity

This activity is modeled after the nursery rhyme "The Itsy-Bitsy Spider." Have the children imitate your motions.

The itsy-bitsy baby,
Reached the table top, (*Mime pulling up to a standing position.*)
Baby lost her balance, (*Flail arms and wobble.*)
And landed with a plop. (*Sit.*)
Baby stretched her arms, (*Stretch arms.*)
And struggled with all her might, (*Scrunch face and mime pulling up again.*)
And the itsy-bitsy baby, (*Slowly get into a standing position.*)
Pulled up and stood upright. (*Stand straight, throw out arms, and say,*
    "Ta-da!")

King Baby, written and illustrated by Kate Beaton (Arthur Levine, 2016).

> King Baby makes many demands of his subjects (his parents): "FEED ME! BURP ME! CHANGE ME! BOUNCE ME! CARRY ME!" When King Baby learns to crawl, stand, and walk, he becomes "a big boy."

"MY FAMILY CAME BACK"

Musical/Movement Activity

This activity is modeled after the camp song activity "My Aunt Came Back." Have the children repeat the lines after you and imitate your motions. Everyone stands.

Leader: My dad came back,

Audience: My dad came back,

Leader: From the shopping mall.

Audience: From the shopping mall.

Leader: He wound up buying,

Audience: He wound up buying,

Leader: A ladder this tall.

Audience: A ladder this tall. (*Hold up one arm high overhead and keep it there the entire activity.*)

Leader: My brother came back,

Audience: My brother came back,

Leader: From the local school.

Audience: From the local school.

Leader: He started acting,

Audience: He started acting,

Leader: Like he was cool.

Audience: Like he was cool. (*While one arm is still overhead, walk in place with a swagger and nod head like you are the coolest person around.*)

Leader: My mom came back,

Audience: My mom came back,

Leader: From the city park.

Audience: From the city park.

Leader: She got chased out,

Audience: She got chased out,

Leader: By bugs in the dark.

Audience: By bugs in the dark. (*Add the slapping of various body parts with the other hand to the previous motions.*)

Leader: My sister came back,

Audience: My sister came back,

Leader: From her favorite playground.

Audience: From her favorite playground.

Leader: She got on a ride,

Audience: She got on a ride,

Leader: That went 'round and 'round.

Audience: That went 'round and 'round. (*Add the motion of turning slowly in a circle to the previous motions.*)

Leader: My family is dizzy,

Audience: My family is dizzy,

Leader: From running 'round town.
Audience: From running 'round town.
Leader: So, I just think,
Audience: So, I just think,
Leader: They'll sit right down.
Audience: They'll sit right down. (*Stop all motions and sit.*)

PICTURE BOOK MATCH

One Big Family, written by Marc Harshman and illustrated by Sara Palacios (Eerdmans, 2016).

> At the end of summer, Grandma and Grandpa say, "Come." During the visit, Brother says, "Swim," cousin Tommy says, "Run," Uncle Jim says, "Sing," Aunt Jayne says, "Wash," and a photographer says, "Smile."

"MY GRANDMOTHER HAD A HOUSE"

Musical Activity

Sing to the tune of "Old MacDonald Had a Farm." Have the children imitate your sounds, making a whistle sound and a snoring sound in place of saying the words "whistle" and "snore."

My grandmother had a house, E-I-E-I-O.
And in this house, she had a clock, E-I-E-I-O.
With a "Tick-Tock" here and a "Tick-Tock" there,
Here a "Tick," there a "Tock," everywhere a "Tick-Tock,"
My grandmother had a house, E-I-E-I-O.
And in this house, she had a teapot, E-I-E-I-O.
With a (*whistle*) here and a (*whistle*) there,
Here a (*whistle*), there a (*whistle*), everywhere a (*whistle*),
With a "Tick-Tock" here and a "Tick-Tock" there,
Here a "Tick," there a "Tock," everywhere a "Tick-Tock,"
My grandmother had a house, E-I-E-I-O.
And in this house, she had a rocking chair, E-I-E-I-O.
With a "Squeak-Squeak," here and a "Squeak-Squeak" there,
Here a "Squeak," there a "Squeak," everywhere a "Squeak-Squeak,"
A (*whistle*) here and a (*whistle*) there,
Here a (*whistle*), there a (*whistle*), everywhere a (*whistle*),

With a "Tick-Tock" here and a "Tick-Tock" there,
Here a "Tick," there a "Tock," everywhere a "Tick-Tock,"
My grandmother had a house, E-I-E-I-O.
And in this house, she had a grandpa, E-I-E-I-O.
With a "Snore-Snore" here and a "Snore-Snore" there,
Here a "Snore," there a "Snore," everywhere a "Snore-Snore,"
With a "Squeak-Squeak" here and a "Squeak-Squeak" there,
Here a "Squeak," there a "Squeak," everywhere a "Squeak-Squeak,"
A (*whistle*) here and a (*whistle*) there,
Here a (*whistle*), there a (*whistle*), everywhere a (*whistle*),
With a "Tick-Tock" here and a "Tick-Tock" there,
Here a "Tick," there a "Tock," everywhere a "Tick-Tock,"
My grandmother had a house, E-I-E-I-O.

PICTURE BOOK MATCH

Grandma's Tiny House, written by JaNay Brown-Wood and illustrated by
Priscilla Burris (Charlesbridge, 2017).
> Everyone meets at Grandma's old house on Brown Street. Will they all fit
> inside? The house quickly fills up until folks move outside to Grandma's
> backyard, "where we all go to EAT."

"THE NEW MY AUNT CAME BACK" ————————

Musical/Movement Activity

This activity is modeled after the camp song activity "My Aunt Came Back." Have
the children repeat the lines after you and imitate your motions. Everyone stands.

Leader: Well, my aunt came back,
Audience: Well, my aunt came back,
Leader: From Old Belize.
Audience: From Old Belize.
Leader: She had some fun,
Audience: She had some fun,
Leader: Swaying in the breeze. (*Raise hands overhead and sway.*)
Audience: Swaying in the breeze.
Leader: Well, my aunt came back,
Audience: Well, my aunt came back,

Leader: From grand Old France.
Audience: From grand Old France.
Leader: She got caught up,
Audience: She got caught up,
Leader: From doing a dance. (*Dance in place while swaying arms overhead.*)
Audience: From doing a dance.
Leader: Well, my aunt came back,
Audience: Well, my aunt came back,
Leader: From Ecuador.
Audience: From Ecuador.
Leader: She got stuck in,
Audience: She got stuck in,
Leader: A revolving door. (*Spin in a slow circle while dancing in place and swaying arms overhead.*)
Audience: A revolving door.
Leader: Well, my aunt came back,
Audience: Well, my aunt came back,
Leader: From Cameroon.
Audience: From Cameroon.
Leader: She got sucked in,
Audience: She got sucked in,
Leader: A big typhoon. (*Blow with gusto while spinning in a slow circle and dancing in place and swaying arms overhead.*)
Audience: A big typhoon.
Leader: Well, my aunt came back,
Audience: Well, my aunt came back,
Leader: From Italy.
Audience: From Italy.
Leader: She hurried home,
Audience: She hurried home,
Leader: 'Cuz she missed me! (*Stop all motions and point to self.*)
Audience: 'Cuz she missed me!

PICTURE BOOK MATCH

The Frazzle Family Finds a Way, written by Ann Bonwill and illustrated by Stephen Gammell (Holiday House, 2013).

The Frazzle Family forgets things. Aunt Rosemary comes to visit with several memory tips. None of them work until the Frazzle Family learns to sing songs to help them remember.

"UNCLE DAVID"

Have the children repeat the lines after you and imitate your motions. Everyone stands.

Leader: My Uncle David likes to bowl, (*Make underhand bowling motions with right hand.*)
Audience: My Uncle David likes to bowl,
Leader: My Uncle David likes to fish, (*Make overhand casting motion with left arm.*)
Audience: My Uncle David likes to fish,
Leader: Bowl, fish. Bowl, fish. (*Make the bowling motion followed by the fishing motion twice each.*)
Audience: Bowl, fish. Bowl, fish.
Leader: My Uncle David likes to punt, (*Make a punting motion with right leg.*)
Audience: My Uncle David likes to punt,
Leader: My Uncle David likes to kick, (*Make a sideways, karate-style kick with left leg.*)
Audience: My Uncle David likes to kick,
Leader: Punt, kick. Punt, kick. (*Make the punting motion followed by the kicking motion twice each.*)
Audience: Punt, kick. Punt, kick.
Leader: My Uncle David likes to twist, (*Do "The Twist" dance movements.*)
Audience: My Uncle David likes to twist,
Leader: My Uncle David likes to skip, (*Skip in a tiny circle.*)
Audience: My Uncle David likes to skip,
Leader: Twist, skip. Twist, skip. (*Make the twist dance motion followed by the skipping motion twice each.*)
Leader: My Uncle David falls in a heap, (*Fall to floor.*)
Audience: My Uncle David falls in a heap,
Leader: He's totally pooped and falls asleep. (*Close eyes.*)
Audience: He's totally pooped and falls asleep.

The Big Ideas of Buster Bickles, written and illustrated by Dave Wasson
(Harper, 2015).
> Buster's uncle invents a "What-If Machine" that transports the two of
> them to a world made of ice cream. "There was even a caramel river."
> The two get into trouble when the machine creates robot dinosaurs, but
> everything eventually returns to near normal.

"WHAT'CHA DOING?"

Movement Activity

Have the children imitate your motions.

Hey there, Friend, what'cha doing?
Looks to me like you're digging a hole, (*Make digging motions.*)
Digging a, digging a, digging a hole.
Hey there, Friend, what'cha doing?
Looks to me like you're eating a cone, (*Mime eating an ice cream cone.*)
Eating a, eating a, eating a cone.
Hey there, Friend, what'cha doing?
Looks to me like you're putting on shoes, (*Sit and mime putting on shoes.*)
Putting on, putting on, putting on shoes.
Hey there, Friend, what'cha doing?
Looks to me like you're doing a dance, (*Dance in place.*)
Doing a, doing a, doing a dance.
Hey there, Friend, what'cha doing?
Looks to me like you're making a friend, (*Everyone nods to each other.*)
Making a, making a, making a friend.

A Perfect Day for Digging, written by Cari Best and illustrated by Christine
Davenier (Two Lions, 2014).
> Nell and her dog Rusty play in the dirt and attract the attention of
> Norman, who hates getting dirty. Norman watches Nell and Rusty dig
> a "tunnel like a mole." Norman eventually joins the fun, getting dirty
> in the process.

FEELINGS

"THE BIG GORILLA"

Sound Effects Activity

Have the children repeat the lines after you.

Leader: The big gorilla says, "Ooh! Ooh! Ooh!"
Audience: The big gorilla says, "Ooh! Ooh! Ooh!"
Leader: "Ooh! Ooh! Ooh!" means "I love you!"
Audience: "Ooh! Ooh! Ooh!" means "I love you!"
Leader: The farmer's cow says, "Moo! Moo! Moo!"
Audience: The farmer's cow says, "Moo! Moo! Moo!"
Leader: "Moo! Moo! Moo!" means "I love you!"
Audience: "Moo! Moo! Moo!" means "I love you!"
Leader: The tiny pigeon says, "Coo! Coo! Coo!"
Audience: The tiny pigeon says, "Coo! Coo! Coo!"
Leader: "Coo! Coo! Coo!" means "I love you!"
Audience: "Coo! Coo! Coo!" means "I love you!"
Leader: The wise old owl says, "Whoo! Whoo! Whoo!"
Audience: The wise old owl says, "Whoo! Whoo! Whoo!"
Leader: "Whoo! Whoo! Whoo!" means "I love you!"
Audience: "Whoo! Whoo! Whoo!" means "I love you!"
Leader: The teeny ghost goes, "Boo! Boo! Boo!"
Audience: The teeny ghost goes, "Boo! Boo! Boo!"
Leader: "Boo! Boo! Boo!" means "I love you!"
Audience: "Boo! Boo! Boo!" means "I love you!"
Leader: The shiny train goes, "Choo! Choo! Choo!"
Audience: The shiny train goes, "Choo! Choo! Choo!"
Leader: "Choo! Choo! Choo!" means "I love you!"
Audience: "Choo! Choo! Choo!" means "I love you!"
Leader: The little baby goes, "Goo! Goo! Goo!"
Audience: The little baby goes, "Goo! Goo! Goo!"

Leader: "Goo! Goo! Goo!" means "I love you!"
Audience: "Goo! Goo! Goo!" means "I love you!"

PICTURE BOOK MATCH

Swish and Squeak's Noisy Day, written and illustrated by Birgitta Sif
(Knopf, 2017).
> For breakfast, one mouse sister goes, "CRUNCH CRUNCH CRUNCH
> CRUNCH." At school, the mice hear "RING RING RING" and
> the "Squeeeeak toot pump um bah ba" of the school band. At
> the end of the day, one sister hears the other sleeping with a
> "ZZZ-Zzzz-ZZzzz-hngGGgghPpbhwzZZ-zzzzz."

"BUT MOSTLY I LOVE YOU"

Movement Activity

Have the children imitate your motions. Everyone stands.

I love, I love the earth below, (*Touch the ground.*)
I love the sky so blue, (*Point upward.*)
I love this world so very much, (*Head back, face upward, arms out, spin
    slowly in a circle.*)
But mostly I love you. (*Point to eyes on "I," point to your heart on "love,"
    and point to someone else on "you."*)

PICTURE BOOK MATCH

Love, written and illustrated by Emma Dodd (Nosy Crow, 2016).
> A mother rabbit tells her little one, "Love is in the morning when you
> wake and smile at me." Their love continues throughout the whole day.
> At nighttime, there are as many reasons to love as "there are stars up
> in the sky."

"EASY-PEASY"

Movement Activity

Have the children imitate your motions. Everyone stands.

You can clap, (*Clap.*)
You can clap, (*Clap.*)

Why, that's so easy-peasy. (*Give a thumbs-up motion.*)
You can smile, (*Give a big smile and keep it going for the next verse.*)
You can smile,
That's so easy-peasy, too. (*Wave hand as if saying, "That was nothing."*)
You can sing, (*Stroke throat with mouth open. Sing these three lines.*)
You can sing,
Why, that's so easy-peasy. (*Give thumbs-up motion.*)
You can love, (*Cross hands over heart.*)
You can love,
That's easy-peasy, too. (*Wave hand as if saying, "That was nothing."*)

PICTURE BOOK MATCH

My Little Sister and Me, written and illustrated by Maple Lam (Harper, 2016).

> A boy is proud when Mom asks him to take his little sister "home from the bus stop—all by myself!" His sister chases dogs and birds and is frightened by a thunderstorm. Big brother reassures her that she is brave.

"IF YOU'RE BRAVE AND YOU KNOW IT"
Musical Activity

Sing to the tune of "If You're Happy and You Know It." Have the children imitate your sounds and motions.

If you're brave and you know it, make a muscle, (*Make a muscle.*)
If you're brave and you know it, make a muscle, (*Make a muscle.*)
If you're brave and you know it, then your heart will surely show it,
If you're brave and you know it, make a muscle. (*Make a muscle.*)
If you're scared and you know it, say Boo-Hoo, (*Say "Boo-Hoo" with an exaggerated crying voice.*)
If you're scared and you know it, say Boo-Hoo, (*"Boo-Hoo."*)
If you're scared and you know it, then your heart will surely show it,
If you're scared and you know it, say Boo-Hoo. (*"Boo-Hoo."*)
If you're brave and you know it, shout, "I'm brave!" (*"I'm brave!"*)
If you're brave and you know it, shout, "I'm brave!" (*"I'm brave!"*)
If you're brave and you know it, then your heart will surely show it,
If you're brave and you know it, shout, "I'm brave!" (*"I'm brave!"*)

I'm Brave, written by Kate McMullan and illustrated by Jim McMullan
(Balzer and Bray, 2014).

> A fully equipped big red engine heads out to battle a fire at the Pine Street
> Warehouse. The engine uses its resources, including the water cannon, to
> put out the fire. When the engine returns to the station and gets cleaned
> up, it proudly states that it is "Brave! That's what. And—good lookin'."

"I'M MAD! STOMP! STOMP!"

Movement Activity

Have the children repeat the lines after you and perform the motions.

Leader: I'm mad! Stomp! Stomp! (*Make a mad face and stomp the floor
repeatedly.*)
I'm mad! Stomp! Stomp!
I'm mad! I'm mad! I'm mad! Stomp! Stomp!
Audience: I'm mad! Stomp! Stomp!
I'm mad! Stomp! Stomp!
I'm mad! I'm mad! I'm mad! Stomp! Stomp!
Leader: I'm mad! Hop! Hop! (*Continue making a mad face and hop in
place.*)
I'm mad! Hop! Hop!
I'm mad! I'm mad! I'm mad! Hop! Hop!
Audience: I'm mad! Hop! Hop!
I'm mad! Hop! Hop!
I'm mad! I'm mad! I'm mad! Hop! Hop!
Leader: I'm mad! Scream! Scream! (*Continue making a mad face. Say
these lines with a higher pitched voice.*)
I'm mad! Scream! Scream!
I'm mad! I'm mad! I'm mad! Scream! Scream!
Audience: I'm mad! Scream! Scream!
I'm mad! Scream! Scream!
I'm mad! I'm mad! I'm mad! Scream! Scream!
(*Pause.*)
Leader: I'm taking control. (*Stand still.*)
Audience: I'm taking control.
Leader: I'm going to freeze!

Audience: I'm going to freeze!
(*Stand motionless for a few seconds.*)
Leader: Whew. (*Wipe brow.*)
Audience: Whew.
Leader: I feel much, much better.
Audience: I feel much, much better.

How Do Dinosaurs Say I'M MAD?, written by Jane Yolen and illustrated
by Mark Teague (Blue Sky, 2013).

> When dinosaurs act mad, do they roar, slam doors, and yell at Mom
> and Dad? When they get mad, do they throw their toys, kick chairs, or
> "fling a mug at the cat"? No, they learn to count, take deep breaths,
> apologize, and give a big hug.

"MY FACE"

Imagination Exercise

Have the children repeat the lines after you and make the appropriate faces.

Leader: My oh my, my oh my, I've got my mad face on! (*Make a mad
face.*)
Audience: My oh my, my oh my, I've got my mad face on!
Leader: My oh my, my oh my, I've got my sad face on! (*Make a sad face.*)
Audience: My oh my, my oh my, I've got my sad face on!
Leader: My oh my, my oh my, I've got my surprised face on! (*Make a
surprised face.*)
Audience: My oh my, my oh my, I've got my surprised face on!
Leader: My oh my, my oh my, I've got my worried face on! (*Make a
worried face.*)
Audience: My oh my, my oh my, I've got my worried face on!
Leader: My oh my, my oh my, I've got my happy face on! (*Make a happy
face.*)
Audience: My oh my, my oh my, I've got my happy face on!
(*Follow up by going through the facial expressions as a drill: "Mad! Sad!
Happy! Worried! Surprised! Mad! Happy! Sad!"*)

PICTURE BOOK MATCH

The Good for Nothing Button!, written and illustrated by Charise Mericle Harper (Hyperion, 2017).

> Yellow Bird has a button that doesn't do anything when it's pressed. He does get upset when Red Bird and Blue Bird are happy when they press the button. Yellow Bird goes through a whole range of emotions before they all realize that the button makes them funny. And Yellow Bird likes being funny.

"NO, NO, NO, NO, NO, NO, NO, YES, YES, YES, YES, YES!"

Movement Activity

Teach the children to say "No!" seven times when you ask a "naughty situation" question and to say "Yes!" five times when you ask a "proper behavior" question, with a special loud "YES!" on the fifth "yes." Have them shake their head "no" or nod "yes" at the appropriate times.

Leader: Should I kick the cat? Should I kick the cat?
Audience: No, No, No, No, No, No, No!
Leader: Should I pet the cat? Should I pet the cat?
Audience: Yes, Yes, Yes, Yes, YES!
Leader: Shall I spit my food? Shall I spit my food?
Audience: No, No, No, No, No, No, No!
Leader: Shall I swallow my food? Shall I swallow my food?
Audience: Yes, Yes, Yes, Yes, YES!
Leader: Shall I write on the walls? Shall I write on the walls?
Audience: No, No, No, No, No, No, No!
Leader: Shall I write on paper? Shall I write on paper!
Audience: Yes, Yes, Yes, Yes, YES!
Leader: Shall I push my parents? Shall I push my parents?
Audience: No, No, No, No, No, No, No!
Leader: Shall I hug my parents? Shall I hug my parents?
Audience: Yes, Yes, Yes, Yes, YES!

Grumpy Pants, written and illustrated by Claire Messer (Albert Whitman, 2016).

> Penguin is in a bad mood. He stomps home, throws off his rain clothes, and is still grumpy. He takes a deep breath and counts, has a nice cold bath where "he hid under the water and made himself a bubble beard," and starts to feel better "little by little."

"THE SMILEY HOKEY POKEY"

Musical Activity

Sing to the tune of "The Hokey Pokey." Have the children imitate your expressions and motions.

You put your SMILE on, (*Give a big smile.*)
You take your SMILE off, (*Look blank.*)
You put your SMILE on, (*Give a big smile.*)
And you shake it all about, (*Move head around in a figure-eight motion while smiling.*)
You do the Hokey Pokey, (*Continue moving head.*)
And you show your great big SMILE, (*Exaggerate smile.*)
That's what it's all about. (*Clap twice.*)
You put your SAD FACE on, (*Look sad. Perhaps stick lower lip out.*)
You take your SAD FACE off, (*Look blank.*)
You put your SAD FACE on, (*Look sad.*)
And you shake it all about, (*Look at ground and shake head back and forth.*)
You do the Hokey Pokey, (*Continue moving head.*)
And you show your poor SAD FACE, (*Look sad.*)
That's what it's all about. (*Clap twice.*)
You put your MAD FACE on, (*Look mad.*)
You take your MAD FACE off, (*Look blank.*)
You put your MAD FACE on, (*Look mad.*)
And you shake it all about, (*Cross arms and shake head back and forth.*)
You do the Hokey Pokey, (*Continue moving head.*)
And you show your poor MAD FACE, (*Look mad.*)
That's what it's all about. (*Clap twice.*)

(*Pause and ask the kids if coming to Storytime makes them sad. Ask them if it makes them mad. Finally, ask them if coming to Storytime makes them happy and sing the "SMILE" verse one more time.*)

You put your SMILE on, (*Give a big smile.*)

You take your SMILE off, (*Look blank.*)

You put your SMILE on, (*Give a big smile.*)

And you shake it all about, (*Move head around in a figure-eight motion while smiling.*)

You do the Hokey Pokey, (*Continue moving head.*)

And you show your great big SMILE, (*Exaggerate smile.*)

That's what it's all about. (*Clap twice.*)

PICTURE BOOK MATCH

Wild Feelings, written and illustrated by David Milgrim (Holt, 2015).

A child is asked if he ever feels "as sad as a lost kitten in the rain," or "as daffy as a duck," or even "really, really, rrrrreally mad." The child is assured that everyone has those feelings. "It's only natural."

IMAGINATION

"ABRA-CADABRA-BIPPITY-BOPPITY" ———————

Movement Activity

Have the children imitate your motions.

Abra-Cadabra-Bippity-Boppity,
Imagine you are holding a pretty butterfly! (*Cup hands together as if holding a tiny butterfly.*)
Abra-Cadabra-Bippity-Boppity,
Imagine you are holding a funny green frog! (*Hold hands just a little farther apart than before.*)
Abra-Cadabra-Bippity-Boppity,
Imagine you are holding a cuddly kitty cat! (*Spread hands even more and make a cuddle motion.*)
Abra-Cadabra-Bippity-Boppity,
Imagine you are holding a heavy pink pig! (*With a surprised look on your face, hold hands out in front of you as if holding a pig.*)
Abra-Cadabra-Bippity-Boppity,
Imagine you are holding a black-and-white cow! (*Make an even more surprised look with your hands upward as if holding something heavy overhead.*)
Abra-Cadabra-Bippity-Boppity,
Imagine you are holding a great big whale! (*Act even more astonished and hold hands way overhead. Have your body slump down under that great weight. Make grunting noises.*)
Abra-Cadabra-Bippity-Boppity,
Now you see them, now you DON'T! (*Clap hands on "DON'T."*)

It Came in the Mail, written and illustrated by Ben Clanton (Simon and Schuster, 2016).

> Liam says "Boogers" because he never gets mail. When he checks the mailbox, he finds "diddly-squat." One day, Liam receives a dragon in the mail. The mailbox keeps bringing other weird objects, like "Pickles! Pigs! A whale with wings! A trombone!"

"CAN YOU CLIMB?"

Musical/Movement Activity

Sing to the tune of "Mary Had a Little Lamb." Teach the children to stand every time there is a word that begins with the letter C and to sit when followed by another word beginning with C. Say the chant slowly to allow for the constant up-and-down movements. An alternative method is to have the children raise and lower their hands.

Can you climb up to a cloud?
To a cloud? To a cloud?
Can you climb up to a cloud?
If so, I'll clap my hands.

I Am Yoga, written by Susan Verde and illustrated by Peter H. Reynolds (Abrams, 2015).

> When the world feels too big, a girl thinks "racing breath: be slow" and states, "I am yoga." She imagines herself soaring among the clouds, dancing with the moon, sailing on the sea, and relaxing. Now, the "world is just the right size."

"FEE FI FO FUM"

Movement Activity

Have the children imitate your motions.

Fee Fi Fo Fum,
I'm not a giant,
I'm a Frog! (*Hop like a frog and make frog noises.*)

Fee Fi Fo Fum,
I'm not a giant,
I'm a Fish! (*Move around as a fish might look swimming.*)
Fee Fi Fo Fum,
I'm not a giant,
I'm a Fly! (*Buzz around the room like a fly.*)
Fee Fi Fo Fum,
I'm not a giant,
I'm a Forest! (*Stand like a tree.*)
Fee Fi Fo Fum,
I'm not a giant,
I'm a Friend! (*Encourage the kids to give each other a high five, smile at each other, etc.*)

PICTURE BOOK MATCH

I'm a Frog!, written and illustrated by Mo Willems (Hyperion, 2013).
Piggie pretends to be a frog by hopping and saying, "Ribbit!" Gerald the elephant is confused. He thought Piggie was a pig. Frog teaches Gerald all about pretending. Gerald pretends to be a cow.

"HEY YOU! HEY ME!"

Movement Activity

Have the kids repeat the lines after you and imitate your motions. Everyone stands.

Leader: Hey you!
Audience: Hey you!
Leader: Hey me!
Audience: Hey me!
Leader: Look'ee here!
Audience: Look'ee here!
Leader: I'm a tree!
Audience: I'm a tree! (*Display "branches" with arms.*)
Leader: Hey you!
Audience: Hey you!
Leader: Hey me!
Audience: Hey me!

Leader: Look'ee here!

Audience: Look'ee here!

Leader: I'm a bee!

Audience: I'm a bee! (*Make flying motions and buzzing noises.*)

Leader: Hey you!

Audience: Hey you!

Leader: Hey me!

Audience: Hey me!

Leader: Look'ee here!

Audience: Look'ee here!

Leader: I'm a chimpanzee!

Audience: I'm a chimpanzee! (*Make ape noises and movements.*)

Leader: Hey you!

Audience: Hey you!

Leader: Hey me!

Audience: Hey me!

Leader: Look'ee here!

Audience: Look'ee here!

Leader: We are WE!

Audience: We are WE! (*Point to each other or do a group hug.*)

PICTURE BOOK MATCH

Ally-saurus and the First Day of School, written and illustrated by Richard
Torrey (Sterling, 2015).

Ally pretends to be a dinosaur throughout her first day of school. Other
kids join the fun. When Ally wakes up the next day, she hops like a
rabbit. "She couldn't wait to get to school."

"IF YOU WERE"

Movement Activity

Have the children follow this two-part movement activity with first an appropriate
sound and then an appropriate movement, however they wish to interpret each
line. Everyone stands.

If you were a monkey . . . you would sound like this . . . and move like
this.

If you were a kitty cat . . . you would sound like this . . . and move like this.

If you were a bird . . . you would sound like this . . . and move like this.

If you were a car . . . you would sound like this . . . and move like this.

If you were an airplane . . . you would sound like this . . . and move like this.

PICTURE BOOK MATCH

Melvin the Mouth, written by Katherine Blanc and illustrated by Jeffrey Ebbeler (Charlesbridge, 2017).

> Mel Blanc was the voice behind Bugs Bunny, Daffy Duck, Porky Pig, Woody Woodpecker, and more. Young Melvin not only moves like he's a dragon, a tiger, and a shark, he also makes "BIG sounds" to accompany his imaginings.

"REPTILES AND AMPHIBIANS"

Fingerplay

Have the children imitate your motions.

Let's pretend we're a little frog,

Sitting on a log in the bog. (*Hold up fist sideways, move thumb up and down, forming a mouth, and make a frog noise.*)

Let's pretend we're a slithery snake,

Sliding through the canebrake. (*Place palms together and move them back and forth.*)

Let's pretend we're a crocodile,

Swimming with a great big smile. (*Place palms together and clap.*)

Now we're lizards in the sun,

Now we dart, now we run. (*Move pointer finger back and forth.*)

Let's pretend we're turtles eating flies,

Now it's time to say a swamp goodbye. (*Make a fist, stick out thumb, wave thumb goodbye.*)

PICTURE BOOK MATCH

Turtle Island, written and illustrated by Kevin Sherry (Dial, 2014).

> A turtle as large as an island is surprised when he gets visitors: a cat, a frog, an owl, and a bear. The animals build a ship to return to their

families, and they leave the turtle behind. The animals return with their families and that "is how Turtle Island started."

"USE, USE, USE YOUR MIND—SOUNDS" ————————

Musical Activity

Sing to the tune of "Row, Row, Row Your Boat." As you sing each verse, pause after the phrase, "Tell me what you say" and let the children fill in with their own animal noises.

Use, use, use your mind,
In a special way,
Imagine that you are a Bee,
Tell me what you say: "Buzz!"
Use, use, use your mind,
In a special way,
Imagine that you are a Coyote,
Tell me what you say: "Howl!" (*or "Yip! Yip!"*)
Use, use, use your mind,
In a special way,
Imagine that you are a Dolphin,
Tell me what you say: "Eee! Eee! Eee!" (*or "Click! Click! Click!"*)
Use, use, use your mind,
In a special way,
Imagine that you are a Donkey,
Tell me what you say: "Hee-haw!"
Use, use, use your mind,
In a special way,
Imagine that you are a Llama,
Tell me what you say: "___" (*Make a pretend spit noise. Entirely optional,
    of course, but the kids will laugh.*)

PICTURE BOOK MATCH

If You Were a Dog, written by Jamie A. Swenson and illustrated by Chris
    Raschka (Farrar, Straus and Giroux, 2014).
        If a kid was like a dog, she might howl like this: "ARRRRR-
    ROOOOOOOOOOOOOO!" She might also make sounds and move like

a cat, fish, bird, bug, frog, or dinosaur. Instead, she goes, "GIGGLE, GIGGLE, GIGGLE!"

"WHAT CAN I DO WITH MY BLANKET?"

Movement Activity

Hold up a baby blanket. Have the children imitate your motions with a pretend blanket.

What can I do with my blanket?
I can wear it as . . . a cape. (*Place blanket around your shoulders.*)
I can wear it as . . . a mask. (*Wrap blanket around your head leaving an open space for your eyes.*)
I can use it as . . . a sack. (*Hold blanket by its corners to make a sack and place a small toy in it.*)
I can use it as . . . a sled. (*Place blanket on floor and sit on it.*)
I can use it as . . . a tent. (*Hold blanket over your head.*)
I can use it as . . . a rug. (*Place blanket on the floor and stand on it.*)
I can use it as . . . a napkin. (*Use a corner of the blanket to wipe the edges of your mouth.*)
I can use it to . . . wave goodbye. (*Flap the blanket in the air.*)

PICTURE BOOK MATCH

Maya's Blanket / La manta de Maya, written by Monica Brown and illustrated by David Diaz (Lee and Low, 2015).

Maya has a special *manta,* a blanket that is blue and green with purple butterflies. It protects Maya from bad dreams. When the blanket is frayed, Abuelita and Maya make it into a *vestido,* a dress. The story line continues until the blanket becomes a magical bookmark. When that is lost, Maya writes the story of *Maya's Blanket / La manta de Maya.*

LET'S MOVE, DANCE, AND SING

"THE ANTS GO DANCING"

Musical/Movement Activity

Sing to the tune of "The Ants Go Marching." Have the children imitate your motions. Everyone stands.

The ants go marching one by one, hurrah, hurrah, (*March in place.*)
The ants go marching one by one, hurrah, hurrah,
The ants go marching one by one,
They twirl and spin and have lots of fun, (*Twirl and spin with teeny-tiny motions, like an ant.*)
As they all go dancing 'round and 'round and 'round.
The penguins go marching one by one, hurrah, hurrah, (*March in place.*)
The penguins go marching one by one, hurrah, hurrah,
The penguins go marching one by one,
They twirl and spin and have lots of fun, (*Twirl and spin with arms at sides and waddling moves, like a penguin.*)
As they all go dancing 'round and 'round and 'round.
The moose go marching one by one, hurrah, hurrah, (*March in place.*)
The moose go marching one by one, hurrah, hurrah,
The moose go marching one by one,
They twirl and spin and have lots of fun, (*Twirl and spin with large movements and hands by head, like a moose.*)
As they all go dancing 'round and 'round and 'round.
The dinosaurs go marching one by one, hurrah, hurrah, (*March in place.*)
The dinosaurs go marching one by one, hurrah, hurrah,
The dinosaurs go marching one by one,
They twirl and spin and have lots of fun, (*Twirl and spin with even larger motions, like a dinosaur.*)
As they all go dancing 'round and 'round and 'round.

Dance Is for Everyone, written and illustrated by Andrea Zuill (Sterling, 2017).

> An alligator shows up for dance lessons at Mrs. Iraina's ballet school. No one is brave enough to send her away. The teacher and human students decide to create a dance just right for an enthusiastic dancer with "a big, swishy tail."

"DIG-A-DIG-A-DIG-A-DIG-A"

Movement Activity

Have the children stand and mime digging a hole with a shovel. With every "Dig-a," they will alternate between a downward motion of the shovel scooping dirt and an upward motion of tossing the dirt over their shoulder. Clap once on "Hole!" Perform this routine slowly to allow the children to get into the flow of the movements. When you get to the section "A Deeper, Deeper, Deeper, Deeper, Deeper, Deeper Hole!," have the children stand straight up and then slowly bend over for the series of "Deeper." Again, clap once on "Hole!" The children stand straight up and bend over a second time before going back to the first set of motions. If the kids pick up the rhythm of the actions quickly, do the entire activity a second time, but faster.

Leader: Let's Dig-a-Dig-a-Dig-a-Dig-a-Dig-a-Dig-a-Hole!
Audience: Let's Dig-a-Dig-a-Dig-a-Dig-a-Dig-a-Dig-a-Hole!
Leader: A Deeper, Deeper, Deeper, Deeper, Deeper, Deeper Hole!
Audience: A Deeper, Deeper, Deeper, Deeper, Deeper, Deeper Hole!
Leader: Let's Dig-a-Dig-a-Dig-a-Dig-a-Dig-a-Dig-a-Hole!
Audience: Let's Dig-a-Dig-a-Dig-a-Dig-a-Dig-a-Dig-a-Hole!

Sam and Dave Dig a Hole, written by Mac Barnett and illustrated by Jon Klassen (Candlewick, 2014).

> Sam and Dave dig a hole looking for something spectacular. They keep digging and digging even though they have run out of chocolate milk and "shared the last animal cookie." At the end of their dig, they decide their adventure was spectacular.

"FASTER, FASTER"

Movement Activity

Have the children imitate your motions.

Blink your eyes very slowly . . . now faster . . . faster! Stop!
Wiggle your tongue very slowly . . . now faster . . . faster! Stop!
Shrug your shoulders very slowly . . . now faster . . . faster! Stop!
Clap your hands very slowly . . . now faster . . . faster! Stop!
(*For an added laugh, take a bow after the clapping routine and thank the children.*)

PICTURE BOOK MATCH

Don't Blink!, written and illustrated by Tom Booth (Feiwel and Friends, 2017). A girl has a staring contest with the reader. She's joined by several animals who try their hardest not to blink. When they do blink, the girl points to the winner and exclaims, "I think YOU won!"

"FLIP, FLOP"

Movement Activity

Have the children imitate your motions.

Flip, Flop,
Drip, Drop,
Time to move,
A little bit funny:
Let me see you move super slow. (*Walk around the room moving in slow motion.*)
Flip, Flop,
Drip, Drop,
Time to move,
A little bit funny:
Let me see you move teeny tiny. (*Move with miniature movements, such as tiny steps and tiny hand gestures.*)
Flip, Flop,
Drip, Drop,
Time to move,

A little bit funny:

Let me see you move backward. (*Model moving backward slowly, even cautioning the children to keep their eyes open and watch where they are going and to go slowly.*)

Flip, Flop,

Drip, Drop,

Time to move,

A little bit funny:

Let me see you (*pause*) sit down! (*Surprise the children by sitting quickly. They'll follow.*)

PICTURE BOOK MATCH

Everybunny Dance!, written and illustrated by Ellie Sandall (Margaret K. McElderry, 2017).

> All the bunnies start dancing with a "twist and twirl, and shake your tail, and wiggle and whirl." Then, the bunnies take turns playing musical instruments and singing until a fox shows up and scares the bunnies. This fox, however, is also musically talented.

"THE FROGGY CHOIR" ———————————————

Poem

Let the children listen to the entire poem. At the very end, ask them to make their favorite frog noises and conduct them like an orchestra for ten seconds or so.

A froggery of frogs
Were looking for a sound.
They hired a frog director,
And this is what they found.
He had the peepers peep high,
And the hop-toads sing low.
The leopard frogs snarled,
They tend to do that, you know.
He taught the fat frogs how to bellow,
And the old ones how to croak.
The baby frogs hollered,
'Cause he gave them a poke.

He made the thin frogs sing "Rib-it,"
The horned frogs blared "Ker-dunk,"
The mud frogs chanted "Knee-deep,"
And the rock frogs sunk.
He showed the drum frogs how to rock,
And the leapfrogs how to roll.
The speckled frogs played jazz,
And the polliwogs, soul.
He told the tree frogs to bark,
And the cricket frogs to chirp.
The river frogs babbled,
And the bullfrog burped.
The sound that was produced
Pleased the frog director's ears.
The beauty of their music
Simply moved those frogs to tears.
And if you have a fancy
To sing down in the mire,
You just might be invited
To join that froggy choir.

PICTURE BOOK MATCH

Ah Ha!, written and illustrated by Jeff Mack (Chronicle, 2013).

> A frog, floating in a pond, sighs with an audible "Aahh!" He sees a rock and goes, "Ah ha!" He climbs on top with an "Aahh!" Frog keeps making noises as he is pursued by a boy, a dog, a turtle, an alligator, and a flamingo.

"HAVE YOU SEEN MY WORM?"

Movement Activity

Have the children imitate your motions.

Have you seen my worm?
I lost my worm,
You'll know it's *my* worm,
'Cause it moves like this . . . (*Move one hand around in a wiggly motion.*)

Have you seen my frog?
I lost my frog,
You'll know it's *my* frog,
'Cause it moves like this . . . (*Jump around the room.*)
Have you seen my fish?
I lost my fish,
You'll know it's *my* fish,
'Cause it moves like this . . . (*Place hands with palms facing backward in front of ears to make fins. Move them, open and shut mouth, and walk around.*)
Have you seen my mole?
I lost my mole,
You'll know it's *my* mole,
'Cause it moves like this . . . (*Hold hands out front as if digging and blink while moving.*)
Have you seen my hen?
I lost my hen,
You'll know it's *my* hen,
'Cause it moves like this . . . (*Tuck arms into body to make wings and strut around the room.*)
Have you seen my penguin?
I lost my penguin,
You'll know it's *my* penguin,
'Cause it moves like this . . . (*Waddle around the room with arms at sides.*)
Have you seen my elephant?
I lost my elephant,
You'll know it's *my* elephant,
'Cause it moves like this . . . (*Lumber around the room with arm swaying in front of nose to represent a trunk.*)
(*At the end, point anywhere in the room and state, "Found it!"*)

PICTURE BOOK MATCH

Don't Move / Ne bouge pas / ¡No te muevas!, written by Anne-Sophie Tilly and illustrated by Julien Chung (Annick, 2017).

> This trilingual board book shows a monkey running, a toucan walking, and a pink flamingo standing on one leg. We also see a rhinoceros, an elephant, a chameleon, a crocodile, and a warthog. An owl takes their picture at the end of the book.

"R-I-N-G-O"

Ask the children if they know anyone famous whose name is Ringo. Tell them about the Beatles' drummer and how he used to wear a lot of rings on his fingers. Have everyone hold up five fingers and wiggle them one at a time for each letter sung. Wiggle the thumb for R, pointer for I, middle finger for N, ring finger for G, and pinkie for O. Sing to the tune of "Bingo." Clap—to simulate Ringo's drums—for each letter that is dropped.

There was a drummer had a band and Ringo was his name-o.
R-I-N-G-O, R-I-N-G-O, R-I-N-G-O,
And Ringo was his name-o.
There was a drummer had a band and Ringo was his name-o.
(*Clap*)-I-N-G-O, (*Clap*)-I-N-G-O, (*Clap*)-I-N-G-O,
And Ringo was his name-o.
There was a drummer had a band and Ringo was his name-o.
(*Clap-clap*)-N-G-O, (*Clap-clap*)-N-G-O, (*Clap-clap*)-N-G-O,
And Ringo was his name-o.
There was a drummer had a band and Ringo was his name-o.
(*Clap-clap-clap*)-G-O, (*Clap-clap-clap*)-G-O, (*Clap-clap-clap*)-G-O,
And Ringo was his name-o.
There was a drummer had a band and Ringo was his name-o.
(*Clap-clap-clap-clap*)-O, (*Clap-clap-clap-clap*)-O, (*Clap-clap-clap-clap*)-O,
And Ringo was his name-o.
There was a drummer had a band and Ringo was his name-o.
(*Clap-clap-clap-clap-clap*), (*Clap-clap-clap-clap-clap*), (*Clap-clap-clap-clap-
     clap*),
And Ringo was his name-o.

PICTURE BOOK MATCH

Drum Dream Girl: How One Girl's Courage Changed Music, written by
   Margarita Engle and illustrated by Rafael López (Houghton Mifflin Harcourt, 2015).
      A girl is told that only boys play drums on her island of music. She finds
      a music teacher who is amazed by her talent. She finally gets to play
      in front of an audience and shows that "both girls and boys should feel
      free to dream."

"STAMP YOUR FEET" ——————————————————

Movement Activity

This activity is inspired by the various "get your wiggles out" exercises that story-tellers use. Have the children imitate your motions. Everyone stands.

Stamp your feet, clap your hands.
Stamp your feet, clap your hands.
Stamp your feet, clap your hands.
Stamp your feet, clap your hands.
Nod your head, wiggle your bum.
Nod your head, wiggle your bum.
Nod your head, wiggle your bum.
Nod your head, wiggle your bum.
Stamp your feet, clap your hands.
Stamp your feet, clap your hands.
Stamp your feet, clap your hands.
Stamp your feet, and sit back down.

PICTURE BOOK MATCH

Ten Tiny Toes, written and illustrated by Caroline Jayne Church (Cart-wheel, 2014).
    It all starts with "Mouth, ears, eyes, nose, arms, belly, legs, and ten tiny toes!" We follow a child and wiggle our ears, touch our belly, open our mouth, wave our arms from side to side, touch our toes, touch our nose, and give a sneeze. We finally "touch our eyes and play peekaboo."

"THE STARS ARE TWINKLING" ——————————

Musical Activity

Sing to the tune of "The Ants Go Marching." Have the children march around the room and wiggle their fingers to represent twinkling stars.

The stars are twinkling one by one, hurrah, hurrah,
The stars are twinkling one by one, hurrah, hurrah,
The stars are twinkling one by one,
They'll twinkle long after storytime's done,
Yes, they all will twinkle on and on and on.

Henry's Stars, written and illustrated by David Elliot (Philomel, 2015).

> Henry the pig sees a constellation in the shape of a pig. He shows it to a flock of sheep, but they see a sheep constellation. A cow sees the "Great Star Cow," a horse sees "a Great Starry Horse," and chickens see "Heavenly Hens." When Henry is finally alone, he once again sees his pig constellation.

"TOPS AND BOTTOMS" ————————————————

Movement Activity

Teach the children the following motions before beginning this activity. When you chant the word "Tops," have the children stand tall and raise their hands over their heads. When you chant the word "Bottoms," have them get down into a squatting position with their hands on the floor. When you chant "Move 'round and 'round," have them stand again and twirl slowly in a circle.

Tops and bottoms,
Tops and bottoms,
Move 'round and 'round, oh,
Tops and bottoms,
Tops and bottoms,
Move 'round and 'round, oh,
Tops and bottoms,
Tops and bottoms,
Move 'round and 'round and
Come to a stop. (*Sit.*)

Bear's Big Bottom, written by Steve Smallman and illustrated by Emma Yarlett (Capstone, 2014).

> Bear's big bottom causes problems. His bottom squishes his friends, it smashes the birthday cake, and it also empties the pool "with one splash." When a fox tries to bite the other animals' bottoms, Bear saves the day. Everyone cheers, "Hooray for Bear's Big Bottom!"

"TWINKLE HERE AND THERE"

Movement Activity

Have the children imitate your motions.

Twinkle standing up, (*Stand and wiggle fingers.*)
And twinkle sitting down, (*Sit and wiggle fingers.*)
Twinkle while you're hopping, (*Stand and hop and wiggle fingers.*)
Around and around and around. (*Hop in a circle and wiggle fingers.*)
Twinkle at the ceiling, (*Stop hopping, and wiggle fingers overhead.*)
And twinkle at the door, (*Point wiggling fingers at the entrance of the program area.*)
Twinkle at each other, (*Wiggle fingers at everyone in the room.*)
And twinkle on the floor. (*Sit while wiggling fingers, then clap for a job well done.*)

PICTURE BOOK MATCH

Touch the Brightest Star, written and illustrated by Christie Matheson (Greenwillow, 2015).
> The reader is instructed to tap the sky beside a tree. A star appears. After we make a wish and swipe the sky, more stars appear. After we touch the brightest star, the Big Dipper is visible. After we close our eyes and open them again, "the magic of the day begins."

"WIGGLE, WIGGLE, WIGGLE"

Movement Activity

Have the children imitate your motions. Everyone stands.

Wiggle, wiggle, wiggle, (*Wiggle entire body.*)
Now wiggle just your head, (*Shake head back and forth.*)
Wiggle up and wiggle down, (*While wiggling head, stand on tiptoe and then crouch.*)
Wiggle 'round and 'round and 'round. (*Straighten up and move in a circle while wiggling head.*)
Wiggle, wiggle, wiggle, (*Wiggle entire body.*)
Now wiggle just your eyes, (*Move eyes back and forth or blink them.*)

Wiggle up and wiggle down, (*While moving or blinking eyes, stand on tiptoe and then crouch.*)

Wiggle 'round and 'round and 'round. (*Straighten up and move in a circle while moving or blinking eyes.*)

Wiggle, wiggle, wiggle, (*Wiggle entire body.*)

Now wiggle just your arms, (*Wave arms all around.*)

Wiggle up and wiggle down, (*While wiggling arms, stand on tiptoe and then crouch.*)

Wiggle 'round and 'round and 'round. (*Straighten up and move in a circle while wiggling arms.*)

Wiggle, wiggle, wiggle, (*Wiggle entire body.*)

Now wiggle just your bum, (*Shake bottom back and forth.*)

Wiggle up and wiggle down, (*While wiggling bottom, stand on tiptoe and then crouch.*)

Wiggle 'round and 'round and 'round. (*Straighten up and move in a circle while wiggling bottom.*)

Wiggle, wiggle, wiggle, (*Wiggle entire body.*)

Now wiggle just your knees, (*Move knees back and forth.*)

Wiggle up and wiggle down, (*While moving knees, stand on tiptoe and then crouch.*)

Wiggle 'round and 'round and 'round. (*Straighten up and move in a circle while wiggling knees.*)

Wiggle, wiggle, wiggle, (*Wiggle entire body.*)

Now wiggle just your feet, (*Sit and kick feet in the air.*)

Wiggle up and wiggle down, (*While kicking feet, move them higher and lower.*)

Wiggle 'round and 'round and 'round. (*Spin in a circle on the floor while sitting and kicking feet.*)

Wiggle, wiggle, wiggle, (*Stand and wiggle entire body.*)

Now wiggle everything, (*Continue wiggling entire body.*)

Wiggle up and wiggle down, (*While wiggling body, stand on tiptoe and then crouch.*)

Wiggle 'round and 'round and 'round. (*Straighten up and move in a circle while wiggling body.*)

I Got the Rhythm, written by Connie Schofield-Morrison and illustrated by
Frank Morrison (Bloomsbury, 2014).

> A little girl walks through the city listening to rhythms all around her.
> She shakes the rhythm with her hips, knocks the rhythm with her knees,
> and stomps the rhythm with her feet. She says, "I got the rhythm and
> you can too."

MY BODY

"BUBBLE BATH"

Fingerplay

Have the children imitate your motions.

Bubbly, bubbly, bubble bath, (*Wiggle all ten fingers.*)
Filled to the top, (*Raise fingers overhead.*)
Listen to the bubbly bubbles, (*Cup hand to ear.*)
Pop! Pop! Pop! (*Clap three times.*)

PICTURE BOOK MATCH

101 Reasons Why I'm Not Taking a Bath, written by Stacy McAnulty and
illustrated by Joy Ang (Random House, 2016).
> A boy's excuses for not taking a bath include that bubbles could get
> in his nose, water makes his fingers wrinkly, his belly button is like a
> self-cleaning oven, and more. Of course, once he's in the bath, he has
> 102 reasons to stay in.

"HIDE AND SEEK"

Fingerplay

Have the children imitate your motions.

One, two, three, four, (*Hold up four fingers on your left hand, one at a time.*)
Hide and seek! (*Spread the four fingers of the left hand and place over your
    left eye horizontally, like half of a mask.*)
Five, six, seven, eight, (*Hold up four fingers on your right hand, one at a
    time.*)
Do not peek! (*Spread the fingers of the right hand and place over your right
    eye horizontally. Both hands form a mask.*)

Nine, ten, ready or not, (*Drop hands from eyes and hold up two thumbs,
   one at a time.*)
Here I come!
I see you, there you are, (*Point at audience.*)
Let's start again with one! (*Hold up one finger. Repeat the entire
   fingerplay, slightly faster.*)

PICTURE BOOK MATCH

Bob and Flo Play Hide-and-Seek, written and illustrated by Rebecca Ash-
   down (Houghton Mifflin Harcourt, 2016).
   Bob the penguin is not very good at hiding during a game of hide-and-
   seek with his friends Flo and Sam. "'You have to hide behind something,'
   said Sam." Bob finally creates a wonderful hiding place.

"I DON'T FEEL GOOD"

Movement Activity

Have the children repeat the lines after you and imitate your motions.

Leader: I don't feel good. (*Make a face.*)
Audience: I don't feel good.
Leader: Wiping my nose. (*Mime wiping nose on left arm sleeve.*)
Audience: Wiping my nose.
Leader: Scratching an itch. (*Scratch your body with your right hand.*)
Audience: Scratching an itch.
Leader: Drinking my medicine. (*Hang tongue out of mouth.*)
Audience: Drinking my medicine.
Leader: Lying down to rest. (*Tip over to your side.*)
Audience: Lying down to rest.
Leader: Falling asleep. (*Close eyes. Snore softly.*)
Audience: Falling asleep.
(*Pause a moment.*)
Leader: I feel great! (*Open eyes and sit back up.*)
Audience: I feel great!
Leader: Time to play! (*Throw arms overhead.*)
Audience: Time to play!

The Day I Lost My Superpowers, written by Michaël Escoffier and illustrated by Kris Di Giacomo (Enchanted Lion, 2014).

A girl dressed in a mask and cape practices "nonstop to develop my superpowers." She makes things disappear, becomes invisible, and communicates with animals. When she falls and hurts herself, her superpowers are finished until Mom gives the girl a magic kiss.

"IF YOU'RE FEELING RATHER ILL"

Musical/Movement Activity

Sing to the tune of "If You're Happy and You Know It." Have the children repeat the sounds after you.

If you're feeling rather ill, cover your mouth, "A-choo!" (*Make a sneeze noise.*)

If you're feeling rather ill, cover your mouth, "A-choo!" (*Make a sneeze noise.*)

If you're feeling rather ill, with an ache and with a chill,

If you're feeling rather ill, cover your mouth, "A-choo!" (*Make a sneeze noise.*)

If you're feeling rather ill, wipe your nose, "Here's a tissue!" (*Mime wiping nose.*)

If you're feeling rather ill, wipe your nose, "Here's a tissue!" (*Mime wiping nose.*)

If you're feeling rather ill, with an ache and with a chill,

If you're feeling rather ill, wipe your nose, "Here's a tissue!" (*Mime wiping nose.*)

If you're feeling rather ill, drink plenty of fluids, "Sip, sip." (*Mime drinking.*)

If you're feeling rather ill, drink plenty of fluids, "Sip, sip." (*Mime drinking.*)

If you're feeling rather ill, with an ache and with a chill,

If you're feeling rather ill, drink plenty of fluids, "Sip, sip." (*Mime drinking.*)

If you're feeling rather ill, crawl in bed, "Zzzz-Zzzz." (*Make a snoring noise.*)

If you're feeling rather ill, crawl in bed, "Zzzz-Zzzz." (*Make a snoring noise.*)

If you're feeling rather ill, with an ache and with a chill,
If you're feeling rather ill, crawl in bed, "Zzzz-Zzzz." (*Make a snoring noise.*)
When you're feeling slightly better, read a book, "Oh yeah!" (*Fashion hands to represent a book and smile.*)
When you're feeling slightly better, read a book, "Oh yeah!" (*Fashion hands to represent a book and smile.*)
When you're feeling slightly better, when you're feeling slightly better,
When you're feeling slightly better, read a book, "Oh yeah!" (*Fashion hands to represent a book and smile.*)

PICTURE BOOK MATCH

I Feel Sick!, written and illustrated by Tony Ross (Andersen, 2015).
> Whenever anyone asks the Little Princess to do anything, like walking the dog or cleaning the cat's box, she tells them that she is sick. She feels much better when she gets an invitation to a friend's party. After eating a lot of food and playing and dancing, the Little Princess says, "Oh, no! I feel sick!"

"I'M CLEAN!"

Movement Activity

Inform the children that they are all cleaned up for a special event and they don't want to get dirty. Have them repeat your lines after you and imitate your motions.

Leader: I'm clean! I'm clean!
I'm clean, I'm clean, I'm clean!
Audience: I'm clean! I'm clean!
I'm clean, I'm clean, I'm clean!
Leader: I'm clean, my muddy sister! (*Hold out hands as if to keep someone away.*)
Don't touch me, I'm clean!
Audience: I'm clean, my muddy sister!
Don't touch me, I'm clean!
Leader: I'm clean, my muddy brother! (*Hold out hands as if to keep someone away.*)
Don't hug me, I'm clean!
Audience: I'm clean, my muddy brother!
Don't hug me, I'm clean!

Leader: I'm clean, my muddy doggie! (*Hold out hands as if to keep someone away.*)
Don't lick me, I'm clean!
Audience: I'm clean, my muddy doggie!
Don't lick me, I'm clean!
Leader: Aargh! You touched me! (*Wipe body frantically.*)
Oh no, I'm not clean!
Audience: Aargh! You touched me!
Oh no, I'm not clean!
Leader: Aargh! You hugged me! (*Wipe body frantically.*)
Oh no, I'm not clean!
Audience: Aargh! You hugged me!
Oh no, I'm not clean!
Leader: Aargh! You licked me! (*Wipe face frantically.*)
Oh no, I'm not clean!
Audience: Aargh! You licked me!
Oh no, I'm not clean!
Leader: I'm dirty, but . . . I'm happy! (*Stop, look at self, and smile.*)
Audience: I'm dirty, but . . . I'm happy!

PICTURE BOOK MATCH

Bears in the Bath, written by Shirley Parenteau and illustrated by David M. Walker (Candlewick, 2014).

> It's time for his bear cubs to take a bath, but Big Brown Bear fails to convince them to get in. The cubs like being dusty, muddy, sweaty, and stinky. They change their mind once Big Brown Bear jumps in the tub.

"MARY HAD A LITTLE COLD"

Musical Activity

Sing to the tune of "Mary Had a Little Lamb." Perform the song as if you have a stuffed nose. Ask the children to join you as you sing the song a second time. Encourage the children to sing it with a "stuffed nose" vocal treatment.

Mary had a little cold, little cold, little cold.
Mary had a little cold, it's hard to sing this song.
'Cuz every time I try to sing, try to sing, try to sing,
Every time I try to sing, I (CHOO)-(CHOO)-(CHOO)-(CHOO)-(CHOO)!

Bob, Not Bob!, written by Liz Garton Scanlon and Audrey Vernick and
  illustrated by Matthew Cordell (Hyperion, 2017).

> Little Louie is sick. His nose is clogged. He calls out "BOB" in his "weird,
> all-wrong, stuffed-up voice," and his dog Bob comes running. That's not
> who Louie wants. He wants his mom, who winds up sneezing at the
> end of the book.

"THE MORE WE BRUSH OUR TEETH" ————————————

Musical/Movement Activity

Sing to the tune of "The More We Get Together." Have the children imitate your
motions.

The more we brush our teeth, (*Mime brushing*)
Our teeth, our teeth,
The more we brush our teeth,
The healthier we'll be.
Brush this way and that way,
And that way and this way,
The more we brush our teeth,
The healthier we'll be.
The more we floss our teeth, (*Mime flossing*)
Our teeth, our teeth,
The more we floss our teeth,
The healthier we'll be.
Floss this way and that way,
And that way and this way,
The more we floss our teeth,
The healthier we'll be.

Alan's Big, Scary Teeth, written and illustrated by Peter Jarvis (Candlewick, 2016).

> Alan the alligator brushes "each of his big, scary teeth for (at least) ten
> minutes at a time." He then walks through the jungle scaring the other
> animals with his teeth. The other animals learn that Alan's teeth are
> false teeth and that he is not very scary without them.

"OW, OW, I BUMPED MY HEAD" ———————————

Have the children repeat the lines after you and imitate your motions. Everyone stands.

Leader: Ow, ow, I bumped my head! (*Hold head.*)

Audience: Ow, ow, I bumped my head!

Leader: Ow, ow, I squashed my nose and bumped my head! (*Hold nose, then head.*)

Audience: Ow, ow, I squashed my nose and bumped my head!

Leader: Ow, ow, I hurt my tummy and squashed my nose and bumped my head! (*Hold tummy, then nose, then head.*)

Audience: Ow, ow, I hurt my tummy and squashed my nose and bumped my head!

Leader: Ow, ow, I landed on my seat and hurt my tummy and squashed my nose and bumped my head! (*Sit and rub bottom, hold tummy, then nose, and then head.*)

Audience: Ow, ow, I landed on my seat and hurt my tummy and squashed my nose and bumped my head!

Leader: Ow, ow, I skinned my knee and landed on my seat and hurt my tummy and squashed my nose and bumped my head! (*Rub knee, then bottom, then hold tummy, then nose, and then head.*)

Audience: Ow, ow, I skinned my knee and landed on my seat and hurt my tummy and squashed my nose and bumped my head!

Leader: Ow, ow, I stubbed my toe and skinned my knee and landed on my seat and hurt my tummy and squashed my nose and bumped my head! (*Grab toe, then rub knee, then bottom, then hold tummy, then nose, then head.*)

Audience: Ow, ow, I stubbed my toe and skinned my knee and landed on my seat and hurt my tummy and squashed my nose and bumped my head!

Leader: I need a kiss! (*Make kissing noises.*)

Audience: I need a kiss!

Leader: All better! (*Big smile*).

Audience: All better!

The Cow Tripped Over the Moon: A Nursery Rhyme Emergency, written
  by Jeanne Willis and illustrated by Joel Stewart (Candlewick, 2015).
     The Storyland Ambulance is having a very busy day. The cow "tripped
  on the moon and fell to the ground." A bird pecked a poor washer maid
  on the nose. Humpty Dumpty fell and "smashed his shell."

"THE TEENY-TINY KID" ————————————————————

Movement Activity

Have the children imitate your motions. Emphasize "teeny" with a high voice. Everyone stands.

When I was a *teeny-teeny-teeny*-tiny kid,
I was just this big! (*Indicate a two-inch space between thumb and pointer
    finger.*)
When I was a *teeny-teeny*-tiny kid,
I was just this big! (*Hold hand flat by knees.*)
When I was a *teeny*-tiny kid,
I was just this big! (*Hold hand flat by waist.*)
When I was a *tiny* kid,
I was just this big! (*Hold hand flat by nose.*)
Some kids want to be *this* big, (*Stand on tiptoes and stretch arms high
    overhead.*)
But I'm the *right-sized* kid! (*Hold hand on top of head.*)

I Don't Want to Be Big, written by Dev Petty and illustrated by Mike Boldt
  (Doubleday, 2016).
     A frog turns down dinner because he doesn't want to be big. He might
  hit his head on things and says, "I'll miss the legroom." The frog finally
  decides that it will be okay to be big, but he refuses to take a bath.

SCHOOL

"BRING A FRIEND TO SCHOOL"

Movement Activity

This activity can be done with stuffed animals as props, or it can be done with just simple actions. Have the children imitate your motions.

Bring a friend to school,
Bring a friend—Clap! Clap! (*Clap twice.*)
Bring a friend to school,
Bring a friend—Clap! Clap! (*Clap twice.*)
I brought a little friend,
My friend is a bunny. (*Hold up a toy bunny or make bunny ears behind your head.*)
Bring a friend to school,
Bring a friend—Clap! Clap! (*Clap twice.*)
Bring a friend to school,
Bring a friend—Clap! Clap! (*Clap twice.*)
I brought a little friend,
My friend is a bear. (*Hold up a teddy bear or say "Grr . . . grrr."*)
Bring a friend to school,
Bring a friend—Clap! Clap! (*Clap twice.*)
Bring a friend to school,
Bring a friend—Clap! Clap! (*Clap twice.*)
I brought a little friend,
My friend is an alligator. (*Hold up a toy alligator or make alligator jaws with arms.*)
Bring a friend to school,
Bring a friend—Snap! Snap! (*Snap twice with arms forming alligator jaws.*)
Bring a friend to school,
Bring a friend—Snap! Snap! (*Snap twice as before.*)

Oliver and His Alligator, written and illustrated by Paul Schmid (Hyperion, 2013).

> Oliver is nervous about school, so he brings along an alligator. When "a
> lady who wasn't his mom" asks his name, Oliver says, "Munch, munch!"
> and the alligator swallows the lady. The alligator swallows the other
> kids. The alligator then swallows Oliver so he can join everyone else.

"FIVE LITTLE FISH HEADING TO SCHOOL" ———————————

Fingerplay

Have the children imitate your motions.

FIVE little fish were oh, so cool! (*Hold up five fingers.*)
These five fish were heading to school! (*Make swimming motion with hands.*)
One little fish swam close to shore, (*Point to thumb.*)
Those five fish are down to . . . (*Hold up five fingers and wiggle them . . .*)
FOUR little fish were oh, so cool! (*Tuck thumb and hold up four fingers.*)
These four fish were heading to school! (*Make swimming motion with
   hands.*)
One little fish went out to sea, (*Point to pinkie finger.*)
Those four fish are down to . . . (*Hold up four fingers and wiggle them . . .*)
THREE little fish were oh, so cool! (*Tuck pinkie finger with thumb and
   hold up three fingers.*)
These three fish were heading to school! (*Make swimming motion with
   hands.*)
One little fish met a fishing crew, (*Point to ring finger.*)
Those three fish are down to . . . (*Hold up three fingers and wiggle them . . .*)
TWO little fish were oh, so cool! (*Tuck ring finger with thumb and pinkie
   and hold up two fingers.*)
These two fish were heading to school! (*Make swimming motion with hands.*)
One little fish jumped to the sun, (*Point to middle finger.*)
Those two fish are down to . . . (*Hold up two fingers and wiggle them . . .*)
ONE little fish was oh, so cool! (*Tuck middle finger with other fingers and
   hold up pointer finger.*)
That little fish was heading to school! (*Make swimming motion with hands.*)
One little fish, it followed its heart, (*Point to heart.*)
That fish in school is oh, so smart! (*Point to head and nod.*)

PICTURE BOOK MATCH

The Pout-Pout Fish Goes to School, written by Deborah Diesen and illustrated by Dan Hanna (Farrar, Straus and Giroux, 2014).

> When Mr. Fish was little, he couldn't print his name, make a rhombus, or do long division. With the help of his teacher, he headed for the room for "brand new fish" and had "a spectacular year."

"IF PIGS WENT TO PIG SCHOOL"

Movement Activity

Have any picture book nearby. Instruct the children to repeat the animal noises, imitate your motions, and shout out "READ A BOOK" with you when they see you hold one up.

If Pigs went to Pig school,
What would they learn?
They'd learn to oink, (*Make "oink" noises.*)
And wallow in the mud, (*Flop on the floor.*)
And READ A BOOK! (*Hold up picture book.*)
If Elephants went to Elephant school,
What would they learn?
They'd learn to eat with their trunks, (*Hold up arm in front of nose.*)
And make trumpeting noises, (*Make elephant trumpet noise.*)
And READ A BOOK! (*Hold up picture book.*)
If Turtles went to Turtle school,
What would they learn?
They'd learn to sun themselves on a log, (*Get down on all fours.*)
And hide in their shell, (*Pull head into shoulders.*)
And READ A BOOK! (*Hold up picture book.*)

PICTURE BOOK MATCH

Maria Had a Little Llama / Maria tenía una llamita, adapted and illustrated by Angela Dominguez (Holt, 2013).

> A little llama follows Maria to her Peruvian school in this adaptation of "Mary Had a Little Lamb." Of course, it was against the rules: "Eso iba contra las reglas." When the teacher sends the llama outside, the llama waits patiently for Maria to appear.

"MONSTER SCHOOL"

Sound Effects Activity

Instruct the audience to pretend they are monsters going to school, and they will respond to everything the "teacher"—the story program leader—asks by waving their arms and shouting "Aarrgghh!"

Teacher: One plus one equals what?
Audience: "Aarrgghh!"
Teacher: What color is the sun?
Audience: "Aarrgghh!"
Teacher: How do you spell *cat*?
Audience: "Aarrgghh!"
Teacher: What is the nation's capital?
Audience: "Aarrgghh!"

PICTURE BOOK MATCH

Monstergarten, written by Daniel J. Mahoney and illustrated by Jef Kaminsky (Feiwel and Friends, 2013).
> A monster named Kevin is worried about attending Monstergarten. He hears that all young monsters are required to be scary. He practices being frightful but is not very good at it.

"PLAYGROUND TIME"

Movement Activity

This activity works best where there is plenty of room for the children to move. There is a lot of up-and-down movement, so read the rhyme slowly with plenty of pauses. Everyone starts by standing in a circle.

All join hands, (*Hold hands with neighbor.*)
Circle around, (*Move in a clockwise direction.*)
Now you have,
A merry-go-round. (*While walking, move up and down.*)
Next sit down, (*Sit.*)
Shout and sing, (*Sing "La-la."*)
Legs out front, (*Straighten legs out front.*)
Arms up—swing. (*Mime going back and forth on a swing set.*)

Hula hoop, (*Stand and swing hips.*)
Bumper cars, (*Bump hips with neighbor.*)
Teeter-totter, (*Pair up and join hands, then move back and forth.*)
Monkey bars. (*Mime swinging on bars with hands overhead.*)
Balance beam, (*Place one foot in front of the other a few steps forward.*)
Slippery slide, (*Sit and hold hands overhead and lean back.*)
Crawl through a tunnel, (*Crawl on all fours a few feet forward.*)
Rocking-horse ride. (*Sit and rock back and forth.*)
Catch a ball, (*Mime catching a ball.*)
Dance and rhyme, (*Dance in place.*)
Imagination,
Playground time! (*Cheer.*)

PICTURE BOOK MATCH

Hop Up! Wriggle Over!, written and illustrated by Elizabeth Honey (Clarion, 2017).

> Several Australian animals wake up, gobble their breakfast, and head over to the playground. There, the kangaroo, koala, wombat, echidna, bilby, quokka, wallaby, and others slide, teeter-totter, and swing before heading back home.

"THE TALENT SHOW ABC"

Movement Activity

Inform the children that they will pretend to be different animals showing a variety of skills for a talent show. Because a lot of the movements might be hard for younger children to fully understand, perform a motion and let them follow your lead.

An Anteater Acting . . . (*Strike noble pose and say, "To be or not to be."*)
A Bear twirling a Baton . . . (*Mime twirling a baton.*)
A Camel doing the Can-Can . . . (*Kick one leg up and then the other.*)
A Duck Disco Dancing . . . (*Strike a pose and point one finger straight up and one down.*)
An Elephant playing an Electric guitar . . . (*Mime playing a guitar.*)
A Frog swinging on the Flying trapeze . . . (*Move back and forth miming holding on to a trapeze bar overhead.*)
A Gorilla striking a Gong . . . (*Take a big swing with hand as if striking a gong.*)

A Hippopotamus Hula dancing . . . (*Mime hula dancing with two hands moving downward in one direction and then the other.*)

An Iguana Ice-skating . . . (*Place hands behind back and mime skating.*)

A Jellyfish Juggling . . . (*Mime juggling balls in the air.*)

A Kangaroo telling Knock-Knock jokes . . . (*Tell your favorite "knock-knock" joke.*)

A Llama performing Lasso tricks . . . (*Mime twirling a lasso overhead.*)

A Moose Miming . . . (*Hold up two palms flat in front of you as if encountering a wall.*)

A Newt doing Needlework . . . (*Mime sewing.*)

An Owl singing Opera . . . (*Lift head, stretch out arms, and sing a loud note.*)

A Porcupine presenting a Puppet show . . . (*Hold up both hands as if you have a puppet on each one.*)

A Quail Quizzing the audience . . . (*Ask the children, "What's the president's name?"*)

A Rhino telling a Riddle . . . (*Tell your favorite kids' riddle.*)

A Skunk Skipping . . . (*Skip.*)

A Tiger walking on a Tightrope . . . (*Mime walking on a rope, one foot in front of the other, with outstretched arms trying to maintain balance.*)

A Umbrellabird riding a Unicycle . . . (*Hold arms out to each side and move back and forth.*)

A Vulture playing the Violin . . . (*Mime playing a violin.*)

A Walrus Whistling . . . (*Whistle a simple tune.*)

An X-Ray Tetra playing the Xylophone . . . (*Mime playing a xylophone.*)

A Yak doing Yo-Yo tricks . . . (*Mime playing with a yo-yo.*)

A Zebra saying, "Zee End!" . . . (*All take a bow.*)

PICTURE BOOK MATCH

Animal Alphabet, written and illustrated by Kay Vincent (Button, 2015).
We find an acrobatic ant followed by a busking bear and a canoeing camel. Other animals join in the fun, including a kicking kangaroo, a jolly jellyfish, and a quick quail. A zig-zag zebra brings the alphabet to a close.

"WHY I'M LATE FOR SCHOOL"

Sound Effects Story

Have the children make the appropriate sounds as they come up in the story. You might have to pause slightly before each one as a cue. The sounds represented in the parentheses are the most common the children make when I tell this story.

Why am I late for school today?
It's all because of my brand-new sneakers.
They're squeaky sneakers. (*"Squeak."*)
I stepped into a puddle. (*"Splash."*)
They are squeaky and squishy sneakers. (*"Squeak-splash."*)
I took one off and blew on it to dry. (*Blowing noise.*)
Suddenly, a crow appeared! (*"Caw!"*)
It grabbed my sneaker and flew off! (*Flapping noise.*)
I ran after it. (*Slap legs.*)
I was too slow.
I jumped onto a motorcycle. (*"Vroom!"*)
I was too slow.
I dove into a police car. (*"Wee-ooh!"*)
I was too slow.
I hopped onto a tricycle.
It had one of those little ringy-bells. (*"Ring-ring."*)
I was too slow.
I ran once again and followed the crow into the zoo.
We went past the lion cage. (*"Roar."*)
We went past the monkey cage. (*"Ooh-ooh!"*)
We went past the parrot cage. (*"Squawk!"*)
We went past the giraffe cage. (*Shrug because there's no noise.*)
I was out of breath. (*Huffing noises.*)
I staggered over to a food stand and gobbled a bag of potato chips.
    (*Crunching noises.*)
I was thirsty. I drank a gallon of lemonade. (*Gulping noises.*)
I burped. (*"Burp!"*)
The crow reappeared! (*"Caw!"*)
It flew high into the sky. (*Flapping noises.*)
I grabbed some helium balloons and went up into the sky. (*"Whoa!"*)
Clouds moved in. It got windy. (*Wind noises.*)
It started to rain. (*Snap fingers.*)

The rain got louder and louder. (*Clap hands rapidly.*)

There was thunder. (*"Boom!"*)

I was scared! (*"Waa!"*)

And then . . . the sun came out. (*"Ahhhhh."*)

The crow dive-bombed me and popped my balloons! (*"Pop!"*)

I fell! (*"Aaiiiiieee!"*)

Luckily, I landed on someone's backyard trampoline. (*"Boing!"*)

In the distance, I heard the school bell. (*"Ring!"*)

I ran as fast as I could. (*Slap legs.*)

And that's why I'm late for school today.

And if you believe that . . . CLAP!

PICTURE BOOK MATCH

A Funny Thing Happened on the Way to School, written by Davide Cali
and illustrated by Benjamin Chaud (Chronicle, 2015).

> A boy is late to school because some ants stole his breakfast and his
> uncle's time machine was not working properly. In between these two
> events, he also was attacked by ninjas at the bus stop, rode in an elephant
> parade, landed in an unusually large spider web, rode in the president's
> private plane, and more.

More
Fun

FOOD

"THE BIGGEST JUICIEST APPLE IN THE WHOLE ORCHARD"

Participation Story

This story was inspired by the folktale "The Enormous Turnip" and was created for all the early childhood educators who need a good apple story to share with their students.

Ask for volunteers to act out the parts of Tree and the animals—Pig, Goat, Llama, Horse, and Worm—while you tell the story. The rest of the audience can chime in on the lines "pulled and pulled and pulled." At the start of the story, the Tree actor stands center stage, facing the audience with arms out. The animal actors stand on the left side of the stage area. The storyteller directs the actors verbally and nonverbally while telling the story.)

The biggest, juiciest apple in the whole orchard started as a small blossom. (*Point to tree branch.*)

It grew until it was the size of a coconut. (*Make bigger and bigger hand gestures.*)

It grew until it was the size of a bowling ball.

It grew until it was the size of a watermelon.

That apple grew until it was as big as Tree itself.

Pig was rooting around the orchard. (*Pig slowly approaches Tree.*)

He saw the apple. His eyes grew wide. His jaw dropped. (*Pig's eyes grow wide and jaw drops.*)

He said, "That must be the biggest, juiciest apple in the orchard! I want it!"

Pig grabbed the apple and pulled and pulled and pulled. (*Pig grabs the imaginary apple and pulls. Audience members also pull from their seats while they say the words.*)

Tree bent over a little . . . (*Tree bends a little toward Pig.*)

. . . but the apple stuck tight to the branch. (*Tree straightens up.*)

Goat wandered into the orchard. (*Pig takes a step back while Goat slowly approaches Tree.*)

Goat saw the apple. Her eyes grew wide. Her jaw dropped. (*Goat's eyes grow wide and jaw drops.*)

She said, "That must be the biggest, juiciest apple in the whole orchard! I want it!"

Pig grunted . . . (*Pig grunts.*)

. . . and said, "I saw it first . . . but I guess there's enough for both of us." (*Goat gets in line behind Pig.*)

Goat pulled Pig, Pig pulled the apple, and they pulled and pulled and pulled. (*The two animals grab the imaginary apple and pull. Audience members also pull from their seats while they say the words.*)

Tree bent over a little more . . . (*Tree bends a little bit more toward the animals.*)

. . . but the apple stuck tight to the branch. (*Tree straightens up.*)

Llama wandered into the orchard from a nearby llama farm. (*Pig and Goat take a step back while Llama slowly approaches Tree.*)

Llama saw the apple. His eyes grew wide. His jaw dropped. (*Llama's eyes grow wide and jaw drops.*)

He said, "That must be the biggest, juiciest apple in the whole orchard! I want it!"

Pig and Goat grunted . . . (*Both make grunting noises.*)

. . . and said, "We saw it first . . . but we guess there's enough for all of us." (*All three animals line up.*)

Llama pulled Goat, Goat pulled Pig, Pig pulled the apple, and they pulled and pulled and pulled. (*The three animals grab the imaginary apple and pull. Audience members also pull from their seats while they say the words.*)

The tree bent over a little more . . . (*Tree bends a little bit more toward the animals.*)

. . . but the apple stuck tight to the branch. (*Tree straightens up.*)

Horse galloped into the orchard. (*Pig, Goat, and Llama take a step back while Horse quickly approaches Tree.*)

Horse saw the apple. Her eyes grew wide. Her jaw dropped. (*Horse's eyes grow wide and jaw drops.*)

She said, "That must be the biggest, juiciest apple in the whole orchard! I want it!"

Pig, Goat, and Llama grunted . . . (*All make grunting noises.*)

. . . and said, "We saw it first . . . but we guess there's enough for all of us." (*All four animals line up.*)

Horse pulled Llama, Llama pulled Goat, Goat pulled Pig, Pig pulled the apple, and they pulled and pulled and pulled. (*The four animals grab the imaginary apple and pull. Audience members also pull from their seats while they say the words.*)

The tree bent over a little more . . . (*Tree bends all the way down to the ground.*)

. . . but the apple stuck tight to the branch. (*Tree straightens up.*)

Worm crawled into the orchard. (*Pig, Goat, Llama, and Horse take a step back while Worm very slowly approaches Tree.*)

Worm saw the apple. His eyes grew wide. His jaw dropped. (*Worm's eyes grow wide and jaw drops.*)

He said, "That must be the biggest, juiciest apple in the whole orchard! I want it!"

The other animals grunted . . . (*All make grunting noises.*)

. . . and said, "You're too puny to help. Scram!"

Worm said, "I'm not too puny" and got in line behind the other animals. (*All animals form a line.*)

Worm pulled Horse, Horse pulled Llama, Llama pulled Goat, Goat pulled Pig, Pig pulled the apple, and they pulled and pulled and pulled. (*The five animals grab the imaginary apple and pull. Audience members also pull from their seats and say the words.*)

The four animals stopped and said to Worm, "We told you to scram!"

Worm let go.

Tree snapped the other direction, sending Pig, Goat, Llama, and Horse through the air and out of sight. (*Tree bends toward the right. The four animals head to the right side of the stage area.*)

Then Tree snapped back, sending the apple high into the air where it did an apple turnover and headed straight for Worm. (*Tree bends to the left.*)

Worm's eyes grew wide. His jaw dropped.

Moments before the apple landed, Worm dug a hole and disappeared. (*Worm drops to the floor.*)

The apple landed with a splat. (*Hold hand over Worm.*)

Worm was trapped!

Did he worry? Did he fret?

No, he was a worm. It was an apple.

Worm smiled the biggest smile a worm can smile . . . (*Worm smiles.*)
. . . and began chewing his way through the apple. (*Worm makes chewing motions.*)
He chewed and chewed and chewed . . . and spent the whole year in the middle of the biggest, juiciest apple in the whole orchard.
(*Have all actors move back to the center to "take a bow to thunderous applause!"*)

PICTURE BOOK MATCH

What's an Apple?, written by Marilyn Singer and illustrated by Greg Pizzoli (Abrams, 2016).

> There are many things to do with an apple. You can pick it, kick it, and throw away the core. You can pretend it's a baseball or a basketball. And you can even give an apple to your teacher.

"DON'T EAT THAT!"

Movement/Sound Effects Activity

Have the children imitate your sounds and motions. Everyone stands.

Hey you! Don't eat that pie!
Don't you know it'll make you cry? (*Make crying noises.*)
Hey you! Don't eat that cheese!
Don't you know it'll make you sneeze? (*Make sneezing noises.*)
Hey you! Don't eat those beans!
Don't you know they'll make you mean? (*Make angry face.*)
Hey you! Don't eat that cake!
Don't you know it'll make you shake? (*Shake entire body.*)
Hey you! Don't eat that veal!
Don't you know it'll make you squeal? (*Squeal like a pig.*)
Hey you! Don't eat that trout!
Don't you know it'll make you pout? (*Make a pouty face.*)
Hey you! Don't eat that grape!
Don't you know you'll act like an ape? (*Make monkey noises and gestures.*)
Hey you! Don't eat that honey!
Don't you know you'll act all funny? (*Bend over laughing.*)

Hey you! Don't eat those onion rings!
Don't you know they'll make you sing? (*Sing "La-la-la."*)
Hey you! Don't eat that peach!
Don't you know it'll make you reach? (*Reach for the sky.*)
Hey you! Don't eat that fruit!
Don't you know you'll look real cute? (*Flutter eyelashes.*)
Hey you! Don't eat that chili!
Don't you know you'll look real silly? (*Flutter eyelashes again.*)
Hey you! Don't eat that ice cream!
Don't you know it'll make you scream? (*Mime a silent scream.*)
Hey you! Don't eat that bun!
Don't you know that we're all done? (*Clap hands.*)

PICTURE BOOK MATCH

I Really Like Slop!, written and illustrated by Mo Willems (Hyperion, 2015).

> Piggie makes a batch of slop complete with bad odors and flies. His friend Gerald changes several colors after he tastes the spicy slop. The two remain friends, but Gerald turns down Piggie's fish-bone dessert.

"LIMA BEANS AND DICED BEETS"

Musical Activity

Sing to the tune of "Apples and Bananas." Teach the children the tune and have them join you for the second line.

Leader: I like to eat, eat, eat lima beans and diced beets.
All: I like to eat, eat, eat lima beans and diced beets.
Leader: I like to ate, ate, ate, lay-may baynes and dayced baytes.
All: I like to ate, ate, ate, lay-may baynes and dayced baytes.
Leader: I like to eat, eat, eat lee-mee beans and deeced beets.
All: I like to eat, eat, eat lee-mee beans and deeced beets.
Leader: I like to ite, ite, ite lie-my bines and diced bites.
All: I like to ite, ite, ite lie-my bines and diced bites.
Leader: I like to oat, oat, oat low-mo bones and doced boats.
All: I like to oat, oat, oat low-mo bones and doced boats.
Leader: I like to oot, oot, oot loo-moo boons and doosed boots.
All: I like to oot, oot, oot loo-moo boons and doosed boots.

No Kimchi for Me!, written and illustrated by Aram Kim (Holiday House, 2017).

> Yoomi loves most of her grandmother's dishes, like "dried seaweed, tiny anchovies, soft egg omelets, even her seasoned bean sprouts." But Yoomi won't eat "stinky spicy kimchi." Grandma finally makes a kimchi pancake, and Yoomi finds it yummy.

"THE SIXTEEN-SCOOP ICE CREAM CONE" ————

Felt Story

Place a cone-shaped felt piece at the bottom of a felt board. Add an appropriately colored "felt ice cream scoop" each time a different flavor is mentioned in the story.)

I love ice cream.
One day, I went to an ice cream store that advertised sixteen different flavors.
I could not make up my mind.
I ordered one of each.
On a sugar cone.
I had a scoop of Raspberry Road, and
A scoop of Rocky Ripple, and
A scoop of Blueberry Bliss, and
A scoop of Magical Mint, and
A scoop of Strawberry Surprise, and
A scoop of Grape Jubilee, and
A scoop of Rainbow Ice, and
A scoop of Chocolate Chunk Chip, and
A scoop of Cardinal Cherry Royale, and
A scoop of Luscious Lime Sherbet, and
A scoop of Black Licorice Delight, and
A scoop of Okey-Dokey Mocha, and
A scoop of Choco-Cherry Caramel Twist, and
A scoop of Marshmallow Banana Butterscotch Blonde Blitz, and
A scoop of Peanut Butter Bubblegum Crème Supreme.
The person behind the counter handed me my ice cream cone.
It had one, two, three, four, five, six, seven, eight, nine, ten,
Eleven, twelve, thirteen, fourteen, fifteen scoops.

"Fifteen scoops?" I said. "I thought you advertised sixteen flavors!"
"We do," said the person behind the counter. "But the sixteenth flavor
  is vanilla.
We keep it in the back because nobody ever orders vanilla."
"Vanilla!" I screamed. "You have vanilla? It's my favorite!
Take back all those other flavors and give me vanilla!"
The person behind the counter took back the
Scoop of Peanut Butter Bubblegum Crème Supreme, and the
Scoop of Marshmallow Banana Butterscotch Blonde Blitz, and the
Scoop of Choco-Cherry Caramel Twist, and the
Scoop of Okey-Dokey Mocha, and the
Scoop of Black Licorice Delight, and the
Scoop of Luscious Lime Sherbet, and the
Scoop of Cardinal Cherry Royale, and the
Scoop of Chocolate Chunk Chip, and the
Scoop of Rainbow Ice, and the
Scoop of Grape Jubilee, and the
Scoop of Strawberry Surprise, and the
Scoop of Magical Mint, and the
Scoop of Blueberry Bliss, and the
Scoop of Rocky Ripple, and the
Scoop of Raspberry Road.
And then the person behind the counter gave me
A vanilla ice cream cone.
A sixteen-scoop vanilla ice cream cone!

PICTURE BOOK MATCH

Gorilla Loves Vanilla, written by Chae Strathie and illustrated by Nicola
  O'Byrne (Barron's, 2016).
> Sam's Sundaes has some very unusual ice cream flavors, like squirmy
> worm ice cream, stinky blue cheese ice cream, fish finger ice cream,
> muddy ice cream, and daisy/grass/dandelion ice cream. Of course,
> Gorilla orders vanilla.

IMAGINARY CREATURES
(Aliens, Dragons, Monsters, and Robots)

"BE KIND TO YOUR BOT ROBOT FRIENDS"

Musical/Movement Activity

Sing to the tune of "Be Kind to Your Web-Footed Friends." Everyone stands, moving their arms up and down stiffly and walking in circles with straight legs, like an old-fashioned mechanical robot.

Be kind to your Bot Robot Friends,
Be careful you don't hit that button, (*Point to imaginary button on self.*)
'Cause if you press on the wrong switch,
It will look and sound a lot like this . . . (*Mime pressing the button on self.*)
(*Spoken*) Oh no! Half power!
(*Sing the next verse with a deep voice very slowly. Move in slow motion.*)
Be kind to your Bot Robot Friends,
Be careful you don't hit that button, (*Point to imaginary button on self.*)
'Cause if you press on the wrong switch,
It will look and sound a lot like this . . . (*Mime pressing the button on self.*)
(*Spoken*) Oh no! Extra power!
(*Sing the next verse with a high-pitched voice in a hurried fashion. Move with fast motions.*)
Be kind to your Bot Robot Friends,
Be careful you don't hit that button, (*Point to imaginary button on self.*)
'Cause if you press on the wrong switch,
It will look and sound a lot like this . . . (*Mime pressing the button on self.*)
(*Spoken*) Oh no! Power's off! (*Everyone slowly bends over and freezes.*)
You may think that this is the end.
Well, it is!

Bitty Bot, written by Tim McCanna and illustrated by Tad Carpenter (Simon and Schuster, 2016).

> While all the bots in the robot town power down, Bitty Bot isn't at all sleepy. He breaks "all bedtime rules," builds a rocket, and flies to the moon. When Bitty Bot's batteries run low, he makes it back in time.

"THE EENSY-WEENSY ROBOT"

Musical/Movement Activity

Sing to the tune of "The Itsy-Bitsy Spider." Have the children imitate your sounds and motions. Everyone stands.

The Eensy-Weensy Robot,
Climbed to the table top, (*Mime climbing with arms and feet.*)
Looked all around, (*Hand over eyes, look in all directions.*)
And gave a little hop. (*Hop once.*)
Walked back and forth, (*Walk stiffly like a robot.*)
And looked so very brave, (*Thump chest.*)
Then climbed into a spaceship, (*Mime climbing again.*)
And gave us one last wave. (*Wave and then thrust arms in the air while making a "whoosh" noise.*)

Rabbit and Robot and Ribbit, written and illustrated by Cece Bell (Candlewick, 2016).

> Rabbit is jealous when he finds his friend Robot hanging out with a frog named Ribbit. When Rabbit and Ribbit quarrel, Robot's Emotion Decoder gets hot and he powers down. Rabbit and Ribbit work together to revive Robot.

"THE FIRE-BREATHING DRAGON"

Musical Fingerplay

Sing to the tune of "The Itsy-Bitsy Spider." Have the children imitate your motions.

The fire-breathing dragon
Flew up a mountain top. (*Flap arms as if flying.*)

Down came the rain, (*Wiggle fingers downward to simulate rain.*)
And put the fire out.
A big bolt of lightning (*Hold out hands and fling fingers to simulate lightning.*)
Fried that dragon's brain, (*Point to head.*)
And that fire-breathing dragon,
Is happy once again. (*Open mouth and blow to simulate blowing fire.*)
(*Note: You may have to explain to young children that the lightning
reignited the dragon's fire.*)

PICTURE BOOK MATCH

Again!, written and illustrated by Emily Gravett (Simon and Schuster, 2013).
Cedric, a small dragon, has a favorite book that his mother reads to him
at bedtime. She reads it and reads it until she falls asleep. Cedric gets
so mad that he shouts, "AGAIN! AGAIN! AGAIN!" and burns a hole in
the book with his fire-breathing ability.

"FIVE BIG GREEN MONSTERS" ————————————

Movement Activity

Have the children imitate your sounds and motions. Everyone stands.

Five big green monsters, (*Hold up five fingers.*)
Gave a loud roar, (*Roar.*)
One got a tickle in its throat, (*Cough.*)
And then there were four.
Four big green monsters, (*Hold up four fingers.*)
Roared loud with glee, (*Roar.*)
One got the hiccups, (*Hiccup.*)
And then there were three.
Three big green monsters, (*Hold up three fingers.*)
Roared a very loud, "Boo!" (*Shout "Boo!"*)
One started sneezing, (*Sneeze.*)
And then there were two.
Two big green monsters, (*Hold up two fingers.*)
Thought roaring was such fun, (*Roar.*)
One got laryngitis, (*Open and shut mouth without making a sound.*)
And then there was one.

One big green monster, (*Hold up one finger.*)
Roared while he spun, (*Roar and turn in a circle.*)
He got too dizzy, (*Sit down.*)
And then there were none.

PICTURE BOOK MATCH

The Nian Monster, written by Andrea Wang and illustrated by Alina Chau
(Albert Whitman, 2016).

> Right before Chinese New Year, Xingling learns that the decorations are
> red to scare away the Nian Monster. "Every monster has a weakness.
> Nian had three—loud sounds, fire, and the color red." Xingling must
> think fast when the Nian Monster returns and tells her that the old
> protections no longer work against him.

"IF YOU'RE A GHOST AND YOU KNOW IT"

Musical/Movement Activity

Sing to the tune of "If You're Happy and You Know It." Have the children imitate
your sounds and motions. Everyone stands.

If you're a ghost and you know it, say "Boo!" (*Shout "Boo!"*)
If you're a ghost and you know it, say "Boo!" (*"Boo!"*)
If you're a ghost and you know it, then your face will surely show it,
If you're a ghost and you know it, say "Boo!" (*"Boo!"*)
If you're a cat and you know it, say "Meow!" (*Say a stretched-out "Meow!"*)
If you're a cat and you know it, say "Meow!" (*"Meow!"*)
If you're a cat and you know it, then your face will surely show it,
If you're a cat and you know it, say "Meow!" (*"Meow!"*)
If you're a bat and you know it, flap your wings. (*Flap arms.*)
If you're a bat and you know it, flap your wings. (*Flap arms.*)
If you're a bat and you know it, then your face will surely show it,
If you're a bat and you know it, flap your wings. (*Flap arms.*)
If you're a skeleton and you know it, rattle your bones. (*Shake entire body.*)
If you're a skeleton and you know it, rattle your bones. (*Shake entire body.*)
If you're a skeleton and you know it, then your face will surely show it,
If you're a skeleton and you know it, rattle your bones. (*Shake entire body.*)

Leo: A Ghost Story, written by Mac Barnett and illustrated by Christian
   Robinson (Chronicle, 2015).

> Leo is a ghost who lives by himself in a house. He moves out when a
> family, who clearly do not like ghosts, move in. He meets a girl named
> Jane who thinks Leo is an imaginary friend. When she learns Leo is a
> ghost, Jane says, "Well, that's even better."

"I'M A MONSTER"

Sound Effects Activity

This activity is modeled after the camp chant "I'm a Beaver." Say the chant once
with the roar at the end. Repeat it a second time with the audience saying the words
and imitating your motions. Everyone stands.

I'm a monster, (*Point to self.*)
You're a monster, (*Point to others.*)
We are monsters all. (*Spread out arms.*)
When we get together,
We do the monster call,
Roar! (*Roar.*)

Quit Calling Me a Monster!, written by Jory John and illustrated by Bob
   Shea (Random House, 2016).

> A monster wants the reader to stop calling him one. He states that he
> is "a monster with excellent manners," before realizing that he just
> admitted he is, indeed, technically a monster. He asks everyone to call
> him by his true name, Floyd Peterson. When children are worried about
> monsters at night, their parents can simply say, "It's just Floyd Peterson."

"R-O-B-O-T"

Sing to the tune of "Bingo." As you and the children sing each stanza, replace a letter with the "clank" sound.

There was a brilliant genius kid,
He built a real cool robot.
R-O-B-O-T, R-O-B-O-T, R-O-B-O-T,
He built a real cool robot.
There was a brilliant genius kid,
He built a real cool robot.
(*Clank*)-O-B-O-T, (*Clank*)-O-B-O-T, (*Clank*)-O-B-O-T,
He built a real cool robot.
There was a brilliant genius kid,
He built a real cool robot.
(*Clank-clank*)-B-O-T, (*Clank-clank*)-B-O-T, (*Clank-clank*)-B-O-T,
He built a real cool robot.
There was a brilliant genius kid,
He built a real cool robot.
(*Clank-clank-clank*)-O-T, (*Clank-clank-clank*)-O-T, (*Clank-clank-clank*)-
O-T,
He built a real cool robot.
There was a brilliant genius kid,
He built a real cool robot.
(*Clank-clank-clank-clank*)-T, (*Clank-clank-clank-clank*)-T, (*Clank-clank-clank-clank*)-T,
He built a real cool robot.
There was a brilliant genius kid,
He built a real cool robot.
(*Clank-clank-clank-clank-clank*),
(*Clank-clank-clank-clank-clank*),
(*Clank-clank-clank-clank-clank*),
He built a real cool robot.

And the Robot Went . . . , written by Michelle Robinson and illustrated by
Sergio Ruzzier (Clarion, 2017).

> A variety of characters assemble a robot with a "Zap! Click! Bang! Boom!"
> When the robot is finally all put together, it tells everyone, "Thank.
> You." and walks into the sunset.

"THERE'S A MONSTER BEHIND ME!"

Fingerplay

Have the children imitate your motions. Close your eyes while reciting the rhyme.

There's a monster behind me, oh golly gee! (*Place one hand behind you
and wiggle all five fingers.*)
There's a monster behind me, golly gee!
Now the monster's on my ear, on my ear, oh dear! (*Move your hand with
the wiggling fingers to one of your ears.*)
Now the monster's on my ear, oh dear!
Now the monster's in my hair, in my hair, beware! (*Move your hand
with the wiggling fingers to the top of your head.*)
Now the monster's in my hair, beware!
Now the monster's by my eye, by my eye, oh my! (*Move your hand with
the wiggling fingers in front of your face.*)
Now the monster's by my eye, oh my!
Hey, that's no monster! (*Slowly open your eyes while making whimpering
sounds. Look surprised and then happy at finding only wiggling fingers
instead of a monster.*)
Golly gee! Oh dear! Beware? Oh my!
Just my fingers!

Don't Push the Button!, written and illustrated by Bill Cotter (Sourcebooks
Jabberwocky, 2013).

> A monster named Larry instructs the reader to not push a big red button.
> When the button is pushed, Larry turns yellow and then yellow with
> polka dots. Larry says, "Push it twice!" and a second Larry appears and
> then more. A shake of the book gets rid of the extra Larrys.

"THREE LITTLE ALIENS"

Fingerplay

Tell the kids that the superhero character Superman came from the pretend planet Krypton, thus making him an alien. He landed on Earth and became one of our most popular comic superheroes. Make a flying saucer with your left hand by making a fist. Hold up three fingers on your right hand and place this hand on top of your left hand. The result should resemble three aliens in a flying saucer. Move both hands around while you recite the fingerplay as if the flying saucer is traveling through space. Have the children imitate your motions.

Three little aliens,
In outer space they flew,
One landed on Jupiter, (*Hold up one finger on right hand and move it far from the left hand.*)
And then there were two. (*Hold up two fingers over the "flying saucer."*)
Two little aliens,
Circled 'round the sun,
One got a bit too close, (*Hold up one finger on right hand and move it far from the left hand.*)
And now there is one. (*Hold up one finger over the "flying saucer."*)
One little alien,
Was definitely not a zero,
We call him Superman,
Our very own superhero! (*Make muscles with both arms.*)

PICTURE BOOK MATCH

Life on Mars, written and illustrated by Jon Agee (Dial, 2017).
> A boy attempts to prove there is life on Mars. He brings a gift of chocolate cupcakes but doesn't find anyone to eat them. The reader, of course, sees a large Martian follow the boy. The boy fails to see the large creature but finds life on Mars—a yellow flower.

"THREE LITTLE DRAGONS" ——————————

Movement Activity

Have the children imitate your motions. Everyone stands.

There were three little dragons, (*Flap arms and move around the room.*)
Flying overhead,
Flying overhead,
Flying overhead.
There were three little dragons,
Flying overhead,
One got tired and went to bed. (*Place hands on head as if sleeping.*)
There were two little dragons, (*Flap arms and move around the room.*)
Flying overhead,
Flying overhead,
Flying overhead.
There were two little dragons,
Flying overhead,
One got tired and went to bed. (*Place hands on head as if sleeping.*)
There was one little dragon, (*Flap arms and move around the room.*)
Flying overhead,
Flying overhead,
Flying overhead.
There was one little dragon,
Flying overhead,
It got tired and went to bed. (*Place hands on head as if sleeping.*)
There were no little dragons, (*Everyone sits and pretends to search in the
    air for dragons.*)
Flying overhead,
Flying overhead,
Flying overhead.
There were no little dragons,
Flying overhead,
Until breakfast was served and they were fed! (*Everyone stands and
    starts "flying" again.*)

Dragon Was Terrible, written by Kelly DiPucchio and illustrated by Greg
Pizzoli (Farrar, Straus and Giroux, 2016).

> Dragon is very terrible. He spits on cupcakes, takes candy from baby
> unicorns, and TP's the castle. A young boy tricks the dragon into hear-
> ing a story about a brave dragon. The kingdom is overjoyed when the
> dragon smiles and settles down.

"WE'RE GOING ON A DRAGON HUNT"

Movement Activity

This activity is modeled after the movement activity "We're Going on a Bear Hunt."
Have the children slap their legs to simulate walking and imitate your motions.
Teach them the chorus before starting. Everyone stands.

Chorus:
Dragons fly and they breath fire, (*Slap legs like a horse trotting during the
    refrain.*)
Dragons fly and they breathe fire,
Dragons fly and they breathe fire,
Be very, very careful!

Let's go on a dragon hunt. (*Stop slapping legs.*)
First, we need to put on our armor.
Put on the lower half. (*Mime putting on armor pants.*)
Put on the top half. (*Mime putting on the top half of armor.*)
Don't forget your helmet. (*Mime putting on helmet.*)
Grab your shield. (*Pretend to hook arm on back of a shield.*)
Walk over to your horse. (*Move awkwardly as if wearing heavy armor.*)
Get up on your horse. (*Mime swinging leg over horse's back.*)
Let's go!

Chorus:
Dragons fly and they breath fire, (*Slap legs like a horse trotting during the
    refrain.*)
Dragons fly and they breathe fire,
Dragons fly and they breathe fire,
Be very, very careful!

We're riding through the fields.
We're riding through the woods.
We're at the foot of a mountain. (*Stop slapping legs and point upward.*)
Dismount! (*Mime climbing down from horse.*)
Let's climb! (*Mime climbing up a mountain.*)
Whew! We're near the top. (*Raise hand to stop.*)
Here's a cave. (*Point.*)
Let's go in. Be very quiet. (*Tiptoe in place and whisper the refrain.*)

Chorus:
Dragons fly and they breath fire,
Dragons fly and they breathe fire,
Dragons fly and they breathe fire,
Be very, very careful!

There's something big and dark in the corner of the cave. (*Stop tiptoeing and peer.*)
I see a little flame over there. (*Point.*)
IT'S A DRAGON! LET'S GET OUT OF HERE! (*Slap legs.*)
Out of the cave!
Down the mountain! (*Stop slapping legs and make climbing down motions.*)
Up on your horse! (*Mime climbing on horse.*)
Ride! (*Slap legs.*)
Through the forest!
Through the fields!
Here we are at the castle! (*Stop slapping legs and point.*)
Oh no! The drawbridge is up! (*Hands on cheeks.*)
We'll have to swim in the moat! (*Point.*)
Throw down your shield! (*Mime throwing down shield.*)
Take off your helmet! (*Mime removing helmet.*)
Take off your armor! (*Mime removing the top and lower sections of the armor.*)
Jump in and swim! (*Jump and mime swimming.*)
Everyone out of the moat and in this side door! (*Slap legs.*)
Oh no! The dragon followed us into the castle! (*Slap forehead.*)
I guess we'll have to move to another castle. (*Tiptoe away from "the dragon."*)

Do Not Bring Your Dragon to the Library, written by Julie Gassman and
illustrated by Andy Elkerton (Picture Window, 2016).

If one brings one's dragon to the library, she will take up ten spaces at
storytime. Or get so excited about reading that "her flame might ignite."
In the end, the librarian comes up with a simple solution.

"WE'RE GOING ON A MONSTER HUNT" ————————

Movement Activity

This activity is modeled after the movement activity "We're Going on a Bear Hunt."
Have the children slap their legs to simulate walking and imitate your motions.
Everyone stands.

Leader: We're going on a monster hunt. (*Slap legs.*)
Audience: We're going on a monster hunt.
Leader: We're going to find a big one.
Audience: We're going to find a big one.
Leader: We're not afraid.
Audience: We're not afraid.
Leader: Oh look! (*Stop slapping legs and point.*)
Audience: Oh look!
Leader: A river of lava!
Audience: A river of lava!
Leader: We can't go through it. (*Hold arm straight out.*)
Audience: We can't go through it.
Leader: We can't go under it. (*Make a down-and-up curve with hand.*)
Audience: We can't go under it.
Leader: We'll have to jump over it. (*Make an up-and-down curve with
hand.*)
Audience: We'll have to jump over it.
Leader: Here we go!
Audience: Here we go!
Leader: Jump! (*Mime pole-vaulting.*)
Audience: Jump!
Leader: Whew, that was hot.
Audience: Whew, that was hot.
Leader: We're going on a monster hunt. (*Slap legs.*)

Audience: We're going on a monster hunt.

Leader: We're not afraid.

Audience: We're not afraid.

Leader: Oh look! (*Stop slapping legs and point.*)

Audience: Oh look!

Leader: Fog!

Audience: Fog!

Leader: We can't go under it. (*Make a down-and-up curve with hand.*)

Audience: We can't go under it.

Leader: We can't go over it. (*Make an up-and-down curve with hand.*)

Audience: We can't go over it.

Leader: We'll have to go through it. (*Hold arm straight out.*)

Audience: We'll have to go through it.

Leader: Everybody hold hands. (*Hold hands.*)

Audience: Everybody hold hands.

Leader: Here we go. (*Mime walking with hands stretched in front of you and eyes squinting to see.*)

Audience: Here we go.

Leader: Whew, that was cold and wet.

Audience: Whew, that was cold and wet.

Leader: We're going on a monster hunt. (*Slap legs.*)

Audience: We're going on a monster hunt.

Leader: We're going to find a big one.

Audience: We're going to find a big one.

Leader: We're not afraid.

Audience: We're not afraid.

Leader: Oh look! (*Stop slapping legs and point.*)

Audience: Oh look!

Leader: A creepy house.

Audience: A creepy house.

Leader: Door's locked. (*Mime trying to turn a doorknob.*)

Audience: Door's locked.

Leader: Can't go through it. (*Hold arm straight out.*)

Audience: Can't go through it.

Leader: Can't go over it. (*Make an up-and-down curve with hand.*)

Audience: Can't go over it.

Leader: We'll have to go under it. (*Make a down-and-up curve with hand.*)

Audience: We'll have to go under it.

Leader: Look, here's a trapdoor to the cellar. (*Point.*)
Audience: Look, here's a trapdoor to the cellar.
Leader: Hold hands again. (*Hold hands.*)
Audience: Hold hands again.
Leader: We're going down some steps. (*Mime climbing down stairs with exaggerated, overly large footsteps.*)
Audience: We're going down some steps.
Leader: It's very, very dark in here.
Audience: It's very, very dark in here.
Leader: Stop!
Audience: Stop!
Leader: I hear something. (*Cup hand by ear.*)
Audience: I hear something.
Leader: It's a monster! (*Point.*)
Audience: It's a monster!
Leader: Back up the cellar steps. (*Mime climbing up stairs with exaggerated, overly large footsteps.*)
Audience: Back up the cellar steps.
Leader: Back through the fog. (*Mime walking with hands stretched in front of you and eyes squinting to see.*)
Audience: Back through the fog.
Leader: Over the river of lava. (*Mime pole-vaulting.*)
Audience: Over the river of lava.
Leader: We're safe!
Audience: We're safe!
Leader: What if it followed us?
Audience: What if it followed us?
Leader: I think I see it! (*Point.*)
Audience: I think I see it!
Leader: I'm scared!
Audience: I'm scared!
(*Leader makes a meowing noise.*)
Leader: We ran from a kitty-cat?
Audience: We ran from a kitty-cat?
Leader: Whew! (*Wipe forehead.*)
Audience: Whew!

If Your Monster Won't Go to Bed, written by Denise Vega and illustrated by Zachariah Ohora (Knopf, 2017).

> Don't let your monster count sheep (it'll eat them) or drink a glass of milk (it'll "stay up all night burping sour, green, dirty-underwear-smelling burps"). Instead, be sure to read your monster "the freakiest, creepiest story" and sing it "Shock-a-Bye Monster."

TRANSPORTATION

"A COW IS DRIVING A CAR" ———————————————

Sound Effects Activity

Have the children repeat each line after you.

Leader: A cow is driving, "Moo! Moo! Moo!"
Audience: A cow is driving, "Moo! Moo! Moo!"
Leader: A flock of ducks think, "Let's drive, too!"
Audience: A flock of ducks think, "Let's drive, too!"
Leader: This is how it sounds to you,
Audience: This is how it sounds to you,
Leader: "Quack! Quack! Quack! Quack! Quack! Quack! Quack!"
Audience: "Quack! Quack! Quack! Quack! Quack! Quack! Quack!"
Leader: A cow is driving, "Moo! Moo! Moo!"
Audience: A cow is driving, "Moo! Moo! Moo!"
Leader: A herd of sheep think, "Let's drive, too!"
Audience: A herd of sheep think, "Let's drive, too!"
Leader: This is how it sounds to you,
Audience: This is how it sounds to you,
Leader: "Baa! Baa! Baa! Baa! Baa! Baa! Baa!"
Audience: "Baa! Baa! Baa! Baa! Baa! Baa! Baa!"
Leader: A cow is driving, "Moo! Moo! Moo!"
Audience: A cow is driving, "Moo! Moo! Moo!"
Leader: A pack of mules think, "Let's drive, too!"
Audience: A pack of mules think, "Let's drive, too!"
Leader: This is how it sounds to you,
Audience: This is how it sounds to you,
Leader: "Hee-haw! Hee-haw! Hee-haw! Hee!"
Audience: "Hee-haw! Hee-haw! Hee-haw! Hee!"
Leader: A cow is driving, "Moo! Moo! Moo!"
Audience: A cow is driving, "Moo! Moo! Moo!"

Leader: A parcel of pigs think, "Let's drive, too!"
Audience: A parcel of pigs think, "Let's drive, too!"
Leader: This is how it sounds to you,
Audience: This is how it sounds to you,
Leader: "Oink! Oink! Oink! Oink! Oink! Oink! Oink!"
Audience: "Oink! Oink! Oink! Oink! Oink! Oink! Oink!"
Leader: A cow is driving, "Moo! Moo! Moo!"
Audience: A cow is driving, "Moo! Moo! Moo!"
Leader: A gang of turkeys think, "Let's drive, too!"
Audience: A gang of turkeys think, "Let's drive, too!"
Leader: This is how it sounds to you,
Audience: This is how it sounds to you,
Leader: "Gobble! Gobble! Gobble! Gob!"
Audience: "Gobble! Gobble! Gobble! Gob!"
Leader: A cow is driving, "Moo! Moo! Moo!"
Audience: A cow is driving, "Moo! Moo! Moo!"
Leader: A swarm of bees think, "Let's drive, too!"
Audience: A swarm of bees think, "Let's drive, too!"
Leader: This is how it sounds to you,
Audience: This is how it sounds to you,
Leader: "Buzz! Buzz! Buzz! Buzz! Buzz! Buzz! Buzz!"
Audience: "Buzz! Buzz! Buzz! Buzz! Buzz! Buzz! Buzz!"

PICTURE BOOK MATCH

Moo!, written by David LaRochelle and illustrated by Mike Wohnoutka
(Walker, 2013).

> A cow drives the farmer's car all around, making several variations of
> the word "Moo" throughout his trip. At the end, the cow puts blame on
> the sheep with the word "Baa."

"THE CRAZY TRAFFIC LIGHT" ──────────────────

Felt Story/Movement Activity

Make a felt traffic light with circles of the following colors for lights: red, yellow,
green, pink, purple, orange, brown, white, and blue. Have the children imitate your
motions in the chorus.

There's a crazy traffic light on a corner in our town,
It has the normal colors, you know yellow means Slow Down, (*Point to yellow light.*)
And green means Go and red means Stop, (*Point to green and red lights.*)
It's all the other colors that'll make your mouth drop.

Chorus:
When you see a pink light, it means hop like a bunny. (*Replace one of the light colors with the pink circle and hop around.*)
When the light is purple, make a face that's funny. (*Replace one of the light colors with the purple circle and make a funny face.*)
When the light turns orange, you should bark like a dog. (*Replace one of the light colors with the orange circle and bark.*)
When the brown light shines, you can oink like a hog. (*Replace one of the light colors with the brown circle and oink.*)
When the white light's bright, you should give a loud roar. (*Replace one of the light colors with the white circle and roar.*)
When the light turns blue, fall asleep and snore. (*Replace one of the light colors with the blue circle, close eyes, put head in hands, and snore.*)

One day the workers came to fix that crazy light,
They tried to make it like all the other traffic lights,
They spent a lot of money tearing out its guts,
They tried to guarantee traffic wouldn't go nuts.
They put in brand new wires, they worked all day and night,
They thought when they were finished that they changed that traffic light,
But when they switched it on after spending all that dough,
It flashed those crazy colors that the kids all know.

Chorus:
When you see a pink light, it means hop like a bunny. (*Replace one of the light colors with the pink circle and hop around.*)
When the light is purple, make a face that's funny. (*Replace one of the light colors with the purple circle and make a funny face.*)
When the light turns orange, you should bark like a dog. (*Replace one of the light colors with the orange circle and bark.*)

When the brown light shines, you can oink like a hog. (*Replace one of the light colors with the brown circle and oink.*)

When the white light's bright, you should give a loud roar. (*Replace one of the light colors with the white circle and roar.*)

When the light turns blue, fall asleep and snore. (*Replace one of the light colors with the blue circle, close eyes, put head in hands, and snore.*)

PICTURE BOOK MATCH

Red Light, Green Light, written and illustrated by Yumi Heo (Cartwheel, 2015).

This interactive toy book teaches children about traffic signs and safety. It follows a car driving down a road and approaching the different colored lights of the traffic light, as well as other road signs.

"I'M DRIVING ALONG"

Movement Activity

Have the children imitate your motions.

I'm driving along,

I'm singing my song,

When suddenly, (*Stick out right foot and mime hitting the brakes. Make a "screech" noise.*)

I spot a rabbit! (*Make rabbit ears, stand, and hop around for a few seconds before sitting back down.*)

I'm driving along,

I'm singing my song,

When suddenly, (*"Screech!"*)

I spot a wolf! (*Throw head back and howl.*)

I'm driving along,

I'm singing my song,

When suddenly, (*"Screech!"*)

I spot a moose! (*Make antlers with fingers and do chewing motions.*)

I'm driving along,

I'm singing my song,

When suddenly, (*"Screech!"*)

I spot an elephant! (*Place arm in front of nose for a trunk and make a trumpeting noise.*)

PICTURE BOOK MATCH

Old MacDonald's Things That Go, written by Jane Clarke and illustrated by Migy Blanco (Nosy Crow, 2017).

> The farm animals join Old MacDonald as he drives a variety of vehicles. A bike has a ding-ding bell and is followed by a truck, a tractor, a combine harvester, and even a plane.

"MY LITTLE ROWBOAT"

Movement/Sound Effects Activity

Make rowing motions throughout this activity. Have the children make the animal sounds at the end of each stanza.

My little rowboat,
Rowing 'round and 'round,
We rowed past a little frog,
It made this silly sound: (*Cup ear.*)
"Rib-it!"
My little rowboat,
Rowing 'round and 'round,
We rowed past a little duck,
It made this silly sound: (*Cup ear.*)
"Quack!"
My little rowboat,
Rowing 'round and 'round,
We rowed past a little goose,
It made this silly sound: (*Cup ear.*)
"Honk!"
My little rowboat,
Rowing 'round and 'round,
We rowed past a little turtle,
It made this silly sound: (*Pause, shrug shoulders, and ask, "Do turtles make a sound?"*)

PICTURE BOOK MATCH

Row, Row, Row Your Boat, written and illustrated by Jane Cabrera (Holiday House, 2014).

A cat and a dog row their boat in the jungle creek to see several animals as the oars go splish-splash-splatter. They encounter birds, mice, elephants, monkeys, butterflies. They also learn that "if you see a crocodile, don't forget to Snap! SNAP! SNAP!"

"MY OLD CAR"

Musical/Movement Activity

Sing to the tune of "This Old Man." Have the children imitate your motions.

My old car's not so good, (*Mime driving.*)
It doesn't sound like a cool car should,
It goes, "Chugga-chugga, Clunk-clunk!" (*Move body up and down and all around.*)
All around the town,
My old car just makes me frown. (*Frown and cross arms.*)
(*Spoken*) Let's take it to the auto shop. (*Stand.*)
Let's lift the hood. (*Lift imaginary hood.*)
I see the problem. (*Peer forward.*)
Let's take this out, (*Mime removing part of the engine.*)
And put a new one in. (*Mime putting in new part of the engine.*)
Tighten it up. (*Pretend to tighten part with a wrench.*)
Close the hood. (*Close imaginary hood.*)
We're all set! (*Brush off hands.*)
(*Sing*) My old car sounds real good, (*Mime driving.*)
It sounds like a cool car should,
It goes, "Vroom-vroom! Vroom-vroom!"
All around the town,
My car makes me smile, not frown. (*Give a big smile.*)

PICTURE BOOK MATCH

This Old Van, written by Kim Norman and illustrated by Carolyn Conahan (Sterling, 2015).

> This picture book also uses the song "This Old Man" to celebrate transportation. An old hippie couple drive along until they reach the "All-State Youth Championships Downhill Derby . . . just in time!"

"THE NEW WHEELS ON THE BUS" ————————————

Musical/Movement Activity

Sing to the tune of "The Wheels on the Bus." Have the children imitate your motions.

The wheels on the sports car go 'round-'round-'round! (*Spin hands around each other very fast.*)
'Round-'round-'round! 'Round-'round-'round!
The wheels on the sports car go 'round-'round-'round!
All around the town.
The horn on the sports car goes, "Meep-meep-meep!" (*Mime hitting the car horn.*)
"Meep-meep-meep!" "Meep-meep-meep!"
The horn on the sports car goes, "Meep-meep-meep!"
All around the town.
The motor on the car goes, "rrrrrrRRRRRRrrrrrr!" (*Look left and make a quiet motor noise. Swivel head getting louder and louder. As your head turns right, make the motor noise small again.*)
"rrrrrrRRRRRRrrrrrr!" "rrrrrrRRRRRRrrrrrr!"
The motor on the car goes, "rrrrrrRRRRRRrrrrrr!"
All around the town.
(*Spoken*) Let's get out of the car and get inside a rocket ship.
The boosters on the rocket go, "Whoosshh!" (*Put hands together and then pull apart as you lift them overhead.*)
"Whoosshh!" "Whoosshh!"
The boosters on the rocket go, "Whoosshh!"
Way up overhead.
The radio on the rocket goes, "GarbleSqwackGarble!" (*Put hand in front of mouth and make garbling noises.*)
"GarbleSqwackGarble!" "GarbleSqwackGarble!"
The radio on the rocket goes, "GarbleSqwackGarble!"
Way up overhead.
The people on the rocket go, "Hey! I'm floating!" (*Lift arms and legs as if they are weightless.*)
"Hey! I'm floating!" "Hey! I'm floating!"
The people on the rocket go, "Hey! I'm floating!"
Way up overhead.
(*Spoken*) Let's land this rocket and get into something even more exciting. A donkey cart!

The wheels on the cart go, "KlippityKlop!" (*Spin hands around each other in slow motion.*)
"KlippityKlop!" "KlippityKlop!"
The wheels on the cart go, "KlippityKlop!"
All around the town.
The driver on the cart says, "Giddyup!" (*Mime shaking reins.*)
"Giddyup!" "Giddyup!"
The driver on the cart says, "Giddyup!"
All around the town.
The donkey on the cart says, "Hee-Haw!" (*Make a donkey braying noise.*)
"Hee-Haw!" "Hee-Haw!"
The donkey on the cart says, "Hee-Haw!"
All around the town.
The kids on the cart say, "That's all!" (*Everyone waves goodbye.*)
"That's all!" "That's all!"
The kids on the cart say, "That's all!"
All around the town.
(*Spoken*) "That's all!"

PICTURE BOOK MATCH

Last Stop on Market Street, written by Matt de la Peña and illustrated by
Christian Robinson (G. P. Putnam's Sons, 2015).
> CJ and his nana take the city bus after church. When CJ wonders about
> how run down this part of the city is, Nana says, "Sometimes when you're
> surrounded by dirt, CJ, you're a better witness for what's beautiful." The
> two arrive at their destination—to help at a soup kitchen.

"SHE'LL BE DRIVING A BULLDOZER" ——————

Musical/Movement Activity

Sing to the tune of "She'll Be Coming 'Round the Mountain." Have the children
imitate your motions. Add the previous motions at the end of each stanza.

She'll be driving a bulldozer when she comes. Push it back! (*Hold hands
out front and make a pushing movement away from the body on each
"Push it back!"*)
She'll be driving a bulldozer when she comes. Push it back!

She'll be driving a bulldozer,
She'll be driving a bulldozer,
She'll be driving a bulldozer when she comes. Push it back!
She'll be running a big digger when she comes. Scoop it up! (*Make a scooping motion with hands on each "Scoop it up!"*)
She'll be running a big digger when she comes. Scoop it up!
She'll be running a big digger,
She'll be running a big digger,
She'll be running a big digger when she comes. Scoop it up! Push it back!
She'll be working a dirt-dumper when she comes. Look out below! (*Cup mouth and shout on each "Look out below!"*)
She'll be working a dirt-dumper when she comes. Look out below!
She'll be working a dirt-dumper,
She'll be working a dirt-dumper,
She'll be working a dirt-dumper when she comes. Look out below! Scoop it up! Push it back!
She'll be on a cement mixer when she comes. Shake it up! (*Shake whole body on each "Shake it up!"*)
She'll be on a cement mixer when she comes. Shake it up!
She'll be on a cement mixer,
She'll be on a cement mixer,
She'll be on a cement mixer when she comes. Shake it up! Look out below! Scoop it up! Push it back!
She'll be steering a steamroller when she comes. Roll it flat! (*Twirl arms around each other on each "Roll it flat!"*)
She'll be steering a steamroller when she comes. Roll it flat!
She'll be steering a steamroller,
She'll be steering a steamroller,
She'll be steering a steamroller when she comes. Roll it flat! Shake it up! Look out below! Scoop it up! Push it back!
She'll be driving a street sweeper when she comes. Clean it up! (*Mime sweeping motions as if using a broom on each "Clean it up!"*)
She'll be driving a street sweeper when she comes. Clean it up!
She'll be driving a street sweeper,
She'll be driving a street sweeper,
She'll be driving a street sweeper when she comes. Clean it up! Roll it flat! Shake it up! Look out below! Scoop it up! Push it back!

PICTURE BOOK MATCH

Bulldozer's Big Day, written by Candace Fleming and illustrated by Eric Rohmann (Atheneum, 2015).

> Bulldozer asks the different types of construction equipment if they know what day it is. He is sad when the other machines are too busy for him. The big machines surprise Bulldozer with a birthday cake and tell him to "Dig in."

WINTER PLAY

"IF YOU'RE HAPPY AND YOU KNOW IT— WINTER STYLE"

Musical/Movement Activity

Sing to the tune of "If You're Happy and You Know It." Have children imitate your motions. Everyone stands.

If you're happy and you know it, clap your mittens, (*Clap.*)
If you're happy and you know it, clap your mittens,
If you're happy and you know it and you really want to show it,
If you're happy and you know it, clap your mittens.
If you're happy and you know it, twirl your scarf, (*Mime twirling a scarf.*)
If you're happy and you know it, twirl your scarf,
If you're happy and you know it and you really want to show it,
If you're happy and you know it, twirl your scarf.
If you're happy and you know it, stomp your boots, (*Stomp feet.*)
If you're happy and you know it, stomp your boots,
If you're happy and you know it and you really want to show it,
If you're happy and you know it, stomp your boots.
If you're happy and you know it, throw a snowball, (*Mime throwing a snowball.*)
If you're happy and you know it, throw a snowball,
If you're happy and you know it and you really want to show it,
If you're happy and you know it, throw a snowball.
If you're happy and you know it, make a snow angel, (*Lie down on floor and mime making a snow angel.*)
If you're happy and you know it, make a snow angel,
If you're happy and you know it and you really want to show it,
If you're happy and you know it, make a snow angel.

First Snow, written and illustrated by Peter McCarty (Balzer and Bray,   ·
    2015).

> Pedro is not happy with snow. He visits his cousins Sancho, Bella, Lola,
> Ava, and Maria and experiences winter snow for the first time. He com-
> plains that it's cold, "And I don't like cold." Once he goes down a hill
> on a sled, Pedro states, "I love the snow!"

"SNOWBALL"

Movement Activity

This activity is modeled after the camp call-and-response chant "Flea Fly Mosquito."
Ask the audience members if they have ever had the experience of snow down
their backs. For those folks living in warmer cities, ask them to imagine an ice cube
running down the back of their shirt. Have the children repeat the lines after you
and imitate your motions. Everyone stands.

Leader: Snow!
Audience: Snow!
Leader: Snowball!
Audience: Snowball!
Leader: Slushy-wushy snowball!
Audience: Slushy-wushy snowball!
Leader: Slushy-wushy snowball sliding down my neck! (*Look panicked
    and slap back of neck.*)
Audience: Slushy-wushy snowball sliding down my neck!
Leader: Slushy-wushy snowball sliding down my back! (*Slap at back.*)
Audience: Slushy-wushy snowball sliding down my back!
Leader: Ooh it's cold, it's oh-so-cold, this snowball down my back! (*Hop
    around.*)
Audience: Ooh it's cold, it's oh-so-cold, this snowball down my back!
Leader: Cold-cold, cold-cold-cold, oh it's very cold! (*Dance wildly in
    circles with arms flailing.*)
Audience: Cold-cold, cold-cold-cold, oh it's very cold!
Leader: Oh! (*Pause.*) It's not cold anymore. (*Stop and shrug shoulders.*)
Audience: Oh! (*Pause.*) It's not cold anymore.

Rabbit's Snow Dance, written by James Bruchac and Joseph Bruchac and
illustrated by Jeff Newman (Dial, 2012).

> Rabbit is impatient and creates a little chant to make it snow even
> though it's still summer. He gets his drum and chants, "I will make it
> snow, AZIKANAPO! I will make it snow, AZIKANAPO!" To the delight
> of some animals and the horror of others, it begins to snow.

"SNOW DUDE, SNOW DUDE"

Movement Activity

This activity is modeled after the movement activity "Teddy Bear, Teddy Bear, Turn
Around." Have the children imitate your motions. Everyone stands.

Snow Dude, Snow Dude, turn around, (*Turn slowly in a circle.*)
Snow Dude, Snow Dude, touch the ground, (*Touch the floor.*)
Snow Dude, Snow Dude, you have no toes, (*Point to toes and shake head
   sadly.*)
But check out Snow Dude's carrot nose. (*Point to nose.*)

The Itsy Bitsy Snowman, written by Jeffrey Burton and illustrated by Sanja
Rescek (Simon and Schuster, 2015).

> A little snowman climbs up a snowy hill in this ode to "The Itsy-Bitsy
> Spider." The snowman slides on a sled past ice-skating children. It dodges
> a snowball fight and heads into town. "Everything was perfect in his
> winter wonderland."

"WINTER NOISES"

Movement/Sound Effects Activity

Have the children imitate your motions. Everyone stands.

Winter noises are so fun.
Make them with me one by one.
Tell me how it sounds when you shovel. (*Mime shoveling and make a
   scraping noise.*)

Tell me how it sounds when a big person uses the snow blower. (*Mime pushing a snow blower and make a roaring noise.*)

Tell me how it sounds when you go sledding down a hill. (*Sit down and rock side to side and make a smack noise.*)

Tell me how it sounds when you throw a snowball at a tree. (*Stand and mime throwing and make a smack noise.*)

Tell me how it sounds when you're outside playing in the snow. (*Everyone laughs and yells.*)

PICTURE BOOK MATCH

Into the Snow, written by Yuki Kaneko and illustrated by Masamitsu Saito (Enchanted Lions, 2016).

> A young child is excited to see snowflakes fluttering down from the sky. The child's sled zooms down with a "Whoosh." The child exclaims "Wheee!" and "Aaagh!" as the sled goes faster and faster. When the wind starts howling, it's time to head back home where Mommy says, "I think it's time for your favorite snow day treat."

The Literary World

BOOKS, READING, AND LIBRARIES

"A BOOK! BOK! BOK!"

Sound Effects Activity

Repeat each verse twice. Have the audience join you the second time.

Leader: A book! Bok! Bok!
A book! Bok! Bok!
A chicken's got a book! Bok! Bok!
All: A book! Bok! Bok!
A book! Bok! Bok!
A chicken's got a book! Bok! Bok!
Leader: A book! Bow Wow!
A book! Bow Wow!
A dog has got a book! Bow Wow!
All: A book! Bow Wow!
A book! Bow Wow!
A dog has got a book! Bow Wow!
Leader: A book! Baa! Baa!
A book! Baa! Baa!
A sheep has got a book! Baa Baa!
All: A book! Baa! Baa!
A book! Baa! Baa!
A sheep has got a book! Baa Baa!
Leader: A book! Buzz! Buzz!
A book! Buzz! Buzz!
A bee has got a book! Buzz! Buzz!
All: A book! Buzz! Buzz!
A book! Buzz! Buzz!
A bee has got a book! Buzz! Buzz!

Chicken Story Time, written by Sandy Asher and illustrated by Mark Fearing (Dial, 2016).

A chicken sneaks into the public library and enjoys storytime with the children. A week later, several chickens show up. The library quickly becomes chaotic with chickens and children interacting.

"COMIN' DOWN TO STORYTIME"

Musical/Movement Activity

Sing to the tune of "She'll Be Comin' 'Round the Mountain." Have the children imitate your sounds and motions.

We'll be comin' down to storytime when we come. Yee ha! (*Shout "Yee ha!" with fist in the air.*)

We'll be comin' down to storytime when we come. Yee ha! (*Shout "Yee ha!" with fist in the air.*)

We'll be comin' down to storytime, we'll be comin' down to storytime,

We'll be comin' down to storytime when we come. Yee ha! (*Shout "Yee ha!" with fist in the air.*)

We will hear a funny story when we come. Ha! Ha! Ha! (*Hold stomach and laugh.*)

We will hear a funny story when we come. Ha! Ha! Ha! (*Hold stomach and laugh.*)

We will hear a funny story, we will hear a funny story,

We will hear a funny story when we come. Ha! Ha! Ha! (*Hold stomach and laugh.*)

We will say a nursery rhyme when we come. Mother Goose! (*Flap arms like wings.*)

We will say a nursery rhyme when we come. Mother Goose! (*Flap arms like wings.*)

We will say a nursery rhyme, we will say a nursery rhyme,

We will say a nursery rhyme when we come. Mother Goose! (*Flap arms like wings.*)

We will make a fingerplay when we come. Itsy Bitsy! (*Make the initial finger motions for the "Itsy-Bitsy Spider" fingerplay.*)

We will make a fingerplay when we come. Itsy Bitsy! (*Make the next set of finger motions for "Itsy-Bitsy Spider."*)

We will make a fingerplay, we will make a fingerplay,

We will make a fingerplay when we come. Itsy Bitsy! (*Make the final set of finger motions for "Itsy-Bitsy Spider."*)

We will sing a little song when we come. La! La! La! (*Hold out arm and sing with gusto.*)

We will sing a little song when we come. La! La! La! (*Hold out arm and sing with gusto.*)

We will sing a little song, we will sing a little song,

We will sing a little song when we come. La! La! La! (*Hold out arm and sing with gusto.*)

We will "Quack" and we will "Moo" when we come. "Quack! Moo!" (*Mime using hand puppets.*)

We will "Quack" and we will "Moo" when we come. "Quack! Moo!" (*Mime using hand puppets.*)

We will "Quack" and we will "Moo," we will "Quack" and we will "Moo,"

We will "Quack" and we will "Moo" when we come. "Quack! Moo!" (*Mime using hand puppets.*)

We will all join hands and move when we come. Skip to My Lou! (*Swing arms in the air.*)

We will all join hands and move when we come. Skip to My Lou! (*Swing arms in the air.*)

We will all join hands and move, we will all join hands and move,

We will all join hands and move when we come. Skip to My Lou! (*Swing arms in the air.*)

We will make a pretty picture when we come. Draw! Draw! (*Mime drawing a picture.*)

We will make a pretty picture when we come. Draw! Draw! (*Mime drawing a picture.*)

We will make a pretty picture, we will make a pretty picture,

We will make a pretty picture when we come. Draw! Draw! (*Mime drawing a picture.*)

We might even get a treat when we come. Yum! Yum! (*Rub tummy.*)

We might even get a treat when we come. Yum! Yum! (*Rub tummy.*)

We might even get a treat, we might even get a treat,

We might even get a treat when we come. Yum! Yum! (*Rub tummy.*)

We will check out lots of books when we leave. Bye now! (*Wave goodbye.*)

We will check out lots of books when we leave. Bye now! (*Wave goodbye.*)
We will check out lots of books, we will check out lots of books,
We will check out lots of books when we leave. Bye now! (*Wave goodbye.*)

PICTURE BOOK MATCH

Froggy Goes to the Library, written by Jonathan London and illustrated by Frank Remkiewicz (Viking, 2016).

At first, Froggy thinks storytime is only for babies. He then learns that it is fun because he can listen to a good story and dance around.

"DON'T SCREAM IN THE LIBRARY"

Imagination Exercise

Instruct the audience to say, "Because we're in the library" whenever you ask, "Do you know why?"

Leader: Don't look now, but I see a polar bear!
Shhh! Be quiet or it'll see us.
And whatever you do, don't scream.
Do you know why?
Audience: Because we're in the library.
Leader: Don't look now, but I see an alligator!
Shhh! Be quiet or it'll see us.
And whatever you do, don't scream.
Do you know why?
Audience: Because we're in the library.
Leader: Don't look now, but I see a snake!
Shhh! Be quiet or it'll see us.
And whatever you do, don't scream.
Do you know why?
Audience: Because we're in the library.
Leader: Don't look now, but I see a spider!
Shhh! Be quiet or it'll see us.
And whatever you do, don't scream.
Do you know why?
Audience: Because we're in the library.

Leader: Don't look now, but I see a monster!
Shhh! Be quiet or it'll see us.
And whatever you do, don't scream.
Do you know why?
Audience: Because we're in the library.

PICTURE BOOK MATCH

The Not So Quiet Library, written and illustrated by Zachariah Ohora
   (Dial, 2016).
> Oskar and Theodore look forward to quiet Saturdays at the library. One
> day, they settle down and then they hear "BOOM! CRASH! GROWL!"
> They must deal with noisy monsters until the librarian announces that
> it is storytime.

"THE GRAND OLD STORYTELLER"

Movement Activity

This activity is modeled after the nursery rhyme "The Grand Old Duke of York."
Have the children imitate your motions. Everyone stands.

The Grand Old Storyteller,
Has many girls and boys,
Some are very good,
Some make LOTS of noise, (*Shout.*)
When they need to move, they jump, (*Jump.*)
When they quiet down, they sit, (*Sit.*)
And sometimes it's good to jump, (*Jump.*)
Then sit, then jump, then sit (*pause*) for the next story . . . (*Sit, jump,
   and sit.*)

PICTURE BOOK MATCH

I Am a Story, written and illustrated by Dan Yaccarino (Harper, 2016).
> Stories were told years ago around the campfire by storytellers. Through
> the years, stories appeared on cave walls and in tapestries, were copied
> into books and "acted out onstage," were found in libraries and in
> modern technology. And, of course, stories are still told by storytellers
> around the campfire.

"HERE IS A BOOK"

Fingerplay

Have the children imitate your motions.

Here is a book, (*Hold out both hands together with thumbs up to represent a closed book.*)
With a story inside,
I can't wait,
To open it wide. (*Open hands to represent an open book.*)
I look at the pictures, (*Look at hands, moving head from side to side.*)
I read for awhile,
I then close the book, (*Put hands back to original position.*)
With a great big smile. (*Smile.*)
It was super good! (*Nod vigorously.*)
It had rhythm and rhyme,
I want to read it again,
Not once, not twice, but three more times. (*Hold up one finger, then two fingers, then three fingers.*)

PICTURE BOOK MATCH

Please, Louise, written by Toni Morrison and Slade Morrison and illustrated by Shadra Strickland (Simon and Shuster, 2014).
> Louise leaves her house and walks down the street one rainy day. She passes by things that concern her, like a barking dog and a scary junkyard. She finds refuge in the public library with books that "are loyal friends."

"IF YOU WANT A FUNNY STORY"

Musical Activity

Sing to the tune of "If You're Happy and You Know It." Have the children imitate your sounds and motions.

If you want a funny story, laugh like this, (*Laugh.*)
If you want a funny story, laugh like this. (*Laugh.*)
If you want a funny story,
If you want a funny story,
If you want a funny story, laugh like this. (*Laugh.*)

If you want a real sad story, cry like this, (*Cry.*)
If you want a real sad story, cry like this. (*Cry.*)
If you want a real sad story,
If you want a real sad story,
If you want a real sad story, cry like this. (*Cry.*)
If you want a romantic story, sigh like this, (*Place hand on heart and sigh.*)
If you want a romantic story, sigh like this. (*Place hand on heart and sigh.*)
If you want a romantic story,
If you want a romantic story,
If you want a romantic story, sigh like this. (*Place hand on heart and sigh.*)
If you want a scary story, scream like this, (*Scream.*)
If you want a scary story, scream like this. (*Scream.*)
If you want a scary story,
If you want a scary story,
If you want a scary story, scream like this. (*Scream.*)

PICTURE BOOK MATCH

The Midnight Library, written and illustrated by Kazuno Kohara (Roaring
Brook, 2014).

There is a special library only open at night for nocturnal animals. While
different animals are reading, a wolf starts crying over a sad book. The
librarian and her assistant owls take the wolf to the storytelling corner
where the wolf hears stories that make her smile.

"MONKEYS READING IN BED" ————————————

Fingerplay

This fingerplay is modeled after the fingerplay "Five Little Monkeys Jumping on the
Bed." Have the children imitate your motions.

One little monkey was reading in her bed, (*Hold up one finger.*)
When she was done, this is what she said,
"I read a book that was very sad, (*Make a sad face.*)
But it ended well and now I'm glad." (*Smile and nod.*)
Two little monkeys were reading in bed, (*Hold up two fingers.*)
When they were done, this is what they said,
"We read a book that gave us a fright, (*Make a frightened face.*)
It was fun, but we'll be up all night!" (*Smile and nod nervously.*)

Three little monkeys were reading in bed, (*Hold up three fingers.*)
When they were done, this is what they said,
"We read a book that was lots of fun, (*Smile.*)
It made us laugh and now we're done!" (*Laugh.*)

PICTURE BOOK MATCH

Putting the Monkeys to Bed, written by Gennifer Choldenko and illustrated
by Jack E. Davis (G. P. Putnam's Sons, 2015).

Sam cannot go to sleep and neither can his toy monkeys. Sam finally
grabs his favorite book and reads to the monkeys. "He turns the pages
and the monkeys yawn."

"MY MONKEY LIKES TO READ TO ME"

Sound Effects Activity

Have any book in your hand as a prop.

My monkey likes to read to me,
She's really very good,
She has me sit, then starts to read,
Like a monkey should.
She goes: "Ooh-Ooh-Ooh-Ooh." (*Hold up the book as if you were reading
it out loud as a monkey would sound. Add different inflections and then
invite kids to make the noises with you.*)
My chicken likes to read to me,
She's really very good,
She has me sit, then starts to read,
Like a chicken should.
She goes: "Bawk-bawk-bawk-bawk." (*Follow the same directions as above
with chicken noises.*)
My piggy likes to read to me,
He's really very good,
He has me sit, then starts to read,
Like a piggy should.
He goes: "Oink-oink-oink-oink." (*Follow the same directions as above with
pig noises.*)
My donkey likes to read to me,
He's really very good,
He has me sit, then starts to read,

Like a donkey should.
He goes: "Hee-haw, hee-haw." (*Follow the same directions as above with donkey noises.*)

Make Way for Readers, written by Judy Sierra and illustrated by G. Brian Karas (Simon and Schuster, 2016).
> Several young animals make their way to hear stories from a flamingo named Miss Bingo. She even has them stretch and dance between stories. "Flap with your wings! Clap with your paws!"

"THE READ, READ, READ CHANT"

Call-and-Response Chant

Teach the children to repeat the leader's lines for the chorus. The leader can rap the lines in between the choruses.

Chorus:
Leader: Read, read, read, let's read!
Audience: Read, read, read, let's read!
Leader: Read, read, read, let's read!
Audience: Read, read, read, let's read!

Leader: Read in the kitchen, read in the park,
Read in the day and read when it's dark,
Read in the tub and read at school,
Read in the fridge 'cause it's real cool.

Chorus:
Leader: Read, read, read, let's read!
Audience: Read, read, read, let's read!
Leader: Read, read, read, let's read!
Audience: Read, read, read, let's read!

Leader: Read to a dog, read to a cow,
Read to a kitty cat, read to a sow,
Read to your Barbie, read to your teddy,
Read to your toys before you go to bed-dy.

Chorus:
Leader: Read, read, read, let's read!
Audience: Read, read, read, let's read!
Leader: Read, read, read, let's read!
Audience: Read, read, read, let's read!

Leader: Read at the gym while shooting hoops,
Read at the restaurant while sipping soup,
Read at the circus, read at the zoo,
The monkeys are reading and so should you.

Chorus:
Leader: Read, read, read, let's read!
Audience: Read, read, read, let's read!
Leader: Read, read, read, let's read!
Audience: Read, read, read, let's read!

Leader: Read a mystery, guess the clue,
Read something scary and then go "Boo!"
Read at the pool, read in a tree,
Read when you're alone and with your family.

Chorus:
Leader: Read, read, read, let's read!
Audience: Read, read, read, let's read!
Leader: Read, read, read, let's read!
Audience: Read, read, read, let's read!

Leader: Read, read, read, let's read!
Audience: Read, read, read, let's read!
All: READ!

PICTURE BOOK MATCH

You Can Read, written by Helaine Becker and illustrated by Mark Hoffman
(Orca, 2017).

> This lyrical text is very similar to my chant above. It encourages kids to
> read in the classroom and park, as well as in the bathroom, on a space-
> ship, in your party clothes, or even in your underpants.

"SHH! SHH! SHH!"

Sound Effects Activity

Instruct the children to put their fingers to their lips and say, "Shh! Shh! Shh!" after you recite each line.

What do we say when teacher's talking in school? "Shh! Shh! Shh!"
What do we say when we're trying to look cool? "Shh! Shh! Shh!"
What do we say when someone's trying to sleep? "Shh! Shh! Shh!"
What do we say when Dad says, "Don't make a peep!"? "Shh! Shh! Shh!"
What do we say in the library? "Shh! Shh! Shh!"
Unless we're in Storytime!

PICTURE BOOK MATCH

The Snake Who Said Shhh, written by Jodie Parachini and illustrated by
Gill McLean (QEB Publishing, 2015).
> Instead of hissing, a young snake makes a "Shhhhhh" sound. The other
> animals in the jungle mock the snake. His mother says, "Don't lisssten
> to them, ssson." The noisy animals soon realize that the snake is telling
> them to be quiet with his "Shhhhhh."

"THE TWELVE DAYS OF STORYTIME"

Musical/Movement Activity

Sing to the tune of "The Twelve Days of Christmas." Let the children know that the word "teller" is a shortened version of "storyteller." Have them imitate your sounds and motions. Everyone stands.

On the first day of Storytime,
The teller shared with me,
A book about a curious monkey. (*Scratch head and armpits while making
monkey noises.*)
On the second day of Storytime,
The teller shared with me,
Two Dr. Seuss, (*Yell out "Green Eggs and Ham."*)
And a book about a curious monkey. (*Scratch head and armpits while
making monkey noises.*)
On the third day of Storytime,
The teller shared with me,

Three fingerplays, (*Hold up hands and wiggle fingers.*)
Two Dr. Seuss, (*Yell out "Green Eggs and Ham."*)
And a book about a curious monkey. (*Scratch head and armpits while making monkey noises.*)
On the fourth day of Storytime,
The teller shared with me,
Four funny poems, (*Hold belly and laugh.*)
Three fingerplays, (*Hold up hands and wiggle fingers.*)
Two Dr. Seuss, (*Yell out "Green Eggs and Ham."*)
And a book about a curious monkey. (*Scratch head and armpits while making monkey noises.*)
On the fifth day of Storytime,
The teller shared with me,
Five animal noises, (*Instruct the children to make any animal noise they'd like.*)
Four funny poems, (*Hold belly and laugh.*)
Three fingerplays, (*Hold up hands and wiggle fingers.*)
Two Dr. Seuss, (*Yell out "Green Eggs and Ham."*)
And a book about a curious monkey. (*Scratch head and armpits while making monkey noises.*)
On the sixth day of Storytime,
The teller shared with me,
Six arts and crafts, (*Mime using scissors, drawing, gluing, etc.*)
Five animal noises, (*Animal noises.*)
Four funny poems, (*Hold belly and laugh.*)
Three fingerplays, (*Hold up hands and wiggle fingers.*)
Two Dr. Seuss, (*Yell out "Green Eggs and Ham."*)
And a book about a curious monkey. (*Scratch head and armpits while making monkey noises.*)
On the seventh day of Storytime,
The teller shared with me,
Seven pop-up books, (*Jump up and hold out arms.*)
Six arts and crafts, (*Mime using scissors, drawing, gluing, etc.*)
Five animal noises, (*Animal noises.*)
Four funny poems, (*Hold belly and laugh.*)
Three fingerplays, (*Hold up hands and wiggle fingers.*)
Two Dr. Seuss, (*Yell out "Green Eggs and Ham."*)
And a book about a curious monkey. (*Scratch head and armpits while making monkey noises.*)

On the eighth day of Storytime,
The teller shared with me,
Eight sing-along songs, (*Hold out arms and sing "La-la-la."*)
Seven pop-up books, (*Jump up and hold out arms.*)
Six arts and crafts, (*Mime using scissors, drawing, gluing, etc.*)
Five animal noises, (*Animal noises.*)
Four funny poems, (*Hold belly and laugh.*)
Three fingerplays, (*Hold up hands and wiggle fingers.*)
Two Dr. Seuss, (*Yell out "Green Eggs and Ham."*)
And a book about a curious monkey. (*Scratch head and armpits while making monkey noises.*)
On the ninth day of Storytime,
The teller shared with me,
Nine nursery rhymes, (*Make hand motions for "The Itsy-Bitsy Spider."*)
Eight sing-along songs, (*Hold out arms and sing "La-la-la."*)
Seven pop-up books, (*Jump up and hold out arms.*)
Six arts and crafts, (*Mime using scissors, drawing, gluing, etc.*)
Five animal noises, (*Animal noises.*)
Four funny poems, (*Hold belly and laugh.*)
Three fingerplays, (*Hold up hands and wiggle fingers.*)
Two Dr. Seuss, (*Yell out "Green Eggs and Ham."*)
And a book about a curious monkey. (*Scratch head and armpits while making monkey noises.*)
On the tenth day of Storytime,
The teller shared with me,
Ten Hokey-Pokeys, (*Put "one arm in and one arm out."*)
Nine nursery rhymes, (*Make hand motions for "The Itsy-Bitsy Spider."*)
Eight sing-along songs, (*Hold out arms and sing "La-la-la."*)
Seven pop-up books, (*Jump up and hold out arms.*)
Six arts and crafts, (*Mime using scissors, drawing, gluing, etc.*)
Five animal noises, (*Animal noises.*)
Four funny poems, (*Hold belly and laugh.*)
Three fingerplays, (*Hold up hands and wiggle fingers.*)
Two Dr. Seuss, (*Yell out "Green Eggs and Ham."*)
And a book about a curious monkey. (*Scratch head and armpits while making monkey noises.*)
On the eleventh day of Storytime,
The teller shared with me,

Eleven puppet shows, (*Hold up hand and move thumb and fingers as if a puppet is talking.*)
Ten Hokey-Pokeys, (*Put "one arm in and one arm out."*)
Nine nursery rhymes, (*Make hand motions for "The Itsy-Bitsy Spider."*)
Eight sing-along songs, (*Hold out arms and sing "La-la-la."*)
Seven pop-up books, (*Jump up and hold out arms.*)
Six arts and crafts, (*Mime using scissors, drawing, gluing, etc.*)
Five animal noises, (*Animal noises.*)
Four funny poems, (*Hold belly and laugh.*)
Three fingerplays, (*Hold up hands and wiggle fingers.*)
Two Dr. Seuss, (*Yell out "Green Eggs and Ham."*)
And a book about a curious monkey. (*Scratch head and armpits while making monkey noises.*)
On the twelfth day of Storytime,
The teller shared with me,
Twelve yummy treats, (*Rub tummy.*)
Eleven puppet shows, (*Hold up hand and move thumb and fingers as if a puppet is talking.*)
Ten Hokey-Pokeys, (*Put "one arm in and one arm out."*)
Nine nursery rhymes, (*Make hand motions for "The Itsy-Bitsy Spider."*)
Eight sing-along songs, (*Hold out arms and sing "La-la-la."*)
Seven pop-up books, (*Jump up and hold out arms.*)
Six arts and crafts, (*Mime using scissors, drawing, gluing, etc.*)
Five animal noises, (*Animal noises.*)
Four funny poems, (*Hold belly and laugh.*)
Three fingerplays, (*Hold up hands and wiggle fingers.*)
Two Dr. Seuss, (*Yell out "Green Eggs and Ham."*)
And a book about a curious monkey. (*Scratch head and armpits while making monkey noises.*)

PICTURE BOOK MATCH

The Library Book, written by Tom Chapin and Michael Mark and illustrated by Chuck Groenink (Atheneum, 2017).

> A child goes down to the library one rainy Saturday. She greets the books and tries to decide which ones to check out. Winnie the Pooh tells her to bring him home, as does Madeline, Pinocchio, the Cat in the Hat, and other literary characters.

LITERARY CHARACTERS

"FOLKLORE CHARADES"

Movement Activity

Perform a form of traditional charades with the children. Act out the following motions, or improvise other motions, and have the children guess the folklore story or characters.

(*Mime eating with a spoon something that's too hot:* "Goldilocks and the Three Bears.")

(*Mime opening a door, the doorknob breaking off, and eating the doorknob:* "Hansel and Gretel.")

(*Mime climbing up something tall:* "Jack and the Beanstalk.")

(*Mime pointing and then making wide eyes with hand circles:* "Little Red Riding Hood.")

(*Mime brushing extra-long hair, bundling it, and then throwing it out a window:* "Rapunzel.")

(*Mime pricking a finger and then rolling your eyes into the back of your head:* "Sleeping Beauty.")

(*Mime huffing and puffing and blowing something down:* "The Three Little Pigs.")

PICTURE BOOK MATCH

Fairy Tales for Mr. Barker, written and illustrated by Jessica Ahlberg (Candlewick, 2015).

> Lucy and her dog, Mr. Barker, climb into a house and try to guess where they are. They see "a broken chair, three bowls of porridge, and a little golden-haired girl" and guess that they are in the cottage of the three bears. They explore other fairy-tale locations and meet the Three Pigs, Jack, and Sleeping Beauty.

"GOLDILOCKS"

Musical/Movement Activity

Sing to the tune of "Over in the Meadow." Have the children imitate your sounds and motions.

Goldilocks went to the home of the bears,
She decided to sample their wares,
She ate their porridge and then she cried,
"It's too hot!" (*Make an expression as if you ate something hot while fanning mouth.*)
"It's too cold!" (*Scrunch face, hug self, and shake whole body as if shivering.*)
And then, "It's just right!" (*Make a circle with thumb and pointer finger and wink.*)
Goldilocks went to the home of the bears,
She decided to sample their wares,
She sat on their chairs and then she cried,
"It's too hard!" (*Rub bottom as if it is sore.*)
"It's too soft!" (*Hold arms overhead and wiggle downward as if sinking.*)
And then, "It's just right!" (*Make a circle with thumb and pointer finger and wink.*)
Goldilocks went to the home of the bears,
She decided to sample their wares,
She crawled into their beds and then she cried,
"It's too hard!" (*Hold body stiff as a board with arms alongside.*)
"It's too soft!" (*Repeat the motions you did for the soft chair.*)
And then, "It's just right!" (*Pretend to fall asleep.*)
Goldilocks slept in the home of the bears,
She didn't hear them climbing up the stairs,
They woke her up and then she cried, (*Pause.*)
"AAAAAAAAAAHHHHHHHH!!!!!" (*Scream.*)

PICTURE BOOK MATCH

Goldy Luck and the Three Pandas, written by Natasha Yim and illustrated by Grace Zong (Charlesbridge, 2014).

One Chinese New Year, Goldy's mother asks her to visit the neighbors and bring them a plate of turnips. When Goldy finds that the neighbors, the Chans (all panda bears), are not at home, she eats their rice porridge, breaks a chair, and sleeps in a futon.

"THE HAPPY, SAD, MAD NURSERY RHYME"
Sound Effects Activity

Choose a nursery rhyme, such as "Jack and Jill," "Humpty Dumpty," or "Hickory Dickory Dock," and recite it three times with the children. The first time, recite the rhyme with a happy voice. The second time, recite it with a sad voice. Recite it the third time with a mad voice. The result is usually laughter. My granddaughter Ruth recently recited "Mary Had a Little Lamb" with a "heavy metal voice."

PICTURE BOOK MATCH

When the Wind Blew, written by Alison Jackson and illustrated by Doris
  Barrette (Holt, 2014).
> The wind blows the rock-a-bye baby cradle. The old woman who lives in the shoe tries to return the baby but sees some mittens and crying kittens. The adventure involves many other nursery rhyme characters, such as Jack and Jill, Mary and her little lamb, Little Bo Peep, and Little Boy Blue.

"LITTLE RED'S BASKET OF GOODIES"
Movement/Sound Effects Activity

Have a basket as a prop. Pretend to take out the food and beverages mentioned in the rhyme. Have the children imitate your motions.

Grandma, those big teeth are neat,
I have a basket full of treats. (*Point to imaginary basket.*)
Grandma, what I have for you,
Is corn-on-the-cob that you can chew. (*Mime chewing corn-on-the-cob.*)
I brought you tea that'll make you flip,
Don't gulp it down, just take a sip. (*Mime sipping from a cup of tea with
     pinkie finger extended.*)
I brought you something good for lunch,
Here's some popcorn you can munch. (*Mime eating from a bag of
     popcorn.*)

Grandma, you will get a kick,
Out of this sucker, take a lick. (*Mime licking a sucker.*)
These are goodies to gobble and slurp,
I just hope they won't make you burp. (*Say "burp" real loud, followed by
   "Excuse me."*)

PICTURE BOOK MATCH

Little Red Hot, written by Eric A. Kimmel and illustrated by Laura Huliska
   Beith (Amazon, 2013).
      A Texas gal named Little Red Hot sets out to deliver a hot pepper pie to
      her ailing Grandma. A wolf named Señor Lobo takes Grandma's place to
      surprise Little Red Hot. The gal saves the day by sticking the hot pepper
      pie into Señor Lobo's mouth.

"TALL-TALE HEROES"

Musical Activity

Sing to the tune of "London Bridge." Have the children imitate your sounds and
motions. Everyone stands.

Tall-tale heroes run real fast, (*Run in place.*)
Run real fast, run real fast.
Tall-tale heroes run real fast,
All over this land.
Tall-tale heroes swim real fast, (*Mime swimming.*)
Swim real fast, swim real fast.
Tall-tale heroes swim real fast,
All over this land.
Tall-tale heroes lift big things, (*Mime straining and lifting a heavy weight
   overhead.*)
Lift big things, lift big things.
Tall-tale heroes lift big things,
All over this land.
Tall-tale heroes eat a lot, (*Mime shoving food in your mouth.*)
Eat a lot, eat a lot.
Tall-tale heroes eat a lot,
All over this land.

Tall-tale heroes yell real loud, (*Yell the lines of the song.*)
Yell real loud, yell real loud.
Tall-tale heroes yell real loud,
All over this land. (*Yell "Hurray!"*)

PICTURE BOOK MATCH

John Henry vs. the Mighty Steam Drill, written by Cari Meister and illustrated by Victor Rivas (Picture Window, 2015).
As a newborn, John Henry clutched "a 10 pound steel-drivin' hammer"
in his hand. He grew up singing, "I was born with a hammer in my hand.
Got me a hammer in my hand, yes, sir." John Henry also helped others.

"THREE LITTLE BILLY GOATS TRIP-TRAP-TRIP" ———————

Fingerplay

This activity is modeled after the fingerplay "Five Little Monkeys Jumping on the
Bed." Tell the kids to pretend that they are the ogre beneath the bridge and that they
hear the Three Billy Goats Gruff overhead. Have the children imitate your motions.

Three little billy goats,
Trip-trap-trip, (*Hold up three fingers and bounce them up and down.*)
One ran across at a real fast clip, (*Hold up one finger and move it quickly
in front of you from one side to the other.*)
Ogre called its Mama and the Mama yipped, (*Pretend to make a phone
call.*)
"No more billy goats trip-trap-trip!" (*Wave finger as if scolding.*)
Two little billy goats,
Trip-trap-trip, (*Hold up two fingers and bounce them up and down.*)
One ran across at a real fast clip, (*Hold up one finger and move it quickly
in front of you from one side to the other.*)
Ogre called its Mama and the Mama yipped, (*Pretend to make a phone
call.*)
"No more billy goats trip-trap-trip!" (*Wave finger as if scolding.*)
One little billy goat,
Trip-trap-trip, (*Hold up one finger and bounce it up and down.*)
He ran across at a real fast clip, (*Hold up one finger and move it quickly in
front of you from one side to the other.*)

Ogre called its Mama and the Mama yipped, (*Pretend to make a phone call.*)

"No more billy goats trip-trap-trip!" (*Wave finger as if scolding.*)

PICTURE BOOK MATCH

The Three Billy Goats Gruff, written and illustrated by Jerry Pinkney (Little, Brown, 2017).

> A selfish troll threatens to gobble each of the goats as they "Trip-trap! Trip-trap!" over its bridge. After the third goat knocks the troll into the water, a large fish threatens to gobble up the troll.

SPOONERISMS

A spoonerism is a fun oral story form that reverses letters and parts of words in a story familiar to many folks. These stories can be read to an audience or memorized and recited. Read each story once for the fun of hearing the silly words and then repeat it, asking the children to translate the story line by line.

"Bean and the Jackstalk"

Once a time upon, Jack lived with his mold other.
She called him a bazy-loans.
She told him, "A waste is a terrible thing to mind."
So, Jack cold his sow for bean threes.
They were bagical means.
They were the greatest bing since sliced thread.
Jack's mold other was mopping had.
She stew her black and bossed the teens.
That night, a great stalkbean grew clouder than the highs.
Jack hooted up the stalk and skid in the cupboard.
He was as bug as a rug in a snug.
Then, Jack stole a gag of bold that belonged to a giant.
I mean, this guy was a mall tan.
He was a really fried weak.
He was a floated bellow.
A befty hulk.
Bat and furly.

He was one wig bopper.
Jack grabbed a harp and chooted a licken that could gay olden legs.
The grover-own mammoth woke up.
Jack said, "Don't cry over milked spill."
The giant said, "I'll bind your groans to break my med!"
Jack beaned the chopstalk and the fig bellow did a felly blop.
He was doored as a deadnail.
Jack gold the sold and they all happed livily after ever.
All except the mumbo jonster.

Translation: "Jack and the Beanstalk"

Once upon a time, Jack lived with his old mother.
She called him lazybones.
She told him, "A mind is a terrible thing to waste."
So, Jack sold his cow for three beans.
They were magical beans.
They were the greatest thing since sliced bread.
Jack's old mother was hopping mad.
She blew her stack and tossed the beans.
That night, a great beanstalk grew higher than the clouds.
Jack scooted up the stalk and hid in the cupboard.
He was as snug as a bug in a rug.
Then, Jack stole a bag of gold that belonged to a giant.
I mean, this guy was a tall man.
He was a really wide freak.
A hefty bulk.
Fat and burly.
He was one big whopper.
Jack grabbed the harp and looted a chicken that could lay golden eggs.
The overgrown mammoth woke up.
Jack said, "Don't cry over spilled milk."
The giant said, "I'll grind your bones to make my bread."
Jack chopped the beanstalk and the big fellow did a belly flop.
He was dead as a doornail.
Jack sold the gold and they all lived happily ever after.
All except for the jumbo monster.

Jack and the Beanstalk and the French Fries, written and illustrated by
  Mark Teague (Orchard, 2017).
> After Jack plants a beanstalk, the only food everyone eats has beans
> in it. "They ate bean salad and bean soup, pickled beans and refried
> beans, baked beans, minced beans, mashed beans, breaded beans, bean
> sprouts, and bean dip."

"Dincerella"

This piece was originally created as a readers' theater script but can be performed
as a straight oral story by one person.

Reader 1: Once a time upon, Dincerella lived with her sticked
  wepmother and her sad misters, who kept her as beezy as a biz.
Reader 2: She had to poke the sots and dipe the wishes.
Reader 3: She had to steep the sweps and flop the moor.
Reader 4: She had to bake the meds and bust the dunks.
All: Everything had to look spack-and-spin.
Reader 1: But grid she dumble?
All: No!
Reader 2: She kept a liff upper stip.
Reader 3: She kept her grind to the nosestone.
Reader 4: She knew that's the way the crumble cookies.
Reader 1: The sticked wepmother and the sad misters bent to a wall
  given by some ditch rude.
Reader 2: Dincerella was mad she got left behind, and she blarted to
  stubber.
Reader 3: Who should appear but her merry god fom.
Reader 4: She made some dancy fuds for Dincerella to bear to the wall.
All: Do you know how Dincerella bent to the wall?
Reader 1: It wasn't in a vini-man.
Reader 2: It wasn't in a dullbozer.
Reader 3: It wasn't in a trickup puck (with fancy flood maps).
Reader 4: It wasn't even in a trump duck.
All: She went in a bandsome huggy made from a pig bumpkin.
Reader 1: At the ball, Dincerella woogie-boogied with the ditch rude.

Reader 2: Never one to spot the hoglight, she dashed out at the moke of stridnight.

Reader 3: The ditch rude told his men to keep their peels eyed for the girl.

Reader 4: He told them . . .

Reader 1: "If the woo fits, share it."

Reader 2: They tried to sit the flipper on the sad misters' finky steet.

Reader 3: Dincerella said . . .

Reader 4: "Hey! Slop that flipper on my fainty deet!"

All: The flipper sit!

Reader 1: Wick as a quink, the two were wappily harried.

Reader 2: As for the sticked wepmother

Reader 3: And the sad misters, they learned that

Reader 4: The eek shall inherit the mirth.

Translation: "Cinderella"

Reader 1: Once upon a time, Cinderella lived with her wicked stepmother and her mad sisters, who kept her as busy as a bee.

Reader 2: She had to soak the pots and wipe the dishes.

Reader 3: She had to sweep the steps and mop the floor.

Reader 4: She had to make the beds and dust the bunks.

All: Everything had to look spick-and-span.

Reader 1: But did she grumble?

All: No!

Reader 2: She kept a stiff upper lip.

Reader 3: She kept her nose to the grindstone.

Reader 4: She knew that's the way the cookie crumbles.

Reader 1: The wicked stepmother and the mad sisters went to a ball given by some rich dude.

Reader 2: Cinderella was mad she got left behind, and she started to blubber.

Reader 3: Who should appear but her fairy god mom.

Reader 4: She made some fancy duds for Cinderella to wear to the ball.

All: Do you know how Cinderella went to the ball?

Reader 1: It wasn't in a mini-van.

Reader 2: It wasn't in a bulldozer.

Reader 3: It wasn't in a pickup truck (with fancy mud flaps).

Reader 4: It wasn't even in a dump truck.

All: She went in a handsome buggy made from a big pumpkin.

Reader 1: At the ball, Cinderella boogie-woogied with the rich dude.

Reader 2: Never the one to hog the spotlight, she dashed out at the stroke of midnight.

Reader 3: The rich dude told his men to keep their eyes peeled for the girl.

Reader 4: He told them . . .

Reader 1: "If the shoe fits, wear it."

Reader 2: They tried the slipper on the mad sisters' stinky feet.

Reader 3: Cinderella said . . .

Reader 4: "Hey! Flop that slipper on my dainty feet!"

All: The slipper fit!

Reader 1: Quick as a wink, the two were happily married.

Reader 2: As for the wicked stepmother

Reader 3: And the mad sisters, they learned that

Reader 4: The meek shall inherit the earth.

PICTURE BOOK MATCH

Cinderella's Stepsister and the Big Bad Wolf, written by Lorraine Carey and illustrated by Migy Blanco (Nosy Crow, 2015).

> Cinderella lives with her stepmother Mrs. Ugly and the two Ugly sisters. A third sister, Gertie, is nice and does Cinderella's chores for her. Mrs. Ugly sends Gertie out to learn lessons from the Wicked Queen from Snow White, the witch from Hansel and Gretel, and the big bad wolf from Little Red Riding Hood.

"Goldibear and the Three Locks"

Once a time upon, there was a Boppa Pear, a Bommy Mare, and the Beeny Weeny Tear.

One morning, their hop was too slot.

Boppa Pear said, "Ow! I've turnt my bung!"

So they went for a skittle lip in the woods.

Soon, there was a dock at the noor.

It was a gritty little pearl named Loldigocks.

To make a short story long, she basically dashed the trump.

Finally, she said, "I could use a snittle looze."

She sent to weep.

She even snarted to store.

When they arrived home, the shurry fammals were mocked.

Boppa Pear said, "Somebody's been oating my eatmeal!"

Bommy Mare said, "Somebody's been pouring my eatidge!"

And the Beeny Weeny Tear said, "Somebody's been souping my slurp!"

They found the chusted bares and headed for the red booms.

Boppa Pear said, "Somebody's been bedding in my nap!"

Bommy Mare said, "Somebody's been taking a natcap in my bed!"

And the Beeny Weeny Tear said, "Somebody's been beeping in my
   sled!"

The bears copped the calls and they all happed livily after ever.

All except for the little smart goldy pants.

Translation: "Goldilocks and the Three Bears"

Once upon a time, there was Papa Bear, Mommy Bear, and the Teeny
   Weeny Bear.

One morning, their slop was too hot.

Papa Bear said, "Ow! I've burnt my tongue!"

So they went for a little skip in the woods.

Soon, there was a knock at the door.

It was a pretty little girl named Goldilocks.

To make a long story short, she basically trashed the dump.

Finally, she said, "I could use a little snooze."

She went to sleep.

She even started to snore.

When they arrived home, the furry mammals were shocked.

Papa Bear said, "Somebody's been eating my oatmeal!"

Mommy Bear said, "Somebody's been eating my porridge!"

And the Teeny Weeny Bear said, "Somebody's been slurping my soup!"

They found their busted chairs and headed for the bedrooms.

Papa Bear said, "Somebody's been napping in my bed!"

Mommy Bear said, "Somebody's been taking a catnap in my bed!"

And Teeny Weeny Bear said, "Somebody's been sleeping in my bed!"

The bears called the cops and they all lived happily ever after.
All except for the little gold smarty pants.

Goatilocks and the Three Bears, written by Erica S. Perl and illustrated by
  Arthur Howard (Beach Lane, 2014).
  > A goat enters the home of three bears and eats the smallest bowl of
  > porridge and "the little spoon, too." Goatilocks also eats Baby Bear's
  > chair and bed, "plus the blanket, two pillows, and a pair of pajamas."
  > The bears come home and find a mess.

"Little Rude Riding Head"

Once a time upon, a gritty little pearl named Little Rude Riding Head
  had a gasket for her branny.
She had . . .
. . . a broaf of homemade lead,
. . . a wottle of bine,
. . . grapples and apes,
. . . three or four belly jeans,
. . . a bag of pollilops,
. . . some shop chewey,
. . . a twelve-inch peese chizza,
. . . some sicken noodle choop,
. . . some plack-eyed bees,
. . . and a bottle of boot rear.
On the way, she met a wolfy wile.
. . . He was cotton to the roar.
. . . He was a party-smants and a skunky stink.
. . . He was a real snattle-rake.
. . . He was the shack bleep of the family.
The wolf tooted through the skimbers while Red walked at a pail's
  snace.
Granny was all bin and scones, but choosers can't be beggy.
The wolf chicked his lops and burped the old gal down in one sight.
Granny found herself in that belly wolf's smelly.
He stuck her kite nap on his head and beeped into led.

Red arrived and said, "What pig beepers you have."
The wolf said, "All the setter to be you, you tweet little shing."
Red said, "What a hig bonker you have."
The wolf said, "All the smetter to bell you, punny high."
Red said, "What lig bips you have."
The wolf said, "Weed them and reap!"
Suddenly, there was a dot in the shark!
A hassing punter saved the day!
And they all happed livily after ever.
All except for the wolf, who learned that humans
"Stick softly and carry a big speak."

Translation: "Little Red Riding Hood"

Once upon a time, a pretty little girl named Little Red Riding Hood had
    a basket for her granny.
She had . . .
. . . a loaf of homemade bread,
. . . a bottle of wine,
. . . apples and grapes,
. . . three or four jelly beans,
. . . a bag of lollipops,
. . . some chop suey,
. . . a twelve-inch cheese pizza,
. . . some chicken noodle soup,
. . . some black-eyed peas,
. . . and a bottle of root beer.
On the way, she met a wily wolf.
. . . He was rotten to the core.
. . . He was a smarty-pants and a stinky skunk.
. . . He was a real rattlesnake.
. . . He was the black sheep of the family.
The wolf scooted through the timbers while Red walked at a snail's
    pace.
Granny was all skin and bones, but beggars can't be choosy.
The wolf licked his chops and slurped the old gal down in one bite.
Granny found herself in that smelly wolf's belly.

He stuck her nightcap on his head and leaped into bed.
Red arrived and said, "What big peepers you have."
The wolf said, "All the better to see you, you sweet little thing."
Red said, "What a big honker you have."
The wolf said, "All the better to smell you, honey pie."
Red said, "What big lips you have."
The wolf said, "Read them and weep!"
Suddenly, there was a shot in the dark!
A passing hunter saved the day!
And they all lived happily ever after.
All except for the wolf, who learned that humans
"Speak softly and carry a big stick."

PICTURE BOOK MATCH

Little Red, written and illustrated by Bethan Woollvin (Peachtree, 2016).
A wolf races ahead and gets to Grandma's house before Little Red. "Which was unlucky for Grandma." Little Red notices something is amiss, "which might have scared some little girls. But not this little girl." Little Red takes care of the situation, "which was unlucky for the wolf."

THE LIBRARY RAPS

I GOT A lot of mileage doing library outreach programs as Rappin' Rob early in my career as a children's librarian. For the first rap, I've known folks to change "Rappin' Rob" to their own name and adjust the rhyme, like "I'm Rappin' Sue and you know what I'll do, I'll tell you all about books." If that doesn't work, you can always say, "I'm a Rappin' guy and I'll tell you why I'm tellin' kids about books" or "I'm a Rappin' gal, your very best pal, and I'm tellin' kids about books."

"THE RAPPIN' ROB LIBRARY RAP"

I'm Rappin' Rob and I got a job, and that's tellin' kids about books.
So, lend me an ear, get over here, and don't give me no dirty looks.
I'm a storyteller, a pretty nice feller, there's no need for you to be wary.
Get your act together, get light as a feather, and fly down to the library.
We g-g-got, We g-g-got, We g-g-got, B-B-B-B-B-Books on . . .
We g-g-got, We g-g-got, We g-g-got, Books-Books on . . .
Boys diggin' holes, boys swallowin' keys,
Chrysanthemum, Minerva Louise,
A Winn-Dixie dog and froggies that flew,
A princess diary and a click clack moo!
Olivia the pig, the Redwall crew,
The Stinky Cheese Man and others—PU!
We got your sideways stories from wayside school,
Or is it wayside stories from a sideways school?
Yo! Yes? Chicka Boom! and a Zin! Zin! Zin!
A Lon Po Po, I Spy! We win!
Hey! Junie B. Jones, you know that we got her,
And how could we ever forget Harry Potter?
Now I've said my rap, gonna take a nap, hope my dreams aren't scary.
'Cause when I wake up all new, I'll find my dreams have come true,
'Cause I'm going to the library! Yeah!

"THE LI-BERRY RAP" ————————————————

Well, I'm Rappin' Rob and that's a fact!
I've come to get you and take you back.
Back on down to the li-brary.
And don't pronounce it li-berry!
We ain't a place for pickin' fruit.
So, don't give me no raspberry toot.
Come check us out, this li-brary,
Just don't pronounce it li-barey!
This place won't break you, won't take your loot,
Come in your jeans, not your birthday suit.
I say-say slide on down to the li-brary,
Just don't pronounce it li-beary!
Corduroy's a bear and although he's real cute,
If you don't pronounce it right, I'm gonna give you the boot!
L-L-L-Li-brary!
L-L-L-Li-brary!
L-L-L-Li-brary!
Yeah, the Library!
Not the Li-berry,
Don't say the Li-barey,
It's not the Li-beary,
It's the Library!
Yeah!

"THE MESSED-UP RAP" ————————————————

I'm Rappin' Rob and I'm confused,
I gotta puzzle with a lot of clues,
I read about forty books last night,
But I got 'em mixed up,
Something's not quite right.
I'm gonna ask ya please to help straighten 'em out,
'Cause I bet ya know books, without a doubt,
Listen carefully now and use your head,
Ready or not, here's what I read:
Thirteen Ways to Eat Fried Worms,

Cloudy with a Chance of Caps for Sale,
Millions of Very Hungry Caterpillars,
Tales of a Fourth Grade Freckle Juice,
The Day Jimmy's Boa Buzzed in People's Ears,
Horton Hatches Blueberries for Sal,
Island of the Blue Jumanji,
The Little Engine That Could Wrinkle in Time,
A Day No Pigs Would Make Way for Ducklings,
From the Mixed-Up Files of Mr. Popper's Penguins,
Animals Should Definitely Not Wear Corduroy,
Brown Bear, Brown Bear, Where's Waldo?
If You Give a Mouse Stone Soup,
The Sweet Valley Babysitters Club,
Ramona, Plain and Tall,
Free to Be . . . A Boy, a Dog, and a Frog.
Nobody Asked Me If I Wanted a Nightmare in My Closet,
The Lion, the Witch, and the Best Christmas Pageant Ever,
Where the Red Fern, Wild Things, and the Sidewalk Ends,
Green Eggs and the Terrible, Horrible, No Good, Very Bad Ham!
That's the Messed-Up Rap, now I'll take a break,
Please straighten these titles, 'cause they give me an ache,
Then when you're done with that, I think it would be fun,
If you took your two favorite books and messed them into one.
That's how you do the Messed-Up Rap,
You read a few books, put on your thinking cap,
Mix the words in a title and give a little snap,
Now you got your own little Messed-Up Rap.

KEY

1. *Thirteen Ways to Sink a Sub* by Jamie Gilson
2. *How to Eat Fried Worms* by Thomas Rockwell
3. *Cloudy with a Chance of Meatballs* by Judi Barrett
4. *Caps for Sale* by Esphyr Slobodkina
5. *Millions of Cats* by Wanda Gag
6. *The Very Hungry Caterpillar* by Eric Carle
7. *Tales of a Fourth Grade Nothing* by Judy Blume

8. *Freckle Juice* by Judy Blume
9. *The Day Jimmy's Boa Ate the Wash* by Trinka Hakes Noble
10. *Why Mosquitoes Buzz in People's Ears* by Verna Aardema
11. *Horton Hatches the Egg* by Dr. Seuss
12. *Blueberries for Sal* by Robert McCloskey
13. *Island of the Blue Dolphins* by Scott O'Dell
14. *Jumanji* by Chris Van Allsburg
15. *The Little Engine That Could* by Watty Piper
16. *A Wrinkle in Time* by Madeleine L'Engle
17. *A Day No Pigs Would Die* by Robert Newton Peck
18. *Make Way for Ducklings* by Robert McCloskey
19. *From the Mixed-Up Files of Mrs. Basil E. Frankweiler* by E. L. Konigsburg
20. *Mr. Popper's Penguins* by Richard Atwater
21. *Animals Should Definitely Not Wear Clothing* by Judi Barrett
22. *Corduroy* by Don Freeman
23. *Brown Bear, Brown Bear, What Do You See?* by Bill Martin Jr.
24. *Where's Waldo?* by Martin Handford
25. *If You Give a Mouse a Cookie* by Laura Joffe Numeroff
26. *Stone Soup* by Marcia Brown
27. The Sweet Valley Twins series by Francine Pascal
28. The Babysitters Club series by Ann Martin
29. Ramona series by Beverly Cleary
30. *Sarah, Plain and Tall* by Patricia McLachlan
31. *Free to Be You and Me* by Marlo Thomas
32. *A Boy, a Dog, and a Frog* by Mercer Mayer
33. *Nobody Asked Me If I Wanted a Baby Sister* by Martha Alexander
34. *There's a Nightmare in My Closet* by Mercer Mayer
35. *The Lion, the Witch, and the Wardrobe* by C. S. Lewis
36. *The Best Christmas Pageant Ever* by Barbra Robinson
37. *Where the Red Fern Grows* by Wilson Rawls
38. *Where the Wild Things Are* by Shel Silverstein
39. *Green Eggs and Ham* by Dr. Seuss
40. *Alexander and the Terrible, Horrible, No Good, Very Bad Day* by Judith Viorst

GOODBYE ACTIVITIES / CLOSINGS

"AIR GOODBYE"

Fingerplay

Have the children imitate your sounds and motions.

Let's play air guitar, (*Mime playing guitar and make guitar noises.*)
Let's give an air high five, (*Mime giving high fives, not touching hands.*)
Let's give an air kiss, (*Blow a silent kiss with a wave of the hand.*)
Let's give an air goodbye. (*Wave hands and say, "Goodbye."*)

"MORE, MORE, MORE"

Movement Activity

Have the children imitate your motions. Everyone stands.

Stand up, sit down,
More, more, more. (*Stand and sit four times before moving on to the next lines.*)
Twirl your hands,
More, more, more. (*Twirl hands over and over four times.*)
Move this way and that way,
More, more, more. (*Step sideways right, then left four times.*)
Twirl your body,
More, more, more. (*Spin in a slow circle four times.*)
Give me an "air five,"
More, more, more. (*Mime giving a high five to everyone in the audience.*)
Wave your hand,
And march out the door. (*Lead the children out of the program area.*)

"THE PENGUIN MARCH" ─────────────────────

Movement Activity

Recite the chant a few times while the children march like penguins—waddling with arms at sides—in a few circles before leaving the story program area.

The penguins march,
A waddling march,
Hut-two-three-four,
Hut-two-three-four,
Hut-two-three-four,
Waddle, waddle, out the door.

"A ROUND OF APPLAUSE" ─────────────────────

Movement Activity

Have the children imitate your motions.

You're so great!
Now please stand, (*Stand.*)
Give yourself,
A great big hand. (*Clap.*)
Clap the floor, (*Touch the floor.*)
Clap the chair, (*Touch any chair in the area or a pretend chair.*)
Clap the wall, (*Run to wall and touch it.*)
And clap the air. (*Bat hand around in the air.*)
Clap your elbows, (*Touch one elbow.*)
Clap your feet, (*Touch both feet.*)
Clap your pinkies, (*Touch one pinkie finger.*)
And clap your seat. (*Slap bottom.*)
Clap with flippers, (*Touch the backs of hands together as if they are seal flippers.*)
Clap with claws, (*Make a lobster claw shape with thumbs far apart from hands and clap hands.*)
Now a big
Round of applause. (*Clap hands in a circle in the air.*)
Clap your neighbor, (*Give neighbor a high five.*)
Don't ask how,
Last of all
Take a bow! (*Take a bow.*)

"THE TRAFFIC LIGHT"

Felt Movement Activity

Cut out a felt traffic light with red, yellow, and green circles. Wear the felt traffic light on your chest or place on a felt board. Cover up the red and green lights and ask audience members to wave their hands in the air slowly. Next, show only the green light and have audience members wave their hands quickly. Show them only the red light and have them stop.

Next, have audience members nod their heads and follow the lights. Show only the yellow and have them nod their heads slowly. Ask them if they are having a good time and show only the green light. Hopefully, everyone will laugh when they realize they've been tricked into nodding their heads vigorously. Show them only the red light to stop.

Next, have audience members clap slowly to the yellow light. Show the red light to make them stop. Continue to alternate between the yellow and red lights a few more times. Finally, show them the green light and take a bow when they clap quickly.)

"WAVE GOODBYE"

Movement Activity

Have the children imitate your motions.

Wave high, (*Wave hand over head.*)
Wave low, (*Wave hand near the ground.*)
I think it's time, (*Point to wrist as if wearing a watch.*)
We gotta go. (*Point to the door.*)
Wave your elbows, (*Wave elbows.*)
Wave your toes, (*Wave toes/feet.*)
Wave your tongue, (*Stick out tongue and wave it.*)
And wave your nose. (*Wiggle nose.*)
Wave your knees, (*Wave knees.*)
Wave your lips, (*Move mouth all around.*)
Blow a kiss,
With fingertips. (*Blow a kiss.*)
Wave your ears, (*Wiggle ears.*)
Wave your hair, (*Shake head.*)
Wave your belly, (*Shake belly.*)
And derriere. (*Shake rear end.*)

Wave your chin, (*Wiggle chin.*)
Wave your eyes, (*Blink.*)
Wave your hand, (*Lift up hand.*)
And wave goodbye. (*Wave.*)

credits

THE FOLLOWING APPEARED in *Animal Shenanigans* (ALA Editions, 2015): "Animal Baths," "Animal Photo Poses," "Animal Sirens," "Animal Snores," "The Ants Go Dancing," "Bring a Friend to School," "A Cow Is Driving a Car," "Dig-a-Dig-a-Dig-a-Dig-a," "The Farm Animals Introduce Themselves," "Five Little Alligators," "Five Little Fish Heading to School," "Five Little Hungry Birds," "Five Little Monkeys Jumping So High," "Flap Your Wings," "Goldilocks," "Have You Seen My Worm?," "Hide and Seek," "I Know an Old Lady Who Had a Pet Fly," "If a Dinosaur Says 'Roar!'," "If Pigs Went to Pig School," "A Little Bear Climbed Up a Tree," "Monkeys Reading in Bed," "The Mosquito Wave," "My Best Friend," "My Little Kitten Ran Away," "My Little Rowboat," "My Monkey Likes to Read to Me," "The Not-So-Itsy-Bitsy Hippo," "Over in the Creek," "Over in the Forest," "A Pig in a Pond," "The Sauropod," "Spider Here, Spider There," "The Talent Show ABC," "This Funny Bug," "Three Little Billy Goats Trip-Trap-Trip," "The Three Little Kittens Weren't the Only Ones to Lose Things," "Tiny Little Frogs," "The Triceratops," "Use, Use, Use Your Mind—Move," "Use, Use, Use Your Mind—Sounds," "We're Going to Explore a Cave," "We're Taking a Walk in the Woods," "What Did I See at the Pond?," "When Bears Wake Up," "While We Sleep," "Who Eats Corn?," "Winter Noises," "The Woolly Mammoth," and "The Zoo Animals Introduce Themselves."

The following appeared in *Family Storytime* (ALA Editions, 1999): "The Bear Cubs' Hunt," "Bubble Bath," "Busy Day," "The Crazy Traffic Light," "Dincerella," "Elephant Hunt," "The Froggy Choir," "If Your Clothes Have Any Red," "Lima Beans and Diced Beets," "The New Wheels on the Bus," "A Round of Applause," "Some of These Stories," "Three Little Smelly Skunks," and "Uncle David."

The following appeared in *LibrarySparks* magazine created by Upstart: "Abra-Cadabra-Bippity-Bop" (Vol. 13, No. 1), "The Baby Bird Choir" (Vol. 12, No. 4), "Be Kind to Your Bot Robot Friends" (Vol. 11, No. 2), "Can You Climb?" (Vol. 7, No. 5), "Dog Commands" (Vol. 8, No. 6), "Don't Scream in the Library (Vol. 9, No. 6), "Dressing for the Weather" (Vol. 10, No. 6),

"The Farm Animals Sing Old MacDonald" (Vol. 7, No. 6), "The Fire-Breathing Dragon" (Vol. 10, No. 7), "Five Big Green Monsters" (Vol. 12, No. 8), "Five Little Cats" (Vol. 7, No. 2), "Five Little Quiet Raccoons" (Vol. 13, No. 1), "Five Wolves in the Bed" (Vol. 8, No. 4), "A Fly Is Buzzing 'Round My Head" (Vol. 12, No. 6), "Guess My Friend" (Vol. 11, No. 2), "Here Is a Book" (Vol. 11, No. 9), "I Was Walking in the Woods" (Vol. 10, No. 1), "If You Want a Funny Story" (Vol. 11, No. 9), "If You Were," (Vol. 6, No. 3), "If You're Brave and You Know It" (Vol. 6, No. 6), "If You're Feeling Rather Ill" (Vol. 12, No. 5), "I'm a Monster" (Vol. 12, No. 8), "The Itsy-Bitsy Baby" (Vol. 12, No. 4), "Monster School" (Vol. 12, No. 8), "More, More, More" (Vol. 12, No. 7), "My Family Came Back" (Vol. 8, No. 6), "My Old Car" (Vol. 12, No. 1), "The Stars Are Twinkling" (Vol. 11, No. 7), "Tall-Tale Heroes" (Vol. 5, No. 5), "Ten Little Fireflies" (Vol. 12, No. 2), "There May Be Wildlife Near" (Vol. 12, No. 5), "There Was Who in the Bed?," "Three Little Dragons" (Vol. 10, No. 7), "Tops and Bottoms" (Vol. 12, No. 6), "Trip-Trap, Trip-Trap, Who's That?" (Vol. 9, No. 6), "Twinkle Here and There" (Vol. 11, No. 7), "The Underwater Parade" (Vol. 9, No. 3), "We're Going on a Dragon Hunt" (Vol. 10, No. 7), "We're Going on a Monster Hunt" (Vol. 6, No. 8), "What Can I Do with My Blanket?" (Vol. 12, No. 7), "What Kind of Sound Does a Cat Make?" (Vol. 7, No. 2), and "What'cha Doing?" (Vol. 11, No. 2).

The following appeared in *More Family Storytimes* (ALA Editions, 2009): "Air Goodbye," "Baby Bear Roars," "Does Your Scarf Hang Low?," "An Elephant Came to Play, Play, Play," "Five Little Kiddos," "Hello Kids," "I Have Fleas," "If You're Happy and You Know It—Winter Style," "If You're Wearing a Shirt," "I'm Driving Along," "I'm Not Sleepy," "Looking for Polar Bears," "The More We Tweet Together," "My Dog Is a Noisy Dog," "My Grandmother Had a House," "The New My Aunt Came Back," "Ow, Ow, I Bumped My Head," "Reptiles and Amphibians," "R-I-N-G-O," and "Snowball."

The following appeared in *Shake and Shout* (Upstart, 2008): "Dogs and Cats and Guinea Pigs," "Happy Birthday in Cow," "The Happy, Sad, Mad Nursery Rhyme," "If You're a Ghost and You Know It," "The More We Brush Our Teeth," "My Face," "The Penguin," "The Penguins All March in a Line," "The Raccoons' Hunt," "Snow Dude, Snow Dude," "Stamp Your Feet," and "The Teeny-Tiny Kid."

The following appeared in *Something Funny Happened at the Library* (ALA Editions, 2003): "The Animals in the Zoo," "Bean and the Jackstalk,"

"The Biggest Juiciest Apple in the Whole Orchard," "Don't Eat That," "Goldibear and the Three Locks," "The Li-Berry Rap," "Little Rude Riding Head," "The Messed-Up Rap," "Old MacDonald Had a Pig," "P-O-R-K-Y," "The Rappin' Rob Library Rap," "The Read, Read, Read Chant," "Storytelling Warmups," and "The Traffic Light."

The following appeared in *Storytime Slam* (Upstart, 2006): "A Book! Bok! Bok!," "The Bundle-Up Dance," "I Know a Cowboy, I Know a Cowgirl," "Old MacDonald Had an Owl," "Playground Time," "The Quacker Choir," "She'll Be Driving a Bulldozer," "The Sixteen-Scoop Ice Cream Cone," and "The Twelve Days of Storytime."

The following appeared in *Welcome to Storytime* (Upstart, 2012): "The Eensy Weensy Robot," "Hey You, Hey Me!" "I Don't Feel Good," "I'm Mad! Stomp! Stomp!," "Mary Had a Little Cold," "R-O-B-O-T," "Shh! Shh!," "The Smiley Hokey Pokey," "There's a Monster Behind Me!," "Three Little Aliens," and "Yawn and Stretch."

The following appeared in *What's Black and White and Reid All Over* (ALA Editions, 2012): "But Mostly I Love You," "A Cow Has a Horn," "Doot Doot Zoo," "Easy-Peasy," "Faster, Faster," "Fee Fi Fo Fum," "Five Little Monkeys Swinging in the Zoo," "Flip, Flop," "Folklore Charades," "The Grand Old Storyteller," "How Much Is That Turtle in the Window?," "Mary Had a Little Zoo," "My Bunny Hops into Its Burrow," "No, No, No, No, No, No, No, Yes, Yes, Yes, Yes, YES," "Old MacDonald ABC," "The Penguin March," "A Rabbit," "Ten in the Field," "There Were Ten Bunnies Hopping," and "Why I'm Late for School."

"Coming Down to Storytime" first appeared as a picture book published by Upstart (2006).

"Wave Goodbye" appeared as a picture book published by Lee and Low (1995).

index